THE LIVING ARISTOPHANES

The
Living
Aristophanes

Alexis Solomos

*Translation and adaptation by Alexis Solomos and
Marvin Felheim*

Ann Arbor
The University of Michigan Press

Foreword

A Foreword can rightly be a history. For me, the beginning of this book, although I didn't know it then, was in 1963. I was finishing an academic stint as Fulbright lecturer in American Literature at the University of Athens. Appropriately climactic, after my classes were finished and just before I was to leave for home, I went to see a performance of Aristophanes at the magnificent theatre at Epidaurus. It was a perfect day. We sailed gaily, as was auspicious for a comedy, from Piraeus. The trip was an adventure, of course. But I could never have anticipated the production. It was *The Wasps*. And I, like my fellow thousands in the evening audience, was spellbound. The precision of the choruses, their movements, their speaking! The absolute hilarity of the gags! The brilliance of the costumes and the inventiveness of the whole production! And when one remembers that all this was in a language not one word of which I could understand!

Afterward, still exhilarated, a friend introduced me to the director Alexis Solomos, bald as Aristophanes, who was sitting quietly in a café watching the crowds. And then we returned to Athens over the water sparkling in the lights like waves of laughter. Soon afterward I left Greece.

Now the scene changes. Even an Aristophanic stage device couldn't have managed this shift. History, imagination, irony? Anyhow, it is some years later; I am back at the University of Michigan in Ann Arbor, when I learn

about a projected Greek Theatre in nearby Ypsilanti. I
get involved in the planning, particularly on the committee interested in the selection of the plays; we decide: a
tragedy and a comedy. Easy enough. The best of each:
the complete *Oresteia* of Aeschylus and *The Birds* of
Aristophanes. I remember Epidaurus and a little dynamic man with dark eyes and an energetic manner.
And suddenly, it seems, Alexis Solomos is in Ypsilanti.
And it is the summer of 1966 and, miraculously, we are
about to open a fabulous, one-summer experiment.

One of the highlights of that experience was, of
course, Solomos' production of *The Birds*. The cast was
headed by comics Bert Lahr and Jack Fletcher. The chorus, of the most enchanting, beplumed birds ever seen in
America (and I include all the Ziegfeld Follies), was a
constant delight. I attended both matinee and evening
performances. For a second time in my experience, Aristophanes, through the skill of Solomos and in two settings
so different as to be accounted for only by the deity of
comedy—the best preserved theatre in the ancient world
at Epidaurus and a converted baseball field on the campus
at Eastern Michigan University—stunned a modern audience with his poetry, his jokes, his satire, his vitality.

Later that summer, Solomos, finished with the exhausting task of directing two major productions, was
looking for something to do. Like his talent, energy flows
from the man in a constant electric current. We decided
to use the afternoons (evenings were still at the theatre,
checking and watching) to translate his book, *The Living
Aristophanes,* into English. What better person to have
written such a work? The man who practically single-
handedly had brought the works of Aristophanes to life in
modern Greece and who now had demonstrated that same
remarkable talent in America. So we sat by the pool at a
motel half-way between Ypsilanti and Ann Arbor and we

knocked off a crude, literal translation of his study, which had first appeared in Greece in 1960.

There follow the dull years of revisions and of checking on references, searching out comments by the scholiasts, rechecking lines from the plays, and so on. The end is now. I sit here in sunshine in a little tree-lined square in the Plaka. Above me towers the rocky north slope of the Acropolis; a few minutes' walk and I am on the Pnyx (that is, if I don't get killed by the wild Athens traffic), I almost wrote Aristophanes' Pnyx. We are at last putting the finishing touches to the text. This is a translation of a book now ten years old; it makes no pretentions to be an up-to-the-minute scholarly work of the kind, say, which Cedric Whitman so well demonstrated in his 1964 publication *Aristophanes and the Comic Hero*. On the contrary, this work is a modest, but a serious and a gay one. It aims to bring the plays of Aristophanes alive where they have always most belonged, in the theatre, and to show how brilliant and successful they are as theatrical pieces; it aims to add a dimension of pleasure to our understanding of the plays, to attach them to the poet's life and times, but as real things from a real world; it aims at reviving Aristophanes as a life-giver.

MARVIN FELHEIM

Acknowledgments

We want to add a brief note of thanks to Professor Cedric Whitman, of Harvard University, and Professors Charles Witke and Gerald Else, of the University of Michigan, for suggestions which have helped us to eliminate some errors; and to Judith T. Manos, of Ann Arbor, whose generosity and charm brightened our days and helped make possible the remarkable Ypsilanti Greek Theatre.

A.S. and M.F.

Contents

Prolegomena

The Theatre of Aristophanes Today

Overtaken by hiccups
Plato, *The Symposium* (185c)

Before we say anything else about Greek Comedy, let us remember Aristophanes' hiccups. It is, without doubt, the most memorable case of hiccups in the history of literature.

At the famous symposium in Agathon's house, the topic of conversation, according to Plato, was Love: a cosmological subject, which the first speakers—Phaedrus, Pausanias, and others—examine with the utmost seriousness, displaying their deep knowledge of philosophy and rhetoric.[1] When Aristophanes' turn comes, he tells the gathering with polite embarrassment that he has the hiccups and that he is, therefore, unable to speak. One of the company, the physician Erixymachus, advises him to hold his breath, gargle with water, and tickle his nose in order to sneeze. Erixymachus then discourses on the relationship between Love and Medicine, while Aristophanes tries to sneeze by tickling his nose.

The interlude of the hiccups is, surely, the most amusing part of the Platonic dialogue and the only de-

Part of the Prolegomena was published in *Le Théâtre dans le monde* (VII, 3) as a lecture given by the author at a meeting of the International Theatre Institute at the Herod Atticus Odeum in Athens in 1957.

scription of Aristophanes-the-man that has reached us. What we joyously note is that Aristophanes-the-man, at least as Plato presents him, remains absolutely true to Aristophanes-the-poet, as we know him from his plays. Listening to the solemn dissertation of the other banqueters, he cannot resist the temptation to satirize. His hiccups are the ridicule of the lofty style, the exaggerated seriousness, and the pompous complacence of his fellow diners. He uses the same ridicule in his comedies to scourge literary systems, social institutions, and human characters, to deplore everything noisy and hollow, deceptive and harmful, grotesquely modernistic or ludicrously obsolete, that he has observed in the symposium of life.

Parody is a very subtle form of satire and Aristophanes' most beloved dramatic tool. In his *Peace,* the beetle which takes Trygaeus to Heaven is a parody of the poets' Pegasus. His *Wasps* deals with the trial of a dog. In *Lysistrata,* the Athenian women take their oath, not with the blood of a sacrificial animal, but with a jug of red wine. The chorus in the *Frogs,* croaking monotonously and idiotically *brekekekex-koax-koax,* may well be a parody of dramatic poets—and dramatic critics, as well.

Schlegel believes that the whole form of tragic synthesis was, for Aristophanes, a subject for parody.[2] And, indeed, the examples that we can draw from his comedies to prove this are innumerable. His songs are very often *kentos* of famous lyric or dramatic verses in incongruous combinations;[3] his musical scores are replete with travesties of well-remembered melodies of Stesichorus, Phrynichus, or Aeschylus; his dances turn the tragic *emmeleia* to ridicule; his actors are asked to perform many scenes of hilarotragoedia, based on the works of the tragic poets;[4] his scenery and costumes caricature more than one notorious tragic show of the day. As a general rule, by using the wrong thing at the right moment, Aristophanes proves Schopenhauer's definition of the comic, as "the logical dis-

cord between an idea and its object." [5] This is most strik-
ingly demonstrated by the animals that abound in his
comedies—a singular zoo of histrionic dogs, pigs, donkeys,
frogs, beetles, bugs, wasps, hoopoes, nightingales, and all
kinds of birds. They testify among other things that Aristophanes had discovered the power of human parody inherent in the behavior of animals, twenty-three hundred
years before Henri Bergson or Walt Disney.[6]

Thus Plato, who appreciated the Aristophanic verve
—much more, it seems, than Aristophanes had ever appreciated the Socratic thought—introduces our comic
writer as a comic character with hiccups; in other words,
as the embodiment of parody.

In these hiccups, however, we should not discern
only parody. There is something else, besides, which is
also an ingredient of Aristophanic comedy: namely, the element of shock and surprise, the sudden stimulant of
thought, the noisy alarm clock, that shakes us out of the
slumber of propriety, routine, and order. Aristophanes'
hiccups are the necessary ingredient of disorder, necessary
to aesthetic balance; because, contrary to what happens in
Tragedy, in Comedy not order but disorder is the primary
factor.

Aristophanes, furthermore, is not only a man of letters, but also a servant of Dionysus, a creator of stage di-
versity and theatrical impressions, in short, an accomplished showman. Naturally enough, in a reunion of
half-drunken intellectuals, the most appropriate theatrical
effect could be no other than the breathing spasm that
accompanies intoxication. The comic poet's hiccups,
therefore, symbolize in the final analysis the presence of
Bacchus in the symposium.

We have started with Aristophanes right away, instead of
defining Attic Comedy in more general terms, because Aristophanes *is* Attic Comedy. His fellow writers of all three

periods—Old, Middle, and New—have all disappeared
under his shadow. We know them only by name and by a
few fragments which have come down to us almost accidentally.[7] Mankind, which wisely banks its intellectual
capital, seems not to have cared about them. It stored up
one fourth of Aristophanes' work and a few slices of
Menander's. Yet, even the master of New Comedy—so
much acclaimed during the centuries of Greek decadence
—is now irrevocably buried in time. We have only been
interested in Menander because we had been excited by
his disciples, Plautus and Terence.[8] Aristophanes, on the
contrary, remains a world apart. He cannot be compared
to nor share his significance with anyone. He is an author
and, at the same time, a period of civilization. A man and
a monument in one.

Despite these facts, the theatrical history of his works
is not rich, when compared to that of his tragic contemporaries. Two main reasons have prevented and to an extent
still prevent his plays from being naturalized in the modern repertoire. The first are his verbal, and sometimes visual, obscenities. The second, his close connection with
people and events of a very remote epoch.

In all probability, the first factor has little weight
with the cultured spectator of today. He knows that the li-
centiousness of many writers, both atheist and Christian,
would make Aristophanes blush like a nun. And, after all,
phallic worship is not a religious affair any longer, as in
the poet's time, and the Church does not openly encourage Priapism.[9]

As for the question of timeliness, it is obvious to
everyone but the very pedantic that Aristophanes' satire is
less concerned with the particular people of his day than
with man in general. The citizen in the times of Cleon or
the Four Hundred is the citizen of all times, and the
world is still full of sadistic judges, irascible policemen,

bad poets, crazy professors, unscrupulous politicians, dynamic wives, and dilapidated husbands, as well as, thank God, militant ideologists. Aristophanes' basic subjects are none other than War, Wealth, Justice, Literature, Politics, Feminism, Utopia, etc., subjects that in our own day and age make front-page news. His many references to contemporary persons and facts can still very well serve their purpose by the simple method of generalization. Timelessness, however, cannot be established by the mere substitution of certain words or names. What is far more important for us is to conceive the right form of theatrical presentation. And this leads us to the question: how to produce Aristophanes today.

There is no safer way of mummifying Greek Comedy than by trying to reproduce the form that it supposedly had in the fifth century B.C. I say supposedly, because our true knowledge of the most fundamental principles of the ancient theatre is exasperatingly limited.[10] What makes things even worse is that our specialists— archaeologists, scholars, or historians of the theatre—are in perpetual disagreement with each other, proposing on the whole a Babel-like reconstruction of the ancient Greek dramatic performance. Matters would not change much even if we were to discover miraculously the exact meaning of all those words which we venerate in the dark, such as *komos, paean, kordax, Lydian melody, parakataloge, hyporchema, mesaulion, thymele, parodos, parabasis, agon* [11]—an endless array of traditional terms, whose coalescence gave ancient performances their special character. Even if we knew the meaning of all the key words, permitting us to restore *mutatis mutandis* a theatrical show of Pericles' times, it is doubtful whether the Greek dramatists—so exacting in questions of quality and style—would approve of our deficient and artless skeleton, made up of dubious and heterogeneous fossils. It is probable that they would not even recognize their own works. By creating a collage of various little facts and facets that we happen to possess, we honor, perhaps, archaeology but not drama. And when we adopt this approach, we deny not only the comic poet's eternal value but also the treasure of our own artistic tradition, the cultural harvest of all the centuries from Aristophanes' days to our own. As for our audiences, it goes without saying that such a spectacle would bore them to the point of riotous indignation.

The modern theatrical craftsman, therefore, must read books in the winter and perform Aristophanes in the summer—never combining erudition and theatre. He must make *tabula rasa* of all arbitrary and controversial theories and scratch all the rust of anti-theatrical scholarship which conceals the brightness of Aristophanes' metal. No matter whether we believe or not—and we must believe—in the educational purpose of art, we have to admit that the public goes to the theatre mainly for entertainment. We should not, therefore, encourage the academic view, that boredom is the prerequisite of classical glory. The spectator's education will accompany, naturally and unobtrusively, his pleasure. Like love, art must please without proclaiming its ultimate purpose. George Bernard Shaw—who might be called the twentieth-century Aristophanes—claims in *The Sanity of Art* that our comic poet, as well as Shakespeare and Ibsen, "are still alive and at home everywhere among the dust and ashes of many thousands of academic, punctilious, most archaeologically correct men of letters and art . . ." [12]

What must be faithfully revived in contemporary productions is not the aspect, but the essence, of ancient drama; not the letter, but the spirit; not a picture, but a vision. We must discover the laws and rhythms, the shapes and colors of the Aristophanic performance in the kaleidoscope of modern popular entertainment. As we shall see

in the last chapter of this book, most of the inventions
and devices which have produced laughter through the
last twenty-three centuries had their roots in his own
Comedy. In fact, the artistic tradition of all those centuries, that we shall draw from to interpret his plays creatively, is none other than his own tradition; for the more
we bring Aristophanes close to our times, the more we discover his particular period. Our basic ambition must be
to offer modern theatre-goers what the Greek poet offered
his audiences. As he created for them an up-to-date performance, so must we build our performance with live and
contemporary materials. This can be achieved without in
the least cheating the author or undermining his dramatic
purpose, provided, of course, that we are in good faith
and that we avoid the temptation—a very common one
among amateurs as well as professionals—to concoct the
parody of a parody: that is to say, instead of laughing at
Life with Aristophanes, to laugh at Aristophanes himself.

To discern his affinity with many genres of modern
popular entertainment is very easy. Were he living today,
he would unquestionably frequent, beside zoos, night-
clubs and music-halls, puppet-shows and circuses; he
would have studied the art of the Fratellinis and the
Marx Brothers, as well as that of Karaghiozes, the Greek
shadow-play of later times; [13] he would be a Donald Duck
fan and a Charlie Chaplin admirer. The mad world of Aristophanes is notably consanguineous with that of modern
broad comedy. The crowd of his odd characters, so clown-
esque in fixed expression and stylized movement (and so
identical with all those hilarious figures that emerge from
ancient vases), have laid in every respect the foundations
for the universe of modern slapstick. Even the facial
makeup of our contemporary clowns is a survival, through
the centuries, of the ancient comic mask.

And this is the best answer, perhaps, to the constant

question about the use or non-use of masks in Greek revivals. The purpose of both mask and stylized makeup being the same, the former becomes superfluous in a modern production, even, perhaps, injurious. Masks have doomed more than one competent performance of our days, thus proving that they have no organic link with the modern theatre. By using them, therefore, we merely imply that we care more about the picturesqueness and the originality of the effect than about the play itself or the human characters it projects. Masks deprive the author of his humanity and raise an artificial barrier between actors and spectators.[14]

Aristophanes' comedy, notwithstanding the playwright's unscrupulous passion for laughter, is fundamentally a serious kind of theatre. And this constitutes the major difference between his kind of entertainment and that produced by modern fun-makers—Chaplin being an outstanding exception. Aristophanes' plays involve three serious elements, unknown to most of our mass-entertainers, namely, poetry, moral purpose, and a determined hero. They combine, in absolute symmetry, light and heavy components, in a manner which is familiar to us through the work of some "engaged" writers of our time, such as Shaw, Mayakovski, Brecht, Genêt, Frisch, Albee, and others, though none of them equals Aristophanes' comic genius. His method is, perhaps, best summed up in two lines of his, written in the years of maturity, as advice from the chorus to the audience:

> Let the wise and philosophic choose me for my wisdom's sake, Those who joy in mirth and laughter choose me for the jests I make.[15]

All that we have said above may be reduced to the well-known aphorism, that the old masters cannot be admired except through modern eyes. Actors no longer inter-

pret Shakespeare in Burbage's wig, nor maestros conduct
Wagner with Liszt's baton. Plato had his way of understanding Aristophanes; Racine, Fielding, or Goethe had
theirs; and the Blacks, who years ago performed *Lysistrata*
in jitterbug rhythms, had theirs too.[16]

For those of us, however, who either were born in
Greece or have lived there, it is obviously a matter of
greater importance. It involves emotions and reflexes connected with everyday life. For a foreign spectator the heroes of Aristophanes are more or less strangers. For those
who have lived in the poet's own land, they are the still
familiar Acharnians, Megarians, or Spartans; his Ilissus
and his Hymettus are still referred to in modern songs; we
see his Propylaea every day; we cross the district where his
frogs croaked to go home; children fly their kites on the
Pnyx. And on the inner slopes of the Dionysiac Theatre,
which owes its existence to the rites of fertility, pregnant
women climb to kiss the Blessed Virgin of the Cave,
whose speciality is to ease childbirth. Under the same sky
which had listened to its ancient flutes, other musical
sounds were heard, and the landscape which served as
background to the *kordax* saw other dances expressing
human joy. When an Aristophanic reveler (*Assembly of
Women,* 1165) says to another: "Move your feet in the
Cretan manner!" what shall we do today? Invent a nonexistent dance, fictitiously "archaic"? Or substitute for it the
vehement dance of the Cretan countryside, a living dance
much beloved by modern audiences? There is another
dance, too, probably of Byzantine origin, which has taken
deep root in the soul of the Greek people: the *khassapikos*
or butchers' dance (named so, either because it was ini-
tially danced by butchers or because its songs usually linger on knives and the slaughter of unfaithful women). In
any case, it is danced by men in the taverns, when they
are alone and they curse the women who have betrayed

them. In *Lysistrata,* when wives and mistresses go on a lovestrike, the angry men carry in logs to burn them, while singing and dancing their indignation with murderous pathos (ll. 256–318). We find ourselves at once in the climate of a familiar *khassapikos,* whose creator is none other than the ancient Athenian poet, still living among us.

These minor and, perhaps, too specific details are among the many which illuminate our approach to Aristophanes. We should always look upon his comic hero as our living contemporary. His home is next to ours; he drinks at the same taverns as we do; he has the same troubles with the Government or the Establishment as we have; he despairs of his wife's over-efficiency or his son's inefficiency, more or less as we do; and enjoys the company of pretty dancing girls, as, perhaps, we ought to do. The *homo aristophanicus* suffers deeply for the afflictions and miseries of his fellow human beings. And yet he laughs no end at their madness and stupidity. His sobs will always be followed by laughing hiccups.

The present book would not call itself *The Living Aristophanes* if the comic poet's immortality were merely based on theorems still to be proved by theatrical experience. I feel a certain pride for having been the first man to bring Aristophanes back to the Epidaurus Theatre—the best preserved monument of ancient dramatic culture—after his long exile of, presumably, more than two thousand years. That happened in the late Fifties; and ever since then he has remained magnificently alive and active, giving a token of his talent every summer and enjoying, *ex equo* with the tragic poets, an immense popularity. In approaching Aristophanes' work, I have used the methods and moods described in these pages. I did not dream of performances inspired by archaeological manuals, but by the very air of our times. My purpose was not so much to present an artificial revival, as to prove a natural survival.

We had always admired the Praxiteles' *Hermes* at Olympia for its striking liveliness and art, without arguing as to what the god was originally holding in his now missing hands. In the same way both artists and audiences let ourselves be conquered by Aristophanes' charm, forgetting our semi-ignorance at the theatre's checkroom. Thus, pure and primitive, we became one with the tumultuous crowd of Peloponnesian peasants who packed the Epidaurus Theatre, bringing laughter back to the ancient dramatic shrine after so many centuries. The comedies of Aristophanes made us see and feel the ancient Greeks as real human beings vibrating with life. They made us realize that the ruined theatres were once temples, not of an awe-inspiring religion only, but also of a warm and merry-making faith.

Antiquities reveal their natural grandeur when trees keep growing around them and ants dig their nests by the old stones. Likewise, when living men sob or laugh in the ancient theatres, the Greek drama prodigiously comes to life.

Chapter I

His Childhood and Inheritance

*O Beloved city of Cecrops, native-born
Attica! . . .*

Aristophanes, *The Farmers,* Fr. 110

Aristophanes was born in Athens, in the very heart of the ancient city below the Acropolis rock. His father was a certain Philip, whom some authors suppose Athenian, others, a native of Rhodes or Aegina, and yet some others, Egyptian.[1] The only positive conclusion that we can draw from these rumors is that Philip did not belong to any illustrious family and that he was a rather obscure member of the middle classes. Furthermore, there is no contemporary information or even gossip about Aristophanes' close relatives, though there is much about Euripides' mother, Aeschylus' brother, or Socrates' wife.

One source gives his mother's name as Zenodora,[2] but modern scholars disagree as to when exactly she brought him into this world. Opinions as to the date of his birth vary from 452 to 444 B.C. It is beyond doubt, however, that our comic poet was born in the very middle of the fifth century, at the time when Pericles was at the height of his power and Athens held supremacy over all Greek city-states. So we shall accept 450 B.C. as the year of his birth—the very middle, that is, of the classic era of Greek arts and letters—historically, the most plausible of all.[3]

The inter-bellum period 470–430 B.C. is popularly known as the Golden Age of Greece. Democracy was flourishing and Peace—one day to become Aristophanes' nostalgic dream—was still something real and solid. Athenians and Spartans were on friendly terms and actually signed a thirty-year treaty (446 B.C.). On the other hand, peace was officially established between the Greeks and their former enemies of Marathon and Salamis (448 B.C.). In such carefree and optimistic days, in which political tolerance was solid and artists could express themselves freely, our comic poet first rose to his feet.

Anyone who is unfamiliar with Aristophanes' works —where the seamy side of classical life as well as its brilliance are laid bare—will be inclined to behold this era in the idealized colors of academic prints glorifying antiquity. Let us view the year 450 B.C. and see what was happening. The Acropolis monuments were under construction and the youthful Socrates was frequenting the Agora. It was not too long since that masterpiece of dramatic art, the *Oresteia* of Aeschylus, had been performed in the wooden theatre of Dionysus. A forty-five-year-old poet, Sophocles, was the uncontested playwright of the day, and a younger one, Euripides, was trying to promote his avant-garde plays. The most brilliant personality at literary reunions was the philosopher Anaxagoras; his theory that intelligence is the highest force governing man was a topic of discussion in literary circles. Another distinguished figure was the sophist Protagoras, who had come from Thrace and had opened a school. He was suspected by conservative Athenians to be an atheist, who, moreover, taught—as teachers should not—for money. Herodotus also had stopped over in the "violet city" to relax from his travels around the world. He was planning to write a history book about the Persian Wars, where, for the first time, the description of past events would not be

in poetry, but in prose. Speaking of poetry, the heroic el-
egies of Simonides had already passed down from the warriors of Marathon to their children, along with other reminiscences of that glorious age. In painting, perspective
had been used for the first time by Polygnotus in his
mythological murals of the Poecile Stoa in the Agora. Statues like the *Discus Thrower* of Myron and the *Spear Car-
rier* of Polyclitus were being created; and sculpture both
in bronze and in marble was a flourishing art.[4]

These are but glimpses of that brilliant world, rich in
immortal names, laurel crowns, victorious anthems, and
Greek "profiles."

If, however, behind this lifeless exhibition, this solemn mortuary poster, we discern the living and breathing
world—the blue or brown eyes of real people, their various accents and idioms, their dusty sandals and untidy
clothes, their sweating efforts to climb up to the Pnyx for
the turbulent People's Assembly, their swearing and spit-
ting, the dirty tricks which robbed the great Sophocles of
a victory and gave it to the inferior Philocles,[5] the riotous
quarrels of the political parties, the bargainings at the
Agora, the flies buzzing around the banquets, the mistakes
Pericles made, or the insults Phidias heard on account of
his public buildings [6]—if we see this world not only as an
idealized or immortal one, but as a human one as well, vibrating with everyday life, then we shall no longer admire it merely out of academic duty. We shall embrace it
wholeheartedly and love the Greeks, not because all of
them were wise and virtuous geniuses, but because they
had faults and weaknesses and vices and spoke of them
daringly to each other. More than anything else, the
works of Aristophanes make us aware of the true Greek
world. He publicly denounced and ruthlessly condemned
his countrymen only because he loved them.

Now let us imagine that a few years have passed since

the middle of the glorious century and that the son of Philip and Zenodora is already a schoolboy. Let us accompany him to school and follow some of his classes.

In school, Aristophanes became first of all acquainted with Homer and Hesiod.[7] These two already ancient poets were the very foundations of elementary education. From their books students learned to read, to spell, and to emulate the physical and spiritual virtues which form the perfect man. They learned, however, the opposite too. They learned to see gods, heroes, and mythological monsters in their private lives, like simple people full of whims and shortcomings, which sometimes made them appear more ridiculous than sublime. The Cyclops Polyphemus, for instance, ceased to be a terrifying superman as soon as Odysseus defeated him by a clever human trick. At once, mythology would turn into farce, to make Aristophanes and his schoolmates laugh. They also laughed at Circe's island, where the witch changed men into pigs. They laughed at the old men of Troy devouring Helen with their eyes. Their youthful frankness would also comment humorously on the illegal union of Ares and Aphrodite, trapped together in Hephaestus' nets.[8]

Aristophanes and his fellow pupils had not been to the theatre as yet. They had not seen a tragedy by Sophocles, a comedy by Magnes, or a satyr-play by the Pratinas family.[9] We find many contrasting opinions about the age when children first began to watch performances at the Dionysiac festivals. At any rate, they must not have been very young.[10] In their fertile brains, however, mythological characters had already taken their final forms, not their solemn forms only, but also their ludicrous ones. The frightened Dionysus of the *Iliad* (VI, 130 f.) who jumps into the sea to save his life is a model for the trembling Dionysus whom we shall meet in the *Frogs*. In the great epic poet, Aristophanes had found a ready-made

comic vision of the world. Even before becoming familiar
with the theatre of his own day, he could clearly see Polyphemus, Heracles, Thersites, and many others, as accomplished comedy characters.

Hesiod's *Works and Days* provided a lesson in realism. It was the first Greek book to abandon heroic
legends to study human beings, namely the ploughmen
with their everyday cares. Perhaps this poetic narrative
gave Aristophanes his first image of the poor old peasants of Attica, who some day will populate his comedies,
the coal-traders, the vine-planters, the farmers, the shep-
herds, the teamsters—people like Dicaeopolis, Trygaeus,
Chremylus—all the humble and heroic, cunning and
penniless rustics, lost in the jungle of the city and overwhelmed by its social marvels and its political monsters.
Hesiod's cosmological vision will also be reproduced,
years later, in the *Birds*,[11] and some of his maledictions
against women will be certainly remembered by the future author of the *Lysistrata*.

It is most likely that students were also supposed to
learn the *Fables* of Aesop, the slave from Asia, that Socrates will recall in his death-cell (Plato's *Phaedo*). The heroes of these tales are mostly animals, and we can well
imagine Aristophanes reciting with zest the famous lines
about "the birds who wanted to elect a king." At any rate,
the tale will be still alive in his brain, no doubt, when he
will sit down to write his own comedy on birds. Besides,
in three other of his comedies he will recall the Aesopian
fable of the beetle and the eagle.[12]

Music and singing must also have taken up a large
part of the school program. The students were taught how
to play the lyre and the flute and how to sing in *choros*.
These choral songs gave the young Aristophanes his first
feeling for group-singing, which was the fundamental aesthetic convention of theatrical art in his days. We can also

trace in his works examples of all the types of lyric poetry, used for various special effects. The entrance-song, for instance, in the *Women at the Thesmophoria* (295 f.) is a *paean,* and the antistrophe (636 f.) in the *Lysistrata* the parody of a *parthenion,* to mention but two cases.

The most vital expression of choral song was the *dithyramb,* a Bacchic oratorio accompanied by dance, which came to Greece with the worship of Dionysus.[13] Originally, the unique theme of the dithyramb had been the life and sufferings of the god himself. And there was a popular belief that the name came from *di* (twice) and *thyra* (door), thus symbolizing the double birth of Dionysus from the womb of Semele and from the thigh of Zeus. Herodotus tells us that "Arion was the first man I know who wrote, named, and taught the dithyramb" (I, 23). That is, he taught the fifty dancers to form a circle and sing, crowned with flowers and ivy. In Athens, the dithyramb was first introduced by the musician Lassus during the sixth century, and after 509 B.C. it became one of the highlights in the Dionysiac festivals. Choruses of boys also took part, a proof that men learned choral singing from a very tender age.

Another form of choral poetry which Aristophanes was acquainted with at school was the *hyporchema.* Pickard-Cambridge believes that the chorus members were divided into two groups and half of them danced what the other half sang.[14] Examples of this technique can be detected in many Aristophanic comedies. We hardly need to enumerate, however, all the kinds of songs that were fashionable in those days, such as *odes, hymns, epithalamia* or *skolia.* With regard to the last mentioned, a scene in the *Wasps* describes how the Athenians used to improvise and sing these drinking-songs at their dinner parties (1222–48).

A great influence exercised on Aristophanes must

have been that of Archilochus; and, more generally, the songs of the *iambic* poets must have been a decisive revelation to the burgeoning satirist. Archilochus, born on the island of Paros in the seventh century B.C., was the inventor of invective poetry. His love affair with a girl and her father's refusal to bless their union mark the beginning of his furious satirical career. So poisonous were the songs he wrote about the girl's family, that, so the legend goes, father, daughter, and sisters hanged themselves for shame.[15]

Aristophanes at once accepted the rare gifts which the Parian writer had bestowed on Greek poetry, namely, his simple popular language, his art for lampooning real living people, as well as the *iambic trimeter,* the verse form which more than any other approached everyday conversation and was the best suited for dramatic dialogue.[16] Along with the mocking verses of Archilochus, Aristophanes came to know, no doubt, the jesting iambs of Semonides of Amorgos and of Hipponax, the choleric poet from Ephesus.[17] The latter was the first to show that the purpose of invective poetry was to purify the State: a doctrine that Aristophanes would always follow in his career of an "engaged" writer.

One wonders why the influence on Aristophanes of another early poet, Alcaeus, hasn't been sufficiently emphasized by scholars. The two of them present many analogies, not only as writers, but also as persons. They both cherished aristocratic—or, at least, conservative—points of view; they both hated demagogues and reacted unceremoniously to the leaders of their respective countries, pouring out their wrath in fiery verses; furthermore, they both paid the price of their temerity.[18] Aristophanes more than once refers to Alcaeus (*Birds,* 1410; *Thesmophoria,* 162). He also uses a verse of the old poet, written against the Lesbian tyrant Myrsilus, almost intact against his own political enemy, Cleon (*Wasps,* 1232). Later in his career,

when Cleon is killed, Aristophanes does not follow the admonition of Archilochus:

"We must not make fun of dead men!"

but, rather, the heartless challenge of Alcaeus:

"Now we must get drunk and rejoice,
for Myrsilus is dead." [19]

He does not, of course, celebrate the death of his opponent at a drinking party; but his theatrical intoxication
tolerates no respect for Cleon's memory.

We have no reason to imagine that Aristophanes attended one of the schools run by sophists. In those schools
—which in the *Clouds* he himself will name phrontesteria
—logic and political science were taught, as well as phys-
ics and astronomy; and discussions were held about all
sorts of important subjects, as, for instance, the orbit of
the sun or the habits of insects. Even if our comic poet
had attended one of them, however, he probably would
not have stayed there very long. The avant-garde teaching
of the sophists—who, one day, were to become his comic
target—could not have been in harmony with the young
reactionary's mentality.

His conservatism, characteristic of all the Attic comic
poets whose profession demanded that they be the critics
and not the eulogists of their times, may be due also in
part to Aristophanes' family environment. We must remember that the years of his childhood were the only
peaceful ones he ever knew. He must have often heard
those typical peacetime conversations where one sees
everything dismal and grim, and yet longs for it when another war breaks in. We may take the liberty to imagine
that Philip and his circle of friends—most of them as conservative, perhaps, as the old men whom we shall meet in
the Aristophanic plays—were against Pericles and his re-

forms, against the sophists and the "new learning," against Euripides and his dramatic extravagances—such as presenting the *Alcestis,* a light tragedy, instead of the traditional satyr-play.[20] Many of those elders had fought at Marathon or Salamis, and were nostalgic about the good old days overflowing with moral and heroic ideals. They admired Cimon, Simonides, Phrynichus, and, of course, Aeschylus. Soon the young Aristophanes began to admire Aeschylus too. Nevertheless, a certain pompous incomprehensibility remained in the back of his mind, even until his years of maturity, when he will serve as literary critic to the tragic patriarch.

In Aristophanes' young days, wages were so attractive that every Athenian wanted to become a senator or a judge or an official of any kind, in order to get payment. To fight this plethora, Pericles was obliged to issue an amendment to his law on wages. Henceforward, only genuine pure-blooded Athenians could be elected to public offices.[21] Did that new decree affect our poet's life in any way?

When we consider the many versions that we have of Aristophanes' nationality—also the charge of being an alien, brought against him by Cleon [22]—we automatically conjecture that perhaps there was, after all, a suspicion of foreign blood in Philip's line of descent. Possibly, he might have immigrated from another state to become a resident of Athens. On the other hand, we know that the family acquired a piece of land on Aegina.[23] This incident occurred about twenty years after Aristophanes' birth and five years before his first arraignment by Cleon. In the summer of 431, the Athenians drove the Aeginetans out of their island, on the pretext that they were friendly with Sparta. Following the evacuation of the island by its inhabitants, they divided the land by lot among Athenian families.[24] A few acres were then allotted to Aristophanes' father. And thereupon our confusion about the family's homeland begins.

It is not against reason to surmise that old Philip, embittered by Periclean Athens, settled in Aegina for good. The ancient *Life* of Aristophanes tells us that the poet, himself, spent most of his time on the island.[25] We are free, therefore, to imagine him living there part of the war years—as Kazandjakis will do during World War II—writing his comedies in the shadow of a fig tree by the sea. In his plays, he does not give us the slightest hint as to where his family came from. He refers to Aegina in three lines of the *Acharnians* (652–55). He declares that "the Spartans will try to conquer the island, in order to kidnap the most precious of poets"—that is, himself.[26] Some have accepted these verses as a genuine evidence of Aristophanes' birthplace; others have neglected them entirely. Mystery will always cover his origin, just as Homer's. It is, ultimately, of no importance. If a poet's home is the place where he writes, then let us call Aristophanes an Aeginetan. If a man's home is the place where he suffers, then let us call him an Athenian. In his old age, he will say: "Home is everywhere a man can have a good time" (*Plutus,* 1151).

If the maxim is true, then his real home was the theatre.

Chapter II

The Festivities of Dionysus

Dionysus who has nurtured me . . .
Aristophanes, *The Clouds,* 519

In Aristophanes' day theatrical activities were strictly connected with the celebrations honoring Dionysus. It was during the festivals dedicated to the god of the earth's fecundity that all satyr-plays, tragedies, and comedies were performed.

This coexistence of religion and entertainment in a single social phenomenon is by no means surprising. Even today, religious ceremonies are very often the major, if not the only, theatrical attractions of many communities. Church services, with the minister preaching and the congregation singing psalms; weddings, with their traditional dialogue between the priest and the marrying couple; funerals, with their homogeneity in dark costumes and sad expressions; liturgies re-enacting Christ's Passion the week before Easter, a custom which still survives in Catholic or Orthodox parishes—all are rituals of faith, which satisfy not only the religious feeling of men, but also their inborn need to be actors and audience.[1]

Among some peoples the phenomenon retains its original primitiveness; among others, it bears the stigmata of civilization. In certain parts of Africa or the Pacific Islands the natives become artists during the most crucial

23

moments of their communication with the divine powers. In those moments, choral singing and collective dancing, the mimetic arts and the poetry of exorcism, come into existence.[2] Similarly, chanting or singing in Christian churches—with its two opposed elements of choir and soloist—is, despite its somewhat artificial mechanism, equally theatrical. In both cases, we have the same spiritual union of people, the same participation in a communal rite, which is an organic necessity to almost every man.

In our time, of course, religious celebrations can only rarely be looked upon as achievements of art. The inherent artistic predisposition of each community will be the determining factor. There are occasions, however, especially in parts of the world not completely converted to western civilization, where religion is still able to produce poetic results. Moreover, in the ceremonies of primitive tribes we discover an important correlative of the Greek bacchanals, namely, the ability of the worshipers to become possessed by the divine spirit and to reach a culmination of physical and spiritual paroxysm.[3] This demoniac state differs but very slightly, I suppose, from the ancient Dionysiac *mania,* which got hold of the celebrants of Bacchus.[4]

The main difference between our religious ceremonies and the dramatic rituals of ancient Greece is that in those days the theatre had its special god, who was also the god of wine. This double responsibility of Dionysus was brought about, we are informed, by some kind of obscure historical evolution. According to the prevailing theory, much contested by modern scholarship,[5] the early Dionysiac festivities practiced by vine-planters gave birth to certain customs, which were molded little by little into laws of a specific art. We vaguely know that the word *tragedy* was derived from *tragos* (male goat), because the intoxicated worshipers of Dionysus used to wear goatskins when they danced about the streets or fields. Aristotle adds that tragedy rose from the *dithyramb* and comedy from the *phallic rites* (*Poetics,* IV, 12). Those singing-and-dancing ceremonies of pretheatrical times were, it seems, the most important liturgies related to Nature's and Man's fertility.

Besides the historical interpretation of Dionysus' two-fold capacity, however, there is a symbolic one too. The intoxicated person and the actor share one common characteristic—the transfiguration of their personalities. In both cases, the individual, unconsciously obeying his inner compulsions, abandons his natural or, at least, socially accepted identity and creates a new one, determined by emotional stress. Dionysiac inebriation and dramatic illusion were, in the Greek mind, almost the same thing.[6]

If now we consider the god's double function through that prism, his mythology becomes clearer to us. The transfigurations of Bacchus into lion, leopard, bull, goat, or snake, as well as the miraculous change of people bewitched by him into animals, plants, or stars, are, in poetic imagery, the distortion of reality provoked by drunkenness.[7] This symbolism comprises also the many aspects that an actor acquires when, being no more himself, he becomes a hero, a titan, a god, or a stupid slave, remaining under the spell of Dionysus and re-enacting the god's legendary transformations.

The actor, however, is only one of the two basic compounds of theatrical alchemy; the other is the public. And the public is also included in the same Dionysiac symbolism because of the spiritual change which the ideal spectator undergoes during an ideal dramatic performance. The man who goes into the theatre is not the same as the one who comes out of it. The message of the play and the identification of the spectator with the hero have transfigured the former's personality.

One more interpretation of the god's metamorphoses

could be suggested. This one concerns the various aspects which the art of the theatre itself takes during its historical development. It is always changing, looking for new ways of expression and craving an ever-renewed fascination over the human masses. As it happened to its guardian-god in his earthly wanderings, the art of the theatre is saved through perpetual transfiguration and immortalized through death and rebirth.

We shall not attempt to explore the labyrinths of Dionysiac mythology. Its innumerable versions vary from age to age and from place to place, and, though they often meet, they never fully coincide. In some legends, Bacchus inherits the characteristics of the Egyptian Osiris, in others, those of the Phrygian Sabazios, in still others he becomes the Triptolemus or the Iacchus of the Eleusinian mysteries.[8] In most, he appears as one of the youngest divinities of Greek religion. Older poets, as Homer and Hesiod, are scarcely concerned with him, and Herodotus tells us that the Greeks invented him much later than the other gods (II, 52).

In Aristophanes' mind, however, the Bacchic religion is already an old one. He knows the various surnames that the god was given, according to his many adventures and activities, and he uses most of them in his comedies. He shows great respect for Dionysus' traditional attributes whenever he happens to reproduce his rites on the stage. He does not seem to adhere to a particular one among the numerous legends. As a poet, he likes them all, because he finds in all the same highly suggestive personification of Nature. Needless to say that nowhere, not even in the *Frogs* where Dionysus is his comic hero, does he seem to doubt the god's omnipotence over the art of the theatre; and his odes to Bacchus often reach an almost Aeschylean exaltation.[9]

The cult of Dionysus had been celebrated of old, it

seems, with dances, disguises, lyrical trances, and jocular turmoil. A procession following the phallus-pole, symbolizing masculine fertility, was the festivity's main event.[10] Licentious jokes and suggestive gesticulations became more and more aggressive as the day passed, and by sunset drunkenness merged all the worshipers into a collective orgy. As in Christian times fasting and penitence express our spiritual participation in Jesus' life of abnegation, so, in pagan days, the excessive satisfaction of all the senses was man's spiritual participation in the stimulating vigor of Dionysus.

Aristophanes knew better than we do, of course, the particular meaning of each costume, mask, or other object used in ritualistic activities and what was actually symbolized by all those beards, horns, sheepskins, feathers, horsetails, or goatfeet, which we still see in abundance on ancient vases. In addition, he may have known when and how the reveling processions of the old festivities were split in two, the loftier ones developing into the dithyramb, the direct ancestor of tragedy, and the earthier ones becoming the *komos,* which engendered comedy. When, a hundred years later, Aristotle will analyze this evolution (*Poetics,* IV, 12), he will not proclaim a discovery of his own; he will merely attest, in scientific style, something well known since Aristophanes' boyhood days, when the *komos* still survived as part of the official festivals.

In the development of both tragedy and comedy, we notice the same gradual rise in importance of the individual actor over the chorus. Among the throng of revelers, the one most talented in singing, dancing, or improvising words and tunes was eventually promoted to the role of soloist. This newborn artist, known as the *exarchon,* is the forefather of all actors.[11]

At this stage of theatrical prehistory, when drama was gradually taking shape in the womb of religious revelry, a new element appeared as a complement to singing and dancing—that of mimicry. The celebrants, no longer satisfied with an abstract commemoration of the Bacchic sagas, wished to see them animated by descriptive movement and re-created emotion. The *exarchon* incarnated thereafter the god himself, while the group represented the maenads, satyrs, and other bacchantes of his company. At that precise moment, when the first individual was raised above the crowd to imitate action and emotion, the art of the theatre was born.

The young intellectuals of 430 B.C. must have known that representational ceremonies of that kind had come from Egypt and had been adopted by the Greeks (Herodotus, II, 48–65). Today, however, we are in a better position to know that fifteen centuries earlier, when not even Homer was born, the Egyptians were already producing religious pageants about the death and resurrection of Osiris.[12]

Contrary to our present custom, when open-air festivals function uniquely in summer, the ancient Greeks never performed their dramas in that period of the year. The Divine Fertilizer had to be celebrated during the months when the earth was preparing her new vegetation. There is also a somewhat plainer explanation. The dates of the various Greek festivities should not coincide, and there was a great number of them, dedicated to almost all of the Olympians, which covered the warm season from April to November. Obviously enough, Dionysus, being the youngest god, had to be satisfied with the remaining months. Still, our Greek ancestors, being astute in their weather predictions, had scheduled their theatrical festivals on dates usually favored by atmospheric conditions; and there is no hint whatsoever to prove that they were ever contradicted by the sun or the moon.

On the other hand, we must not forget that present-day open-air performances are given, as a rule, in the evening, whereas the ancient Athenians, having no other light source than the sun, performed from dawn to twilight. That is why the winter months were better suited to their purpose. Anyone who has lived in Greece during the summer months knows that to attend a day-time theatrical séance under the blazing sun is humanly impossible.

Four major Dionysiac festivals are mentioned as being celebrated in the fifth century.[13] The season opened in December with the Rural Dionysia that seem to have been only secondary in importance, as far as drama was concerned. Nonetheless, all the theatres that emerged in the Greek countryside owed their existence to these celebrations. Even if dramatic competitions of original plays were not held, some theatrical activities must have been connected with them. The Epidaurus theatre, for instance, which in present-day festivals is packed with country folks as well as tourists from all over the world, gives us a lively and convincing idea of the "provincial" theatrical entertainments of those times.[14]

Of all the descriptions that we possess about this Dionysiac country-fair, the one that Aristophanes has left us is by far the most vivid. In a sequence of the *Acharnians* (237–79), he gives us a miniature performance of the festival itself. A young girl, called *kanoephoros* or basket-holder, opens the procession, carrying offerings to the god. The *phallophoroi* or phallus-carriers follow, holding their big pole which they stick into the earth.[15] Food is then prepared for everybody, the sacrifice takes place, and when the banquet is over all the men sing the traditional phallic song—while women and children sit aside—inviting the god to come and drink with them. When his divine presence has been assured, they let themselves go into a more or less obscene carousal, during which, according to Aristophanes, stout serving-maids are always

the male celebrants' target. The comic poet's description
is, of course, a pastiche of the traditional ritual. Parody,
however, is never based on anything but reality.

Before we talk about the Lenaea, second in order
among the year's bacchic celebrations, let us get acquainted with the older festival of the Anthesteria, which
lasted three days at the end of February.

On the first day the jars were opened and the wine
tasted. On the second all the participants devoted themselves to absorbing wine. There was even a drinking competition, the winner of which was offered as a prize . . .
more wine! A replica of this game can be found in the
Acharnians (1000 f.) where Dicaeopolis is acclaimed as the
winner. And in the *Frogs* (218–19) the chorus whimsically
recalls these libations, as they were enjoyed in times of
peace. On this day a special procession may have taken
place—the statue of Dionysus sailed, or rather say rolled,
around the town in a boat on wheels all covered with vine
leaves and grapes.[16] The last day was a kind of All Souls,
devoted to the dead, whose spirits were supposed to fly
around. Notwithstanding this mournful mood, an allegorical wedding took place, uniting Dionysus and the wife of
the archon basileus. This pageant commemorated the
union of Athens and viticulture.[17] It is also probable that
a competition between comic actors was held, which led
to the selection of those who would perform, a month
later, at the Great Dionysia.[18] The only first-hand description that we have of the Anthesteria, however, is the afore-
mentioned Aristophanic one in the *Acharnians*. All other
data are confused and very often contradictory.

The Lenaea was celebrated in January, when the
weather did not encourage sea-travel and the presence of
foreigners was rare. The festival was, consequently, a local
Athenian affair.[19] We must bear in mind, when dealing
with Aristophanes' playwriting career, that to produce a

play at this festival was an achievement of less prestige than to appear at the City Dionysia. Still, the Lenaea offered a special advantage to comic poets—they could be more spontaneous and more outspoken with their fellow Athenians. "No foreigners are present today," Aristophanes will tell his Lenaean audience, "so let us wash our dirty linen in public!" (*Acharnians*, 502–8).

Pericles introduced comic competitions at the Lenaea in 442 B.C., most likely to satisfy the increasing demand for that kind of entertainment.[20] He probably had another reason too. Plays challenging or damaging to the State's reputation—or his own—would be presented thereafter in this local festival devoid of international repercussions.

Originally, five comic poets participated, each with one play. Later, owing to the financial restrictions imposed by the war, the number of comic productions was reduced to three.[21]

Because of their inferior status, the Lenaea were not presided over by the archon eponymos, but the archon basileus. They too included processions, sacrifices, songs, dances, and invocations, but their chief importance lay in the creation of new plays, especially comedies. Tragedy was later added to the schedule, but it never challenged comedy's predominance in this particular festival; only two tragic poets competed, each with two tragedies and no satyr play. There, in 416 B.C., Agathon will win his first victory and celebrate it with a literary party, the famous symposium that Plato will describe. There is no direct information, only presumptions, as to the theatrical building where the Lenaean productions were held, though the most reasonable is to suppose that there was but one official theatre in Athens, that of Dionysus below the Acropolis. Plays were performed only twice a year, covering not more than five or six days altogether; so, why would there be a need for a second theatre? Besides, Aristophanes, as well as the tragic poets, use the same stage-technique regardless of the occasion they are writing for.

The most spectacular and intellectually significant among Athenian festivals were the Great or City Dionysia, which, presumably, Pisistratus had inaugurated in the sixth century.[22] They were celebrated in the early spring, during the last week of March or the first of April. With them, the annual celebrations of Bacchus came to a climax and to an end.

The City Dionysia were a nation-wide festival and attracted visitors from everywhere. Those who took part, as poets, actors, chorus masters, or producers, would at once become famous throughout the civilized world. They were for drama what the Olympic Games were for athletics, or the Pythian for music: the official center of a special cult.

The sacred event commemorated by that important festival was the arrival of the wine god in Athens. Opinions varying, it is not easy to trace the mythical itinerary of Dionysus—and, consequently, that of the viticulture— from the god's uncertain birthplace to Greece. His legendary wanderings carry him from Libya to India and from Phrygia to the island of Naxos, with memorable intermediate stops at Thrace, Thebes, and elsewhere. It is more or less agreed that the vine and its divine protector were born and bred on Mount Nyssa; but the mountain bearing that name has often traveled from Africa to Greece and from Greece to Asia and back again. We ignore, therefore, what the exact nationality of Dionysus was before he adopted the Greek one.[23]

According to one cycle, toward the end of his wanderings, the god decided to conquer Athens. The inhabitants, however, would not let him in. The only person to welcome him was a certain Icarius, who may have been, in reality, the first vintner or the first wine-trader in Attica.

He gave him hospitality and was rewarded thereof with the secret recipe for wine-making. The story goes that when the Athenians tasted the beverage, they went mad and killed Icarius.[24] The next man to help Dionysus enter the city, disregarding the superstitious hostility of the natives, was Pegasus, from the village of Eleutherae on Mount Cithaeron; but again the people of Athens would not allow him in. In the end, the wine god made his triumphant entrance with the help of a Delphian oracle. Athens was stricken by disease, and Apollo advised the inhabitants to use wine as a remedy. So they promptly agreed to swallow the malignant potion only for the sake of their health; and, having recovered, they glorified Dionysus ever after.[25]

On the morning of the eighth day of the month Elaphebolion, before sunrise, the festival began with an official procession of people carrying the wooden statue of Bacchus out of the city, along the road to Eleutherae. The day's second event was the *proagon,* or literary press conference, as we would probably call it today. The dramatists selected to take part in that year's competition appeared in front of the public, surrounded by their actors and dancers, and made a speech. Possibly excerpts of the plays were also read.[26]

In the same evening, a solemn march of citizens and foreigners holding lighted torches and waving the official Dionysus emblem of green pine-cones, called *thyrsus,* re-enacted the god's legendary arrival in the city. They accompanied his statue from the Eleutherae road to his theatre in Athens. And there, in his own home, Bacchus the "ivy-maned king" remained standing, like a spectator who could not find an available seat, to watch patiently the performance of fifteen plays.

The following day a ceremonial array of worshipers led a garlanded bull before the god's temple for sacrifice.

A panorama of multicolored costumes, golden diadems, ivy crowns, shining spears, and swaying *thyrsi* moved along the Acropolis slopes to Bacchus' temple adjoining the theatre. As was the custom in many festivals, girls of the best Athenian families opened the procession, holding baskets, pitchers, basins, and other paraphernalia for libations and offerings. Songs and chants were heard throughout the march.

After a break at midday for food and drink, the revelers attended the dithyramb contest, in which about five hundred dancer-singers of all ages took part. By sunset, the festival was ripe for its most special demonstration: the *komos.* The worshipers, abandoning their heavenly exaltation, came back to earth. Throwing away official costumes, they dressed up in every imaginable kind of droll or weird disguise. They revived, each one guided by his personal whim, the tradition of the primitive *komos,* which was the protoplasm of comedy.

We are visually familiar with that antique carnival, thanks to many well-preserved vase-paintings, where we see a crazy host of masqueraders with bird-feathers and cockscombs, of men disguised as horses, of warriors riding on dolphins and so forth.[27] From these pictures we also get the right feeling about the strangely allegorical choruses used by the poets of Athenian Comedy even before Aristophanes' debut: such, for instance, as the *Beasts* and the *Birds* of Crates, the *Goats* of Cratinus or the *Satyrs* of Ecphantides.[28]

With the *komos* the festival's second day ended and everybody, or nearly everybody, went to bed exhausted. On the morning after, the dramatic competition began. It lasted three days and constituted the principal feature of the whole program.

At dawn, officials known as the *peristiarchi* purified the theatre-area by killing a young pig and spilling its blood around. Then the order in which the plays would appear was decided by lot. The City Dionysia was primarily a festival of tragedy and so three days were devoted to it; three poets participated and each had a day for himself. In the case of comedy, the time of the performances was more vague. Some scholars believe that the comic plays were shown in the afternoons, following the tragic performances; others think that a fourth day was scheduled for them. Both theories are satisfactory, though both are sometimes contradicted by Aristophanes, who likes to be very precise about time in his plays. As no artificial lighting was used, theatrical time and real time should, despite dramatic convention, correspond to a certain extent. So when he speaks of dawn or dusk or brings in choruses with lighted torches, he only makes the riddle of the performances' time more difficult to solve.[29]

The three tragedies, presented by each poet, were usually followed by a satyr-play, a dramatic form which flourished in the first decades of the fifth century. In the period of Phrynichus, Choerilus, or Aeschylus, the three tragedies and the satyr-play belonged to the same legend and told one single story. Sophocles, according to the *Suda,* a tenth-century lexicon, was the first to liberate the four plays from the bonds of mythological unity. Each play became, thereafter, independent. Finally, the last stroke came when Euripides broke with the tradition completely by replacing the satyr-play with a light tragedy, the *Alcestis* and the *Helen* being typical examples. He was, in that respect, the originator of a dramatic genre, which in later years was destined to become famous as sentimental comedy or bourgeois drama: in other words, a new play-form that is neither tragedy nor comedy.

Tragic competitions had started in 534 B.C., when Thespis, the semilegendary forefather of all tragic poets and actors, won the first prize: a goat and a basket of figs (later, the ivy crown was established as the emblem of dramatic victory). Twenty-five years later, *dithyramb* was added to the program, and, in still later times, comedy. The first comic victory was won in 486 B.C. by Chionides.[30]

The two remaining days of the City Dionysia were less entertaining and, consequently, more relaxing. The Pandia [31] on the sixth day was a religious ceremony of purification and absolution. On the seventh, a great convention of all the citizens was held in the theatre, where accusations were brought and penalties inflicted upon all those who had misbehaved during the festival. The Athenians had accepted the worship of Bacchus, but had subdued—almost domesticated—his pagan orgies. In Pericles' civilized years, the god had lost his primitive animosity by which he savagely dismembered Lycurguses and Pentheuses.[32] He had learned to carouse and to enjoy his drinking mania only when human laws allowed him to.

Was not this, after all, the ultimate social purpose of the Dionysiac festivals: to provide an organized and controlled outlet for man's primitive impulses? By instituting on religious pretexts a well-scheduled orgy, the state let men run wild in the streets and fields, free to masquerade, to get drunk, to make love, to exhaust their muscles in dance and their vocal chords in song, in other words, to spend all their resources of energy—lust or madness—during those fixed days, so that during the rest of the year they could calmly and patiently attend to their daily work. Dionysiac festivals were an indispensable emergency exit to man's primitive urges; they were also a counterbalance to the exasperating dullness of his everyday life. This, in spite of its aura of poetic mysticism, did not differ much from our modern holiday systems, when, in a similar way, people try to get rid of the year's monotony. Today, as in ancient times, men satisfy their animal-like

cravings and their god-like aspirations on officially scheduled days, so as to resign themselves in the long months to
come to their simple human destiny.

Being part of such holidays and existing only in rela-
tion to them, the Greek Theatre had to reach as high as
man's physical and mental paroxysm; it had to be the flow
rather than the ebb of the general festivity. That is why
tragedy dealt with exceptional men and women, capable
of superhuman passions. Conflicts between such characters
were strenuous and relentless, like the clash between the
very elements of nature. Their *moira* or destiny of doom,
overburdened by incest, revenge, suicide, matricide, and
physical torture, shook its audience through pity and fear.
The revelers, enraptured as they were by the orgy, would
have been totally unable to respond to any emotional vi-
bration tuned in a minor key.

Comedy's purpose, on the other hand, was to project
a similar superhuman exaggeration of the laughable side
of life. Jokes had to be solid and huge, almost primitive in
their absolute lack of refinement. Grotesque politicians,
delirious intellectuals, antediluvian policemen, and Me-
gatherian generals had to be its favorite targets, as well as
Herculean men or Omphalian women [33] and other such
familiar monsters of everyday life. In the stage action
there ought to be plenty of jumping, running, rambling,
beating, kicking; plenty of uninhibited sexual gestures or
postures, plenty of drinking, eating, and blissfully displaying the consequences of digestion. The theatre air had to
be filled with laughs, screams, wails, animal voices, and incongruous dialects. All the peculiarities of the human
fauna had to be enormously magnified, to match with the
gaping and grimacing theatrical masks. They should be
overstretched and ghoulishly real, like the long phantom-
like shadows which the Athenian sunset cast on the orchestra.

Chapter III

Attic Comedy

Comedy was produced by democracy as antidote to its own overdose of liberty.
Werner Jaeger, *Paideia* (p. 364).

At eighteen or so, Aristophanes finished school and was registered as an Athenian citizen. This new identity entailed two serious privileges: to vote and to go to the war.[1]

We know nothing about his military activities; but if he was born, as we have assumed, around 450 B.C., the outbreak of the Peloponnesian War (431 B.C.) almost coincides with the beginning of his career (427 B.C.), and not until his late forties shall he enjoy peace again. Nevertheless, it is very probable that he would never have become so successful a dramatist had he not been at grips during most of his lifetime with that infamous war. His ancient biographer says that he was still an adolescent when he presented his first play.[2]

At the outbreak of the war, the most popular authors of comedy were Cratinus and Crates, Telecleides and Pherecrates; perhaps also old Magnes and Ecphantides were still alive.[3] What we deduce, however, from Aristophanes' works is that he did not simply attend contemporary performances. He must have read all the comedies previously produced and absorbed any information he could get from his elders concerning the origins of the comic art. His knowledge was not only vaster than ours, but must have exceeded that of Aristotle who, a hundred years later, made this extraordinary confession: "Comedy, for lack of study, has passed out of our knowledge . . . And we do not know who was the first to create characters and dialogues or to establish the number of actors" (*Poetics*, V, 2, 3).

As an Athenian, Aristophanes adhered, no doubt, to the theory that the word comedy derived from *komos* (revelry), and not from *kome* (town), as the Dorians of Greece and those of Sicily asserted. According to the Dorian point of view, comedians were so called because originally they used to stroll in small towns. A third explanation might be also suggested: that comedy derived from *koma* (sleep), not because it sometimes sends its audience to sleep, but because originally it had the form of a nocturnal serenade, sung in the streets when the town was sleeping.

The origin of the name, however, is not half as important as the origin of the art itself. And in that respect the Dorians had some paternal rights, because the first attempts toward a comic theatre were made on Dorian soil and in the Doric dialect. That occurred, primarily, in four cities: Sparta, Corinth, Megara, and Syracuse.

The Spartan pioneering in comedy is, historically speaking, the most uncertain of the four. The first actors made their appearance probably in the seventh century, during the days of Terpander (fl. 670 B.C.) or Alcman (fl. 630 B.C.) and the brief boom of Laconian arts. They were called *deikelistai* and belonged, we may well suppose, to groups of local mountebanks who used mimicry, improvised speech, and a rustic kind of humor. Dorian humor was never much appreciated by the more sophisticated Ionians or Aeolians, and the Athenian playwrights refer to it in terms of contempt.[4]

A similar theatrical activity must have taken place in Corinth, during the years which succeeded those of the great tyrants (ca. 580 B.C.). Here we have an important source: the Corinthian ceramics of the sixth century, which display various farcical characters. As likely as not, the incongruous masks, as well as the padded costumes with the phallus attached, made their first appearance in those primitive shows.[5]

Among the early dramas of the pre-Athenian period the most famous was that of Megara. They were always called dramas, and not comedies, because the latter word was forever connected with the higher genre of Attic Comedy. Megarian drama or farce was still active, we may suppose, during Aristophanes' days, because he and his fellow playwrights often use the adjective *Megarian* for vulgar or insipid humor. Strolling players of Megara used to visit Athens, perhaps, from time to time to perform; and the situation might have been analogous to one of more recent times, when Molière's company played next door to the slapstick Comédie Italienne. We notice that in both cases the highbrow school exploited to its great advantage the comic inventions of the lowbrow. Aristophanes himself owes the Dorian farce a great deal, in spite of his declarations that he always tried to avoid "laughter stolen from Megara" (*Wasps,* 57).

Not a single line has come to us from the drama practiced in Sparta, Corinth, or Megara, not even by third or fourth hand. We only know that the actors "imitated a thief . . . or a foreign doctor," using common language, jumping and kicking . . .[6] We are inclined to suppose, therefore, that plays were performed unwritten, based on a very rudimentary draft of a plot, which left almost everything to the off-hand perspicuity of the actors—a method still used today by many night-club or television comedians.

Contrary to the "orphan" plays of the mother country, those of Magna Graecia had famous fathers. Syracuse, especially, produced written drama, much admired by the ancient Greek world. The most famous among Sicilian playwrights was Epicharmus, an immigrant from the island of Cos, who lived between the sixth and fifth centuries and probably died about the time when Aristophanes was born. Because of the fact that the Hyblaean Megara was his adopted city, the Megarians of Greece prided themselves on being the inventors of comedy.[7]

Epicharmus wrote two kinds of plays—mythological allegories and contemporary comedies "of manners." We possess many titles and fragments of his works. He did for the Dorian farce what many centuries later Carlo Gozzi will do for the Italian. He took the established comedy types—the drunkard, the cunning slave, the soldier, the grumbling old man—and adjusted them to well-organized plots and elaborate dialogues. He merged, in other words, the Dorian tradition of low theatre with the Ionian tradition of high literature. In many of his fragments we meet the gluttonous Heracles, the popular Dorian hero, who orders his meals in a thunderous voice, as well as other stock characters of mythology, such as Odysseus or the Cyclops. Elsewhere, Epicharmus appears more philosophic. His play *Logos and Logina* (where *Logina* signified perhaps feminine commonsense and *Logos,* the masculine) prophesied the method of allegorical personification, dear to all Attic playwrights and used by Aristophanes himself in the *Clouds.* Plato will raise the Sicilian playwright to Homer's level, by declaring those two poets as the originators of comic and tragic poetry, respectively.[8]

Sicilian dramaturgy, as elaborated by Epicharmus, differed radically from the Athenian. Its plays were neither as lyrical nor as spectacular. They lacked the Dionysiac flavor which linked comedy to public festivity. They hardly touched political topics or mentioned real people. They did not thrust violent messages before the public. And, most significant of all, the *comic chorus* was something they completely ignored. Whether they used music, singing, or dancing we do not know; but, even if they did, they gave little importance to those purely theatrical elements. After all, there is no information as to whether those dramas were performed or simply read, though the authors of this book adhere to the theory that the ultimate purpose of every literary work in dialogue form is to be performed.

The second famous author of the Doric colonies was Phormis (sixth–fifth centuries B.C.). Five of his farces, all of them taken from mythology, are mentioned in the *Suda*. Syracusan, as well, but younger than the other two, was Sophron (fifth century), much loved by Plato, whose name has always been connected with the mime-play (*mimos*), a form of short comedy that will reach its apogee under the Alexandrians and the Romans.[9] One cannot help suspecting a possible affinity between the work of this author and that of Aristophanes, because many titles of Sophron's plays remind us of the Attic poet's beloved feminine intrigues. We could mention as such the *Women at the Isthmia,* the *Seamstresses* and the *Women Who Say that they Will Make the Moon Rise.* Unfortunately, the dates of Sophron's career are too uncertain to help us come to any definite conclusions.

We have already suggested that Athenian Comedy was much indebted to these Dorian playmakers, both the famous Sicilians and the anonymous ones of Megara. Although they can be hailed as its forerunners, they were not its creators. As we have said, the comic art of Attica had its roots in the feasts of Dionysus and its chorus was nothing less than the stylized survival of the *komos* revel-

ers. Their symbolic presence in the performances affiliated Attic Comedy to the primitive religious mysteries
and put upon it the seal of nonrepresentational art. It was
thus liberated, as a Nietzsche might have said, from the
bonds of phenomenality. "When the poetic spirit gets into
action," Artaud writes, "it always leads to a boiling anarchy, to an essential dissolution of reality by poetry." [10]

Strange as it may seem, over the panorama of everyday reality offered by the comic poets of Athens, there lingered a charming spell of unreality. This poetic trait, this
predominance of the abstract, is what distinguishes Old
Attic Comedy from Dorian Drama. It also distinguishes it
from the Middle and the New Comedy, as well as from all
their descendants. In fact, the evolution of the world's
comic theatre begins with the primitive farce of the Dorians, proceeds almost directly to the Middle Comedy
of Athens and its contemporary *Phlyax*-plays of Magna
Graecia,[11] passes to Menander and to the authors of the
New Comedy, is taken over by Plautus and Terence,
and, through them, reaches Renaissance writers, such as
Ariosto or Machiavelli, to be successively exploited by
Shakespeare, Molière, Congreve, Goldoni, Marivaux, and
hundreds of others, down to the present-day drawing-bedroom comedy. It is a continuous flow, a natural process.
The Old Attic Comedy, on the contrary, does not belong
to that millennial tradition; it stands apart; its style cannot
be adjusted to the normal orbit of theatre history; it is a
mythological monster without parents and without seed;
it resembles the Satyrs and the Centaurs, the Sphinx and
the Gorgons, in being half human and half supernatural.

We have seen in the preceding chapter that comedy
was officially inaugurated in the City Dionysia in 486 B.C.
What remains a mystery is when it actually appeared in
Athens, because we cannot imagine that Athenians had
no light theatrical entertainment before that year. Theat-

rical history, in its effort to solve this riddle, created a robot with the name of Susarion. According to the *Parian marble,*[12] a comedy-chorus from Icaria, a village in Attica, was once led by a certain Susarion, "who received a basket of dry figs and a flask of wine." Upon this discovery, the scholastic machine got to work, collecting every possible bit of information relating to that name. That is how Susarion the Megarian suddenly emerged as the first producer of comedy in Athens. If there is any truth in all this, then we have the necessary bridge between Dorian farce imported from Megara and Athenian Comedy. All the same, we cannot help suspecting the authenticity of it all. It is rather difficult to explain why no Greek author or grammarian, between 570 B.C. (when Susarion supposedly flourished) and 270 B.C. (when the *Parian marble* was inscribed), mentions this comic writer. To accept that there once lived a comedian with that name is quite reasonable, but to consecrate this almost fictitious character as the initiator of the art of comedy is beyond reason.

The oldest known comic playwright, winner of the first contest in the City Dionysia, was Chionides. We have but a few fragments from his plays, the *Heroes* and the *Poor,* which do not teach us much about the style or ideas of their author.[13] Younger than Chionides but a pioneer too was Magnes, who had amassed eleven first victories. Aristophanes must have often heard of Magnes' past glory, because the old poet's downfall made a tremendous impression on him (*Knights,* 520–25). He may even have seen with his own eyes the playwright being hissed by a savage audience of younger Athenians, who mercilessly rejected the veteran poet's dried-up humor, thoroughly oblivious of his artful comedies and of the benefit of laughter that he had offered Athens for so many years. "He was expelled from the theatre," Aristophanes tells us, "because his invective was good no more." This compassion of the young man for his older fellow craftsman gives to the *parabasis* of the *Knights* an unexpectedly tragic taste. He also mentions there some of the most remarkable creations of the versatile Magnes: the songs of his *Barbitos-players,* the flutterings of his *Birds,* the Lydian melodies of his *Lydians,* the buzzing of his *Gnats* and the croakings of his *Frogs.* We cannot say to what degree, or whether at all Aristophanes himself was influenced by Magnes' plays, because we do not know them. It is obvious, however, that at least two of them he never forgot.

The third comedy writer of the old guard was Ecphantides. He is known primarily for an aphorism of his against Doric-made farce: "I'd be ashamed to write a Megarian drama!" We do not possess enough fragments of his plays to determine whether he stood by his word, or if he succumbed to Megarian humor, as did many of his fellow poets, Aristophanes included. The only known titles of Ecphantides' plays are the *Experiences* and the *Satyrs,* which won a prize in 445 B.C.

Now we come to Cratinus, to whom Aristophanes owes, though he will never admit it, the rules of his art and the orientation of his whole career. Cratinus was the true creator of the Old Attic Comedy as we know it; and, had Aristophanes never been born, the older poet would have, no doubt, been immortalized in his place by Alexandrian scholars, Byzantine monks, and Italian printers, as the greatest exponent of Greek Comedy.

Cratinus was the first to merge effectively the spirit of *iambic* poetry with the *komos* of the religious celebrations and to produce a politically conscious type of play. He was also, we may suppose, the first to shape comedy into its definite form: *prologos, parodos, agon, parabasis, komos, exodos.* According to Tzetzes, who in the twelfth century A.D. copied older information, he raised the number of comic actors to three and gave playwrights the serious purpose of a public scourge.[14]

The poet's own fragments offer us a clear impression

of his talent, which, as we have said, may have equaled
that of Aristophanes. There was, however, a great difference between them, which explains perhaps why grammarians kept the latter alive and entombed the former.
Aristophanes was the merrier of the two. Cratinus' satire,
like that of Archilochus and Hipponax which led people
to suicide, overflowed with poison and hatred. Aristophanes' satire, on the contrary, bursts with love for gay living,
peace, and happiness. He, too, scourges, but he does so
laughingly. His laughter resounds in the theatre, from
the first iambic trimeter of the prologue to the last creto-
lydophrygian stanza of the *exodos*.

When Aristophanes invaded the theatrical arena,
Cratinus was already an old man (born ca. 520 b.c.) and
his muse had almost abandoned him. His eight victories
were far behind him, and wine, his beloved companion,
could not give him back his former verve. Such a venerable drunkard, however, who reached the winter of life
still writing and producing comedies as well as acting in
them, is the best proof that Bacchus, god of wine, really
"nurtures" his servants (*Clouds,* 519). Cratinus himself
confesses in one of his plays that "drinking water makes
no man wise." Aristophanes also tells us that his senior
rival was a valiant warrior of the theatre, "uprooting, like
a torrent, oaks, plane-trees and enemies" (*Knights,*
527–28). Petty politicians, opportunists, and parasites of
public life were badly injured by his poisonous arrows.
His main target, however, was Pericles. He could not forget the beautiful days of Cimon's rule, or even Solon's
times which he had not known himself. In his plays, the
Riches, the *Laws,* and the *Chirons,* he dreams of Athens as
having returned to those palmy days.

When the Lenaea opened their gates to comedy, Pericles was so badly traumatized by the playwrights' attacks
that he issued a law, known as the Morychidean Decree,

forbidding all personal invectives in the theatre.[15] We can be almost sure that among the bilious comedies that made the law necessary was Cratinus' *Chirons*. It contained the famous comparison between Zeus the *Cloud-raiser* and Pericles the *Head-raiser,* because of his big head and his still bigger helmet (Fr. 240). In his *Thracian Women,* Pericles appeared "wearing his Odeum on his skull" (Fr. 71). In a third comedy, Pericles' concubine, Aspasia, suffered damaging blows, being called, among other names, "bitch-eyed" (Fr. 241). It was more than natural, therefore, for the democratic leader to fret and, quite undemocratically, to deprive the comic poets of their freedom of speech. The law, however, did not remain in effect more than two years. And when poetic freedom was restored, the playwrights' counterattack on Pericles and his entourage, including Aspasia, Phidias, and Anaxagoras, was merciless. Perhaps the *Dionysalexandros,* the best known of Cratinus' comedies, was written in those days. It is a parody of the story of Helen of Sparta, and its comic hero, the god Dionysus, presumably symbolized Pericles, while Helen, herself abducted by Dionysus, symbolized the city of Athens.[16]

Another well-known comic poet during Aristophanes' childhood, Crates, had begun his career as an actor in Cratinus' plays. Later, dissatisfied with the political comedy practiced by his master, he left him and became the leader of a countercurrent. Choosing Epicharmus as his model, he introduced mythological allegory to the comic stage. Fiction and mock-heroic burlesque were more important to him than political preaching or propaganda on contemporary topics. Aristotle will tell us that "Crates was the first to leave the iambic idea and create plots and dialogues" (*Poetics*, V, 3).[17]

The mild Crates must have been Pericles' favorite playwright; and one or more of the three victories attributed to him was probably won in the years when the militant poets were temporarily silenced by the law. Nevertheless, since three victories are but a moderate success in an Attic poet's career, we can assume that, on the whole, Crates was less popular than his "engaged" rivals, for the simple reason that the Athenian audience was a politically minded animal. According to Aristophanes, he was an able cook of rather naïve plays, full of comic devices (*Knights*, 538–39).

We need not make special mention of other comedy writers of the time, such as Hermippus, the most anti-Periclean of all, Telecleides, an imitator of Cratinus, or Pherecrates, a lesser Crates. We shall probably meet them again along the way, together with the younger generation of Ameipsias, Phrynichus, Eupolis, and others.

Summing up all that we have said in the last two chapters, about the elements which helped in the creation of Old Attic Comedy, we can easily trace the three simultaneous cultures which produced the rich crop of the Aristophanic art. The ancient vine had its root in the *komos* tradition and the phallus rituals. When grafted with the bitter satire of the *iambic* poets, it produced Cratinus' poisonous grape. Regrafted with Crates' Sicilian-born plant of fantasy, it gave the incomparable wine of Aristophanes as its final product.

A more detailed description of the three separate traditions merging into the Aristophanic Comedy might be of some help.

A. Elements inherited from Dionysiac Rituals:
   a) Choral singing and dancing
   b) Spectacular and ceremonial elements
   c) Musical instruments
   d) Animal disguises
   e) The *komos* and its orgiastic character

B. Elements inherited from Iambic Poetry:
   a) The political and social purposes of satire
   b) Personal invective
   c) The *parabasis,* or address to the people
C. Elements inherited from the Doric Drama:
   a) The traditional costume and padded belly
   b) Stock characters
   c) Low-comedy gags
   d) Mythological parody
   e) Scenes imitated from life

The importance of each of these elements will become more clearly apparent when, in the following chapters, we shall observe Aristophanes in the composition and in the staging of his plays.

The material side of ancient Greek play production is lost in a mist of uncertainty. Our knowledge about how the Athenian stage functioned in the years of its artistic preeminence is but an array of question marks.[18] Did the Oceanides actually make their entrance in a winged chariot? How did the scenery shift from Delphi to Athens? Where did Medea vanish with her dragon? On what pyre did Evadne throw herself? How did Perseus kill the sea-monster?[19] Or, to limit ourselves to comedy, how was the equestrian chorus of the *Knights* represented? From what machine was the Socrates of the *Clouds* suspended? How did Trygaeus fly to heaven in the *Peace* and where was the colossal statue of Peace hidden? How was the rowing to Hades in the *Frogs* effected? In what guise did the choruses in Magnes' *Gnats,* Cratinus' *Androgynes* and *Chirons,* Crates' *Beasts,* Eupolis' *New Moons,* or Pherecrates' *Ant-like-men* appear? There is no end to it. More generally speaking, in what kind of a theatre did the Athenian spectators sit and what stage-building, if any, were they accustomed to behold?

In spite of the prevailing darkness, we must, in order to visualize Aristophanes' plays as live and colorful events, agree on certain basic principles and risk a few suggestions concerning the aspect of the Athenian theatre of the classic period:

1. The theatre was *wooden*. This applies to the stage-edifice and the back-stage areas. As for the seats, the general tendency is to accept that, during Pericles' time, they were already built of stone. (The remains of the Dionysus Theatre of Athens are no evidence, for they belong to the first century A.D.).[20]

2. There was *no elevated stage,* as in later periods; only, perhaps, a slightly elevated platform adjacent to the orchestra. Contrary to what was commonly believed until 1885 (that the ancient actors performed on the stage and the chorus danced in the orchestra)[21] the excavations made in the Theatre of Dionysus in Athens by Hoepken and Doerpfeld[22] have proved that in the fifth-century theatre there were no separate domains and that the actors mingled with the chorus in the orchestra. This view is shared today by many scholars and theatre-historians, who found enough evidence in the Greek plays to corroborate it. To restrict ourselves to Aristophanic passages, let us mention the chorus' attack on Dicaeopolis (*Acharnians,* 280 f.) or similar battles between hero and chorus (*Wasps,* 403 f.; *Birds,* 343 f.), the common efforts of Trygaeus and the peasants to liberate Peace (*Peace,* 459 f.), Philocleon dancing the *kordax* with the chorus ensemble (*Wasps,* 1516 f.), or the Athenian women following Lysistrata in and out of the stage-building representing the Acropolis.

Perhaps we could add two more arguments in favor of this view. First, in the Epidaurus theatre, which among all Greek theatres has best retained the shape and dimensions of the fifth century Dionysus Theatre of Athens, the spectator cannot comfortably watch what happens on an erected stage, like those sometimes used in modern revivals, while, on the other hand, the orchestra is perfectly visible to him from any part of the *koilon*. Second, the circular shape of the Epidaurus orchestra is something complete in itself (and unique in Greek theatres). The eye of the spectator is naturally attracted to it and his concentration is focused on whatever is happening within the ring. Both visually and acoustically, the circular orchestra outweighs every other part of the theatre. It has a tremendous hypnotizing power, like an enormous snake's eye, that captivates all our senses. When Le Corbusier says that there exist *"des lieux mathematiques de consonnance, que j'appellerai des lieux d'acoustique visuelle,"* he may not be completely oblivious of the magic circle of the ancient orchestra. This "consonnance" in itself excludes, in our opinion, any suspicion of a "stage." [23]

3. Scenery (*skenographia*) came into existence either with Sophocles' advent (468 B.C.) or with Aeschylus' *Oresteia* (458 B.C.). We can be more or less sure that in Aristophanes' time the *proskenion* (stage-facade, probably adorned with pillars) was already there as a permanent set, undergoing minor changes according to each play's demands.[24]

4. The top of the *proskenion* offered a second story for elevated scenes. It was called the *theologeion* (from *theos*—god and *logos*—speech). We can easily claim that it was indispensable to Aristophanes: (*a*) In the *Acharnians*, Dicaeopolis' wife watches the Dionysiac revels from the balcony (262); (*b*) In the *Wasps*, Philocleon tries to escape from the roof (144, 206); (*c*) In the *Assembly of Women* a window or high balcony is necessary for the "hag-scene" (961).

5. The stage-crane, called *mechane* or *geranos,* had probably been functioning since Euripides' early plays. It was placed "by the left *parodos*" (Pollux, IV, 128) and de-

posited gods and flying heroes on the *theologeion*. Euripides made excessive use of it—hence Aristophanes' parodies—usually bringing a god from heaven to end his drama (*deus ex machina*). The best example of this device is to be found in the *Women at the Thesmophoria* (1098 f.).

6. The *ekkyklema* was definitely in use in 425 B.C. and possibly at an even earlier date (cf. *Acharnians*, 408–9), since it was already a subject of parody. According to Pollux, it was a wooden rostrum placed at one of the doors of the *proskenion*. By revolving on its wheels, it revealed an "interior scene" to the spectators. The author of the *Onomastikon* warns his readers that they should not confuse the *ekkyklema* with a similar device, the *exostra*, which did not revolve, but simply brought into view the corpses of people slain back-stage (Pollux, IV, 127–29).

7. The *pinakes* were wooden or cloth panels of painted scenery, attached between the pillars of the *proskenion*. Traces of the *pinakes* have been found in the Amphiaraeon Theatre, near Oropos, but they only date from the third century B.C.

8. The *periaktoi* were wooden triangular prisms, erected in front of the *proskenion* and having their three sides painted. By revolving on their axis, they would indicate a change of scenery. There is no positive evidence in Aristophanes' plays either that he himself had ever recourse to the *periaktoi* or that they were used at all in his times.[25]

9. The theatrical elements of the earliest period of Greek Drama—such as pillars, statues, altars, etc.—were, naturally, still present in Aristophanic productions. The same applies to stage-furniture and props—such as thrones, couches, stretchers, lanterns, torches, food, trees, chariots, armaments, phallus-poles, and, especially, *masks*. The masks of the fifth century, however, were not the ex-

aggerated ones preserved in Hellenistic or Roman art; they were smaller in size and plainer in their features.[26]

The little that we know or can surmise, however, about all these technical terms and their use, would be altogether futile, even misleading, if we overlooked the fact that theatre production in ancient Greece was not an illusory art. Artifice and machinery were not meant to deceive the spectator. The audience saw and heard, quite realistically, the functioning of every stage-effect, without being in the least annoyed or disturbed. This is manifest at least in Attic comedy, where Aristophanes is our eloquent guide.[27]

Chapter IV

The Peloponnesian War

*Both sides were full of enthusiasm for
war; and no wonder, for all men are
more energetic at start.*

Thucydides, II, 8

In the autumn of 432 B.C. Aristophanes was looking forward to his life as an Athenian citizen, though in a war-
pregnant atmosphere. Athens and Sparta continued their
diplomatic relations "without a herald but not without
suspicion," says Thucydides, because the previous months
had seen repeated hostile undertakings on both sides.[1]
The most serious hostility, in Aristophanes' mind, was the
punishment inflicted by his countrymen upon Megara, consisting in that city's exclusion from all ports and markets
of the Athenian Alliance. He considered this political
measure one typical of Pericles' imperialistic extravagances and strongly sympathized with the Megarians, who
suddenly were faced with famine. His indignation was so
fierce that it even survived Pericles' death and inspired
the virulent passage about the causes of the Peloponnesian War, in the *Acharnians* (530–34), seven years
later:

The Olympian Pericles
thundered and lightened, and confounded Hellas,

enacting laws which ran like drinking songs,
that the Megarians presently depart
from earth and sea, the mainland and the mart.

Trans. B. B. Rogers

Aristophanes was the first to propound the view, accepted today by many historians, that the "Megarian Decree" was the real *causus belli.* Thanks to it, the old antag-
onism between Athens and Sparta at last exploded. We
are not obliged, of course, to embrace his version in full
or to accept his suggestion that the blockade was brought
about because the Megarians "had abducted two whores
of Aspasia's retinue" (*Acharnians,* 527). That is merely
the comic poet's variation on the theme.

In March, 431 B.C., at the festival of the City Dionysia,
Euripides, Sophocles, and Euphorion, Aeschylus' son,
competed in tragedy. Euphorion received the first prize,
Sophocles the second, and Euripides with his *Medea* the
third.[2] Evidently, this was the last peaceful festival. A
month later war was declared, breaking the thirty-year
treaty between Athens and Sparta in its fifteenth year.

This is, in brief, how it all started. One night in
spring the Theban army invaded the small city of Plataea,
an old ally of Athens. The two great powers were immediately called upon—Sparta by the Thebans, Athens by the
Plataeans. Eventually, all the Greek states were mobilized,
most of them unwillingly, as there was nothing in that
war to spur patriotic feelings. It was not the Aeschylean
"supreme struggle" against the invader, but a political
clash between two parties, the Democrats and the Aristo-
crats or Oligarchs. Not infrequently in the course of the
following years, hostilities between pro-Athenians and
pro-Laconians would cause many a state disastrous civil
strife.

In May, the Spartans and their allies marched against

Attica. They announced that they had no intention other than to free Greece from Athenian domination; in reality, they were seeking to take Athens' place as the supreme power of Greece. The great Doric army, headed by the Spartan king Archidamus, camped by the Corinth Isthmus to wait for the Athenians. They waited in vain. Pericles had decided that the people of Athens should shut themselves within the walls of the city and that the war should be fought only at sea. Accordingly, he ordered all the peasants of Attica to abandon their villages, send their cattle to Euboea, and take refuge for themselves inside the city. Aristophanes saw his hometown packed with refugees from all the nearby areas. Those who had relatives in Athens found hospitality. Others improvised their lodgings in backyards, in public places, in the streets, and even on the ramparts. The noble city of Cranaus was transformed into a crowded and unwholesome gypsy-camp.

Then, in midsummer, news arrived that the enemy had left the Isthmus and was invading Attica. Meeting not a single armed man on their way, the Peloponnesians began sacking the deserted villages. They looted, ravaged the fields, set fire to storehouses. Finally, they installed themselves at Acharnae, ten miles from Athens, establishing there their provisional headquarters. They believed that the Acharnians, sheltered in Athens, would be induced to leave the security of the city to fight for their lands, thus accepting the challenge of war on Attic soil.

This is exactly what the Acharnians were about to do, when Pericles vetoed their project. In vain they implored him to let them defend their homes. No prayer, no argument, no menace could make him abandon his original plan. A month later, no battle fought, the Spartans and their allies were obliged to withdraw. Then the country people of Attica left their shelter, to face the damage done to their hometowns. They invoked curses upon the enemy; but they were more indignant against Pericles, whom they held responsible for the calamity that had befallen them.

During these days (winter 431–430 B.C.) the Athenians attacked Aegina as a pro-Spartan island, banished all the inhabitants and shared the land between themselves by lot. It was on this occasion, as we have already conjectured, that old Philip and his family, harassed by the miseries of the first year of the war, decided to move to that island, on which Aristophanes would for the rest of his life seek refuge whenever he wished to write a play or to escape his political and literary foes.

In the spring of 430 B.C. the first wartime Dionysia were celebrated. They must have been poor, both in pomp and mirth. And the *komos,* if celebrated at all, must have been a sad affair. A month later, two more disastrous events took place: the second invasion of the enemy in Attica and the first intrusion of the plague. This strange illness, which lasted two years, took the lives of 5,000 Athenian soldiers and a still greater number of immigrants and slaves, not to mention women, children, and old men. Plague-stricken people usually died on the seventh or ninth day; a few recovered, to remain invalids. It was such a terrible disease, Thucydides tells us, that dogs and vultures, which are usually attracted by corpses, would not even touch them; and if they did, they died on the spot.

In this infernal atmosphere, with the foe at the city's gate and the plague at his threshold, Aristophanes created his comic art. While breathing the poisonous air and listening to the moan of the dying, he composed his first exercises in dramatic hilarity.

He will never mention the plague in his plays. It is one of those things an entertainer should not recall to his audiences, who may have lost parents, children, or even their own eyes as a result of it. The Attic playwright should awaken his public only to calamities which were brought about by their own faults, not to those sent by the gods. For the latter, they are not responsible and, consequently, they do not need counsel or reprimand. Besides, his first and foremost purpose is to make his audience laugh and forget their sufferings. Greek Comedy, in spite of its corrosive insistence on disagreeable truths, was in its very essence a theatre of escape.

We cannot help observing that Aristophanes' mission was by far more heroic than that of the older comic poets. They had entertained their fellow citizens during calm and unclouded times, when happiness was only disturbed by some repugnant law or financial trouble. He, on the contrary, began his career during some of the darkest years of Greek history. The plays he wrote had a double purpose: to show Athenians the right policy to pursue and to relieve them of their agonies by carefree laughter. His drama came to Athens, as Dionysus' wine had come in legendary times, as a godsent remedy.

We do not know what comedies or tragedies were presented during the festivals of 429 B.C., or whether performances were held at all, with the risk of having the actors collapse plague-stricken in the orchestra. It is more likely that public gatherings had been canceled because of the disease, with the one exception, of course, of the People's Assembly on the Pnyx. It was there that Pericles delivered his last speech. He tried to overcome the defeatism of his countrymen and inspire them with only one thought—the salvation of Athens. He urged them not to be influenced by the pacifists. (Was Aristophanes in the Assembly on that day?) Love of peace, he concluded, is impotent if not accompanied by action.

The great statesman's last year of life was a very dark one. It is true that, up to the end, he would take pride in seeing that the Athenians were following his plan of action. He knew, however, that he had lost their love. For a long time the reactionaries had been objecting to his innovations, and comic poets were shooting their venomous arrows at him and his kinsmen. He had shed tears before the court to rescue his mistress; he had seen his philosopher friend, Anaxagoras, flee Athens to save his life; and his sculptor friend, Phidias, imprisoned for sacrilege and embezzlement.[3]

On the notorious "Pheidian fraud" and on the efforts of Pericles to conceal it, Aristophanes will base another of his extravagant variations on the War. In the *Peace* (605–11) almost ten years later, he will tell us:

Pheidias began the mischief, having come to grief and
    shame,
Pericles was next in order, fearing he might share the
    blame,
dreading much your hasty temper, and your savage bull-
    dog ways,
So before misfortune reached him, he contrived a flame to
    raise,
by his Megara enactment setting all the world ablaze.
Such a bitter smoke ascended while the flames of war he
    blew,
that from every eye in Hellas everywhere the tears it drew.
                                    Trans. B. B. Rogers

The Athenians did not hesitate to accuse Pericles himself of the embezzlement of public funds. And the first to throw the stone at him may have been Cratinus or Hermippus or some other of Aristophanes' choleric forerunners, whose baleful aphorisms had a very strong effect on public opinion.[4] Thus, the man who for thirty years had been the democratic reformer of Athens was condemned, in his last days and at the most crucial moment of his mis-

sion, to pay a fifty talents' fine! It was a reaction of the Democracy, which he himself had struggled to establish.
Thucydides sums up the Greeks' eternal mentality in two
ironic sentences. He says that no one stopped shouting
until they had fined Pericles, and then, "as is the usual
habit of the people, they re-elected him and bestowed on
him the supreme presidency over all public matters! . . ."
(II, 65).

Pericles died, of an illness that was not exactly the
plague, two-and-a-half years after the beginning of the
war. His death saved him, as we may well suppose, from
Aristophanes' relentless blows. The author of the *Knights*
proudly declares in his *parabases* that he always aimed
higher than his fellow playwrights and that fear never soft-
ened his impetus to flog. As we have seen, he attributes
to Pericles the entire responsibility for the Peloponnesian War. His attacks, however, end there, because the
"Olympian" leader belongs already to the past. Besides, as
soon as Pericles leaves the political stage, Cleon the Tanner makes his appearance. And this demagogue is destined
to overshadow any other victim of Aristophanes' political
or aesthetic indignation.

A few months after Pericles' death—in the spring of
428 B.C.—Euripides presented his *Hippolytus* and won one
of his rare first prizes.[5] It was, perhaps, the fourth production of the dramatic reformer that Aristophanes had witnessed so far. He was as ever impressed by Euripides'
mania for stage machinery, especially by that convenient
crane, which deposited on the upper-stage the god who
brought the dramatic denouement.[6]

About the same time, Aristophanes wrote his first
play, the *Banqueters.*[7] Still in his early twenties, he set out
on the adventurous career of an engaged dramatist. He
proved from the beginning that he possessed the three
specific virtues of a good Attic playwright—education,

judgment, and a sense of humor. We should not forget, as we go through the stages of Aristophanes' life, that comedy was not only a major theatrical entertainment but also the counterpart of modern journalism. The only form of social or political editorial the citizens could benefit by was the voice of the poet from the stage. The Pnyx and the Theatre were the two major expressions of public opinion in ancient Athens.

The theme he chose in his first play was the clash between the old and the new mentality, between the solid values of perennial tradition and the fickle way of modern living. Thus, a special kind of dramatic conflict was created, destined to hold strong from the fifth century B.C. down to the age of beatniks and angry young men. It seems worth noting, however, that in this controversy between conservative traditionalism and anarchical radicalism, Aristophanes sided with the former. Contrary to all dramatists, before or after him, who supported the revolt of a young Haemon, Don Carlos, Eugene Marchbanks, or Jimmy Porter against convention, the young author of the *Banqueters* did not glorify the new spirit but adhered passionately and stubbornly to the old. This negative attitude toward social or intellectual progress he will never abandon. It will lead him as far as refusing Euripides and misunderstanding Socrates. The choler of the *Clouds* and the *Frogs* was already present in Aristophanes' first play.

I don't think that enough attention has yet been given to this surprising phenomenon. Why did the great comic poet sympathize with the so-called Marathon generation of Simonides, Pindar, and Aeschylus and not, as it would have been more natural, with that of Euripides, Socrates, and his own? Could an explanation be sought, by any chance, in his feelings toward his own father? . . . We know nothing about Philip that would enable us to come to any conclusions. Throughout Aristophanes' ca-

reer, however, elderly fathers will never cease to be his beloved heroes and choruses—old men who whimper, longing for their glorious young days forever lost.

In the *Banqueters,* he bitterly exposes the *jeunesse
dorée* of those times—the affected, precious, and supercilious generation of dandies, wearing golden curls over
their foreheads, interested only in drinking, gambling,
prating outlandish words, aping the intellectual snobism
of the sophists, and never washing with cold water. Alcibiades, who was the same age as Aristophanes, is the most
typical example of that lost generation. Such is also the
young hero in this comedy.

From the extant fragments [8] we gather that the plot
deals with an old father who has two sons, one studying in
Athens, the other working in the fields. They are, as it
were, the town-mouse and the country-mouse of the fable.
When the first, Thrasymachus, returns to his home town,
the collision of viewpoints begins. The poor father, who
admires Homer and the old Greek ideals, is overwhelmed
by the transformation of his son. "But he learned nothing
of what I sent him to Athens for!" he exclaims. "He has
learned only how to sing abominably, to eat like a Syracusan, to carouse like a Sybaritan and to drink Chian wine
from Samian pitchers!" He has also learned the sophists'
method of fake perspicuity and pseudointellectual repartee. As painted by Aristophanes, he is not a harmless fop
of the golden age, an inoffensive man of the world, he is
the poisonous spawn of modern education, a dangerous
monster of civilization, who does not hesitate to tell his
own father that he is good only for the grave.

It seems that the daring young author was rather
timid as a producer. That is why he chose to present his
first play under another man's name—a trick that was to
remain a useful subterfuge to him ever after. This method
was obviously original, for Aristophanes would later apol-

ogize and explain why he used it, modestly admitting that "producing a comedy is a very difficult job" (*Knights,* 515 f.). The producer he chose and who also served him as a straw-man was a certain Callistratus, probably a medio-cre fellow writer but a competent *didaskalos,* an expert in coaching actors and staging a play. In those days, the training of the chorus in singing and dancing was still the poet's job. Callistratus is, therefore, the first professional producer-director to appear in history.

It was he, and not Aristophanes, who applied to the archon basileus for a chorus and who procured the per-mission to present the play at the Lenaea in January, 427 B.C. The archon commissioned a rich Athenian, Antima-chus, to become the *choregus,* i.e., the financial sponsor of the production. This contribution to public welfare was one of the obligatory duties of all the wealthy citizens. An-timachus had to hire the twenty-four members of the cho-rus, the musicians, and the stage-hands, and pay for their lodging and food during rehearsals. Only the actors—three in number—were paid by the state.[9]

Preliminaries over, Callistratus began rehearsing. He taught the chorus the various positions, gestures, and steps that he thought appropriate for the play and trained them in singing, chanting, or declaiming. He also explained to them the metric system of each *stasimon* or choral inter-lude and the kind of melody that it called for. He may also have taken part in the production as an actor.

Aristophanes' play received the second prize, and our young playwright must have been delighted with his early success.[10] Only one thing spoiled his pleasure—that Anti-machus the *choregus* forgot to invite him to the tradi-tional dinner which was given after the performance. He will still remember this insult two years later and will pray to Zeus, consecrating a whole *stasimon* of the *Acharnians* (1153 f.) to his rancor, to inflict upon Antima-chus the cruelest of punishments. "May he hanker for a dish of the subtle cuttlefish," he says. "As he reaches forth his hand for the meal the Gods provide him, may a dog snatch and carry off the spoil—off the spoil!" (trans. B. B. Rogers).

Meanwhile, the war went on. During this same winter (427 B.C.) the heroic exodus of the Plataeans took place, after a year's siege by the combined armies of Sparta and Thebes. A few months later the town of Plataea had completely vanished from the map.

In the summer, the civil war in the island of Coroyra between Democrats and Oligarchs reached its tragic climax. Even more desperate were the conditions in revolted Mytilene, obliged to surrender to the Athenian fleet after waiting in vain for the help promised by Sparta. When the Athenians gathered on the Pnyx to decide the penalty to be imposed on the Mytileneans, Cleon the Tanner made his spectacular debut as Pericles' successor. His brutal and uncompromising oratory convinced the Athenians to vote for the extermination of the whole male population of the island. A ship left the port of Piraeus to carry the order. But such was the horror of a great number of Athenians, that, on the following day another meeting, overruling Cleon, voted the revocation of the death penalty. Without delay, a second trireme left the port, to overtake the first one already sailing across the Aegean, and the Mytilenean envoys stimulated the sailors with wine and money to make them double their speed. The outcome of the affair was comparatively happy. The inhabitants were spared their lives and only a few outstanding citizens were executed to serve as an example.

Cleon, with his warlike fanaticism and dictatorial tendencies, initiated a period of terror. In this Cleonic Thermidor, Aristophanes wrote his second play. The sub-

ject he dealt with was the Athenian allies, those of Co-
rayra, Plataea, Mytilene and all the rest, who suffered for
no other reason than the glory of Athens and Sparta. He
wished his second play to carry its message further than
the first. He told Callistratus, therefore, to apply to the archon eponymus for participation in the major festival of
the year, the City Dionysia. He wished to exhort his fellow citizens before a panhellenic audience. His subject
was this time political and had a nation-wide significance.
Furthermore, his main target was none other than the
state's new leader, Cleon.

The ambitious young playwright appears already as a
"poet with determined orientation," a compliment that
Engels will pay him one day.[11] And scholars, praising his
courage, by no means overrate it. We must remember,
nevertheless, that boldness was his job and that he could
not do otherwise. His elder playwrights had not hesitated
to attack a man as great as Pericles. How could he spare a
"dirty tanner"? . . . On the other hand, we cannot help
sharing Gilbert Murray's [12] admiration for the equally heroic Callistratus, who signed this flaming pamphlet, the
archon who offered a chorus for the City Dionysia, and
the choregus who sponsored the show. These three Athenians, after all, did not enjoy the poet's creative pride,
which more or less counterbalanced his possible qualms.

Aristophanes called his second comedy the *Babylonians,* maintaining the custom of naming the plays after
their choruses. In Herodotus (III, 159) the Babylonians
were slaves in King Darius' court. In Aristophanes'
comedy they are slaves once more, but here they symbolize the allied states.

From the play's fragments, we surmise that the god
Dionysus was the hero. From other sources, we learn
something about the play's political thesis. It attacked

state officials, Cleon first and foremost, and urged the citizens not to let demagogues clamp an iron rule on their allies.[13]

With the *Babylonians,* Aristophanes had found the pulse of his countrymen. The play was enthusiastically applauded and the judges, no less courageous than those responsible for the production, gave him the first prize.[14] In reality, the person crowned with ivy before thousands of Athenians and foreigners, was Callistratus, while the genuine victor probably watched his triumph peeping through a hole of the *paraskenia.* By now, however, all the members of the audience, except the most thick-headed, must have known who was the real father of that daring comedy. Those who were still ignorant of it at the theatre's exit, would soon learn it in the courtroom, where Cleon would soon indict Aristophanes and make him pay for his temerity.

An exhausting litigation began, thereafter, between the democratic leader and the young playwright—a real-life *agon* which enhanced the comic poet's prestige as a great ideologist. And even more than two thousand years later, when the French prime minister, August Thiers, issued a law abolishing the freedom of the Press, the poet Alfred de Musset recalled none else than Aristophanes and wrote to his chief of state: "You should read him, Monsieur Thiers; he is a powerful genius! . . ."[15]

Chapter V

The *Acharnians*—Comedy and Ideology

In his plays he tried to show that the Athenian state was free and by no tyrant oppressed.

Ancient *Life* of Aristophanes

The *Babylonians* was produced five years after the outbreak of the Peloponnesian War and almost three after Pericles' death. Following the production of this play, Cleon brought an action against Aristophanes for insulting the State "in the presence of foreigners." [1] In his next play, the *Acharnians,* the poet will recall:

> . . . what I myself endured
> at Cleon's hands for last year's comedy.
> How to the Counsil House he dragged me off,
> and slayed and lied and slandered and betongued me,
> roaring Cycloborus-wise; till I well nigh
> was done to death . . .[2]

Justice triumphed, however, and Aristophanes was exculpated. Yet this trial was only the first round of a long fight. The powerful demagogue re-attacked the young author some time later on the ground of his supposedly alien descent and his illegal claim to Athenian citizenship. "Twice and thrice accused," his biographer says, "he was at last acquitted of all charges." [3]

The *Acharnians,* besides being our most authentic

document on Aristophanes' feud with the political leader of his day, is also the oldest surviving Greek comedy. As such, it represents the earliest known technique of comic playwriting. We find in it 1235 lines of verse.[4] The *parabasis* is situated in the very middle, dividing the play into two equal parts. Here is a structural analysis of the comedy's form:

A. The first part is composed of:
   a) The *prologue*—a long comic sequence, with five speaking characters and many extras
   b) The *parodos*—the entrance of the chorus and the first choral song
   c) The *agon*—the clash between protagonist and chorus
   d) Two comic *episodes*

B. The *parabasis,* which comes next, is a choric interlude, containing the poet's message to the audience. It suspends the action half way through the performance.

C. In the second part there are:
   a) Four comic *episodes,* separated by
   b) Three *stasima* or choral songs
   c) The *komos*—general revelry of the chorus, glorifying the triumphant hero
   d) The *exodos* of hero and chorus, singing and dancing

The sequence described above was not a canon, an obligatory pattern for the writers. The Aristophanic *agon,* for instance, is a movable part; some of his plays have a second *parodos* (*metastasis*); others, no *parabasis* at all; and very often four or five short *episodes* succeed one another between two *stasima.*

In this play, written in the summer of 426 B.C., the poet continued his antiwar campaign begun in the *Babylonians.* Up to this year many unsuccessful attempts had been made by Athens and Sparta to bring hostilities to an end; but, whichever of the two states happened to be the more favored on the battlefield at a given time would obstinately refuse to accept the peace terms proposed by the other. It seems that in the spring of that year it had been the turn of the Peloponnesians to show friendly dispositions. Aristophanes, therefore, becomes once more the advocate of Peace and, navigating against the current of Cleon's politics, urges his countrymen to vote for an armistice.

Callistratus, the faithful accomplice, willingly adopted Aristophanes' spiritual offspring and applied for the City Dionysia. Then, quite unexpectedly, a negative answer fell like a thunderbolt on both father and foster-parent. The archon eponymus, succumbing, no doubt, to pressure from Cleon, refused to grant the requested chorus, thus excluding the comic poet from the great international festival. The cause of this expulsion was none other than the previous year's rebellious comedy involving the State's defamation "in the presence of foreigners," something that the irascible demagogue was unable to forget. And, since the playwright had been legally discharged, Cleon conceived this new counteroffensive.

One can well imagine Aristophanes' dismay upon hearing the news. For an up-and-coming dramatist, who had only recently won his first victory at the Great Dionysia, to content himself with the lesser Lenaea must have been distressing beyond measure. The only thing that may have cheered him up a little was the fact that his Lenaean rivals would be Cratinus, the grand sire of Attic Comedy, and Eupolis, a promising craftsman of the younger generation. These three comedy champions— whom Horace will squeeze one day into a famous verse (*Satires,* I, iv, i)—were facing each other for the first time. The eminence, therefore, of the contestants gave extra glamor to the local festival.

Cratinus' *Chimazomenoi* (*Winter Men*), Eupolis' *Nu-*

meniai (*New Moons*) and Aristophanes' *Acharnians* were presented in early February 425 B.C. before, no doubt, a sparse audience, the war keeping many Athenians away from the theatre.

Aristophanes' hero—Dicaeopolis or Just Citizen—is the poet himself under a theatrical mask. More than once the hero refers to the author's political tribulations as if they were his own; and the famous legal battle with Cleon is narrated in the first person. In this respect, the *Acharnians* forecast the *Knights,* where the autobiographical element will be even more conspicuous.[5]

The prologue of the play is a miniature parody of the People's Assembly. The Just Citizen is the only Athenian to be on the Pnyx in time. The others arrive belated and spiritless. Their indifference to the fate of their city is more than exasperating. The session opens. Every time that Dicaeopolis or Amphitheus—another citizen who is a pacifist only because he is half-witted—attempt to condemn the war, the archers violently hush them up in the middle of a sentence. The Assembly has more important matters to attend to: the ambassadors have returned from abroad and will report on their missions. With mellifluous words they tell how laboriously they have been serving Athens in foreign countries—eating, drinking, and pocketing their fat fees for an indefinite length of time. "During the fourth year of my mission in Persia," one of them says, "I arrived at last at King Xerxes' capital; but the monarch had gone, at the head of an enormous army, to excrete on the Golden Mountains, where he remained defecating for eight months" (80–82). The only tangible consequences of the ambassadors' deft diplomacy as far as military and financial aid to Athens is concerned, are some ludicrous Odomantian soldiers and a grotesque Persian prince, called the Royal Eye. The former, "the most war-like Thracian tribe" (153), prove at once the excellence of their war tactics by stealing Dicaeopolis' garlic. The latter is even more frank, as he admits in his broken Greek: "No penny for Athenian bastards!" (104) This monstrous, possibly one-eyed, foreigner belongs to the humorous gallery of Aristophanes' non-Attic characters, who use either an imaginary Graeco-barbarian language (such as the Triballus of the *Birds* or the Scythian of the *Women at the Thesmophoria*) or an exaggerated provincial dialect (such as the Megarian and the Boeotian in the present play).

While the Assembly exhausts its energy in various unnecessary deliberations, Dicaeopolis finally realizes that there will be no discussion about Peace. He decides, therefore, to send Amphitheus to Sparta, to conclude a private treaty with the Lacedaemonians. Amphitheus goes and presently returns, with a speed that is the very parody of theatrical time, bringing the Just Citizen of Athens a private thirty-year-peace with Sparta; Peace appears in the form of a wine jug. In utter delight, our hero hurries home to gather his family, to celebrate with them the Rural Dionysia—their beloved fête champêtre of the serene, bygone days.

When the hero leaves the orchestra, the chorus makes its entrance (204), a flute-player opening the march. This chorus is composed of twenty-four elderly coal-traders of Acharnae. They probably wear blackened chitons and lean on rough sticks. They march in single or double columns and arrange themselves geometrically inside the orchestra circle.[6]

In both comedy and tragedy, the basic arrangement of the chorus in the orchestra had a rectangular shape; three columns of five dancers in tragedy, four columns of six dancers in comedy; it was accordingly called *"square chorus,"* in contrast to the *"circular"* of the dithyramb. Yet the mention of a circular dance is very common in drama too, especially in those cases where religious feeling gives the stasima a dithyrambic flavor.[7]

Why did Aristophanes use the inhabitants of Acharnae as chorus? The reason is obvious. Those peasants of Attica were among the most fanatic enemies of the Spartans, who had destroyed their homes. Besides, they took a great pride in being the worthy descendants of the Marathon warriors. So, by opposing them to his peace-loving hero, the playwright enhanced the tension of the dramatic conflict in order to make the Just Citizen's final victory more effective.

In a fiery succession of trochees and dactyls, the chorus voice their hatred for the rascal, who "made peace with the loathsome enemy." Their song is sadly reminiscent of tragic historical events, because Aristophanes had pitied the Acharnians in the time of their woes. Comedy, however, cannot stand to see its audience in tears. Consequently these chorus dancers are humorously pugnacious old men, who, for no other reason than their own stupidity, support the cause of war. Their mask and costume, their dance and mimicry emphasize the ridiculous. What the spectators see is a bunch of old gargoyles, with stuffed bellies, grimacing faces and, possibly too, leather-penises swinging like time-worn pendulums. No matter how desperately they moan, the public cannot help laughing at them. What they have already suffered from the war was a fatal calamity; but to ask for more such misfortunes is, the playwright believes, sheer idiocy.

When the *parodos*-song is over, Dicaeopolis and his family are seen coming out of their house, presumably through one of the two lateral doors of the *proskenion,* to celebrate Dionysus in the countryside.[8]

We have already made a point of the importance of this Aristophanic parody on the Rural Dionysia, in which the reveling company dances and sings the joys of Peace

around the phallus-pole. The old Acharnians of the chorus watch all these activities in bewilderment. Soon, however, they recover from their stupor and begin to throw
stones at the "traitor." As it happens in all war-dances of
primitive tribes, their movement is rhythmically syn-
chronized with the stimulating repetition of the trochaic
"beat him, beat him, beat him, beat him!" This physical
clash is followed, as is more or less the rule in Greek
Comedy, by a clash of ideas, known as the *agon.* Here the
author's credo, expressed by the hero, is set against public
prejudice, embodied in the chorus. The Acharnians accuse Dicaeopolis of having concluded peace with people
who are vile and false, to which the Just Citizen replies:
"The Spartans are no more responsible for our misfortunes than we are" (309–10).

We praised young Aristophanes' boldness for attacking Cleon in the *Babylonians.* That boldness fades, however, when compared to this new, almost suicidal one: to
urge the war-stricken Athenians to "love their neighbors,"
those neighbors who during five whole years had been
killing their sons, burning their harvests, and wishing
them every possible ill. In fact, the whole *agon,* as well as
the hero's *long speech* (497–556), have no other reason
but to prove to the Athenian people that they are more
guilty of this destructive war than the Spartans. We are almost inclined to wonder why the spectators did not rise to
liquidate not only the actor incarnating Aristophanes'
idea of the just citizen but also the anonymous author
who was hiding back stage. They refrained from doing it,
because, in the first place, they respected a theatrical performance as a tribune of free speech. Furthermore, there
must have been among them some adherents of peace,
who probably hushed the protesting war-lovers. Last—
and this is, I believe, the most important reason—by theatrical convention the chorus represented public opinion;

consequently, the twenty-four Acharnians, who reacted to Dicaeopolis' arguments with insults and stones, fulfilled the unexpressed desire of every warlike spectator.

The Just Citizen, like many future Aristophanic heroes, is a militant ideologist with plenty of guts. He does not run away from the public turmoil with his private peace treaty in his sack. He stubbornly remains there to make the roaring chorus see reason. He is so sure of the just cause of his *agon* that he even agrees to have his own throat cut, in case he fails to convince them. "Although," he adds, "I love my poor life!" (357).

As a shrewd entertainer, Aristophanes loosens for a while the tension of his political debate with two interludes of a somewhat lighter mood. Both of them are inspired by the Euripidean tragedy *Telephus,* produced thirteen years earlier. It must have been a very popular play, since the comic poet expected his audience still to appreciate comic allusions related to it. The first inserted episode (325–37) is a typical tragic parody. In the play of Euripides, Telephus had kidnapped the infant Orestes, threatening to kill him. Here, Dicaeopolis steals an Acharnian coal-sack and prepares to stab it, unless the noisy old men will let him speak his mind. The reaction of the chorus to this feat consists of a mock-heroic version of the traditional tragic lamentation (*kommōs*).

The second interlude (393–479) has larger dimensions, provokes a change of scenery, and introduces an important new character. In order to win the sympathy of the chorus, the Just Citizen decides to borrow a pitiful disguise from Euripides' reputed or, rather, disreputable theatrical wardrobe of shabby costumes. It was, it seems, one of the major innovations introduced by that poet to the Greek theatre: dramatic characters should not look like the imposing statues of the Aeschylean tradition, but rather like human wrecks.

Dicaeopolis knocks at Euripides' door, the central, most probably, of the proskenion. A servant appears, declaring in Euripidean language that his master is composing a play and that no one is allowed to interrupt him. Thereupon, our hero shouts at the invisible tragic master that, since he cannot leave his room, he may as well appear *in* it. Euripides is at once convinced and appears *in* his room. In other words, thanks to a mechanical device, known as the *ekkyklema,* the central part of the proskenion makes a 180-degrees revolution and reveals the interior of the poet's house. Aristophanes' aim is none other than to satirize the excessive "mechanomania" of his tragic colleague. How else could Euripides appear on the stage, if not equipped with one of his pet machines? Needless to say this scene offers theatre historians an almost irrefutable argument that the *ekkyklema* was functioning at least since 425 B.C.[9]

In that year, the youngest of the three tragic masters was in his middle fifties and had already produced more than fifty plays, including such imposing dramas as *Medea* (431 B.C.) and *Hippolytus* (428 B.C.). For Aristophanes, however, he is a preposterous personage. In a later chapter we shall examine more carefully what our comic author approves or disapproves of in him, because this first appearance of Euripides in the theatre will by no means be his last. Its success will establish the tragic poet as a permanent stock-character in Aristophanic comedy.

The *ekkyklema* has revealed the dramatist in his study, his feet on the table, surrounded by papyri, tablets, masks, costumes, wigs, and a thousand little household utensils, indispensable to the realistic atmosphere of his plays. Dicaeopolis begs him to lend him some rags. "What rags?" Euripides shouts. "Those of Oeneus, Phoenix, Bellerophon, Philoctetes, Thyestes, Ino? . . ." Obviously, his ragged heroes are so many that it is not easy to choose. At last the rags of Telephus are discovered and the Just Citizen wraps them around him, while the machine sweeps the "patchwork poet" back into his adytum.

Now the comic interludes are over and Dicaeopolis is standing alone in mid-orchestra, facing the chorus. Well disguised in his disarming rags, he whispers to himself: "Do you realize what an adventure you are up to? . . . To defend the Spartans! . . . Courage, my soul! . . ." (481–83). Let us try to imagine this crucial moment in the ancient performance, when all of a sudden laughs are muffled and in a deathlike silence all eyes are fixed on the hero, anticipating his apology.

Dicaeopolis' "long speech" is a masterpiece of rhetoric. After an introductory warning that he will say "things disagreeable but just," he mischievously adds: "Cleon will not accuse me again of offending the State in the presence of foreigners, for we are at the Lenaea, strictly among ourselves" (501–6). He then attacks the main theme of his discourse by identifying himself with his audience. "I hate the Lacedaemonians as much as you do, for they destroyed my vineyards too!" He proceeds with vehemence to further arguments, striving to prove that he—and, consequently, Aristophanes—is neither pro-Spartan nor a traitor. Having thus secured the attention and, to a certain extent, the trust of his listeners, he delivers his own version of the war-chronicle:

> (Some) men of ours—I do not say the State;
> remember this, I do not say the State—(515–17)

He does not slander the State; there is no fear, therefore, of a new action of Cleon against him. So he continues:

> . . . Some young tipsy cottabus-players, went
> and stole from Megara-town the fair Simaetha.
> Then the Megarians, garlicked with the smart,
> Stole, in return, two of Aspasia's hussies.

From these three wantons, o'er the Hellenic race
burst forth the first beginnings of the War! . . . (524–28)

The narrative is concluded in a more serious mood, by the repetition of the *leitmotiv* of the oration—the proclamation of the enemy's right:

. . . Had some Laconian, sailing out,
denounced and sold a small Seriphian dog,
would you have sat unmoved? Far, far from that!
Ye would have launched three hundred ships of war! . . .
(541–45)

Dicaeopolis' bravura speech has an immediate effect —or better say, half-effect—on the chorus: half of the Acharnians are convinced of the rightness of his cause, while the other half continue to react. Aristophanes thus presents a microscopic view of the customary political disputes, which separated most of the Greek cities into two enemy camps. He also provides a natural explanation for the traditional separation of the chorus into the so-called *half-choruses,* opposing each other.

A war dance between the two parties follows, in which we should imagine more action taking place than the text actually describes. The manuscripts that we possess are mostly the works of Christian copyists who had never set foot in a theatre; this accounts for the numberless omissions and misinterpretations suffered by Greek drama. Dancers "imitated through rhythm, the characters, sufferings and actions" of men, Aristotle will state half a century later (*Poetics,* I, 5). In the Aristophanic comedies, more specifically, we often perceive that the author demands that his chorus add movement between the lines to illustrate the events by mimicry. They ought to create that *"elasticité joyeuse"* that Jacques Copeau dreamed of for his own theatre.[10]

In the violent battle between the two Acharnian semi-

choruses we have a *ne plus ultra* ironic outcome: the pacifists fight better than the bellicose and finally win! Thereupon, the vanquished ones call Lamachus, the Athenian
general, to come to their rescue. Punctually, through the
third door of the stage-building, the high-crested warrior
emerges as terrifying as lightning and thunder (572).

This historical personage owes his immortality more
to Aristophanes' caricature than to his portrayal by Thucydides. As a stage character, he descends directly from the
vociferous Heracles of the Doric Drama, having also some
contingency with the arrogant general of the famous Ar-
chilochian epigram. Through the *Acharnians,* he becomes
the legitimate progenitor of all the braggart soldiers, who
will storm the theatre in later ages—from the *alazon* and
the *episeistos* of New Attic Comedy and the Roman *miles
gloriosus* to the *capitano* and the *scaramuccia* of later European farces—whose living scion is, prosaically enough,
the tough sergeant of modern films.[11]

The peace-loving little man beholds the tempestuous
general and whispers:

That's what I loathe: that's why I made my treaty—
when grayhaired veterans in the ranks I saw,
and boys like you, paltry, malingering boys,
off to some Thrace, their daily pay three drachmas! . . .
                                              (599–602)

And, gradually, the old underdogs of the chorus, the poor
Acharnian *sans culottes,* who not too long ago glowed
with Marathonian ambitions, have to admit that Dicaeopolis is right in every word he said. The two so-far hostile
semichoruses unite in one common ideal: Peace. Then,
walking toward the spectators, they deliver the *parabasis*
(526 f.).

"The man has the best of the wordy debate, and the
hearts of the people he is winning to his plea for the

truce," they say. By "man" they are referring, of course, to Dicaeopolis, who has convinced them. But they are also referring to their playwright, who has convinced, or at least so he hopes, the crowd of the Dionysus Theatre. In the *parabasis* the chorus was by tradition the author's claque: enunciated his message and sang his own praises.

This most original and, one might say, irrational dramatic particle of Greek Comedy—the *parabasis*—had a triple character: it was a eulogy, a libel, and a sermon all in one. Scholars see in it seven parts: [12]

1. The *kommation* (a short introduction, appeal or invocation)

2. The *parabasis proper* or the *anapaests* (where the poet advises his fellow citizens, attacks his enemies, and exalts himself)

3. The *pnigos* or *makron* (a long epigrammatic sentence, which can be either a vow, an oath or a curse)

4. The *ode* or *strophe* (lyrical passage, usually nostalgic, sung by the semichorus)

5. The *epirrhema* (resolution or admonition, sometimes serious, sometimes sarcastic, spoken by one chorus leader)

6. The *antode* or *antistrophe,* and

7. The *antepirrhema*

In the convention of the *parabasis,* Schlegel saw [13] "something incongruous with the essence of dramatic representation; for in the drama the poet should always be behind his dramatic personages, who again ought . . . to take no perceptible notice of the spectators." Theatregoers of the middle twentieth century are in a much better position to understand the parabasis than those of the last one. Our dramaturgy has rediscovered, either purposely or accidentally, much of the spirit of the Aristophanic address to the public and has produced numerous variations on it. We, today, acquainted with the expressionistic and epic drama, as well as with many individual experiments by nonrealistic playwrights, feel more akin to the Attic *parabasis* than to many a fashionable theatrical genre of the imitation-of-life repertory.

The ancient method of performing a *parabasis* is, of course, *terra incognita* for us. We can no more than guess which parts were delivered by the whole chorus and which by one or two leading soloists, where the flute was used and where it was not, where the chorus sang or chanted, danced or walked. The modern director, therefore, can give the *parabasis* any theatrical form he likes, provided that he formally suspend the dramatic action and that he let the company address the audience. The concentration of the Athenian spectator on this lecture (of one hundred or more lines) was doubtless guaranteed by a visual and auditory variety of impressions. That is the purpose of the metrical versatility and multiple form of expression characteristic of the *parabasis*.[14] The *Acharnians* provides us with at least one argument that the *anapaests* were danced by the whole chorus. The leader orders the group to take off their outer garments and make their bodies more fit for dancing (627). The same order occurs in other Aristophanic plays. (Cf. *Lysistrata*, 662, 686.)

The present *parabasis* is also a fine example of Aristophanes' sense of balance between the sublime and the ridiculous. Serious arguments are succeeded by jocular ones in equal proportion. His aims are both objective (to propagandize for Peace) and subjective (to comment on his own career, as that of a comic poet worthy of his mission). Every time, however, that he reaches a climax of earnestness, he purposely brings on an anticlimax. For example, when he prophesizes that foreigners will be visiting Athens hereafter "only to meet the poet, who was courageous enough to tell the citizens what is right," he adds the gasconade that the king of Persia is sure the Athenians will win the war, since they have Aristophanes as their adviser! (643–51)

The *parabasis* over, the chorus withdraws to let the play resume its action. There is no information as to where the dancers stood, or sat, during the episodes. As far as comedy is concerned, I am inclined to imagine that during their moments of inaction they arrayed themselves in a semicircular line, parallel to the circumference of the orchestra, thus becoming the innermost row of spectators. At least that is how they are placed in the Epidaurus productions, and the device seems quite satisfactory. For the audience, they are part of the show; for the actors, part of the audience.[15]

The two episodes that follow—the Megarian's and the Boeotian's—present two contrasting examples of the effects of the war on men, as symbolized by an impoverished Greek and an enriched one. The timid Megarian (729 f.) is so hungry that he is enticed to exchange his two daughters for some salt or garlic from Dicaeopolis' free market. Yet, who would ever buy two skinny girls, as those whom the poor man is dragging behind him? As he happens to come from the hometown of Dorian farce, a farcical trick—a "Megarian machination"—will help him out: he will sell his daughters as if they were pigs. He immediately disguises the girls in pig's attire and orders them to pronounce no other word but *"koi koi"*—thus creating the first item in Aristophanes' rich dictionary of animal sounds.[16] It is also the first of many animal disguises that we shall meet in his comedies and which should be seen as survivals of the old *komos* tradition. Dicaeopolis agrees to buy the pig-girls and the Megarian goes away blissfully exclaiming: "I wish I could sell my mother and my wife too!"

The Boeotian, who comes next (860), is in every way

the opposite of the previous visitor—fat, prosperous, ebu-
lient, gay, and loaded with baskets of goods. He lacks,
however, the other man's ingenuity, which, after all, was a
direct symptom of his misery. The Boeotian does not
come to buy; he has everything that a *bon vivant* can ask
for. On the contrary, he comes to sell some of his prod-
ucts. As Dicaeopolis delights over a fat eel of Lake Copais
—a symbol of terrestrial happiness—the Theban proposes
to exchange it for something that his city lacks and which
abounds in Cleon's Athens—an informer. Going from
word to action, Dicaeopolis captures a notorious stool-
pigeon, Nicarchus, wraps him in straw and gives him to
the visitor in exchange for the eel.

In the meantime Lamachus, the lofty-crested general,
who is also a hungry man, enviously eyes Dicaeopolis'
market. He sends his aide to buy some food, but the Just
Citizen will not sell a single thing to a warmonger. On the
contrary, he is delighted to offer some peace-ointment to a
newly-wed bride, who wishes to keep "the bridegroom's
penis away from the battlefront." He helps her, because
she is a woman and, therefore, not responsible for the war.
This passage gives us the first hint of Aristophanes' attitude toward women. On many occasions he will mock
them, but he will never become their enemy. He laughs at
them, but admires them too. As mothers or mistresses,
they hate war and belong to his own camp. This bride is a
sister of tomorrow's Lysistrata and, consequently, she deserves peace.

The Anthesteria (1000 f.) is the second Dionysiac festival reproduced in the *Acharnians*. As most of these traditional festivities must have been annulled during the
war, Aristophanes makes a generous display of their
charms. He intensifies his antiwar message with arguments
of nostalgia. The play will close, as a matter of fact, with
Dicaeopolis' victory in the drinking bout of the Anthesteria and his acclamation by the chorus.

Before we come to the comedy's conclusion, we ought to mention two important episodes in which the blessings of peace confront the misery of war. The pacific Dicaeopolis and the bellicose Lamachus are juxtaposed in a wildly vivid *stichomythia:*

> L. Boy, bring me out my soldier's knapsack here!
> D. Boy, bring me out my supper basket here!
> . . . .
> L. Now bring me here my helmet's double plume!
> D. Now bring me here my thrushes and ring doves!
> . . . .
> L. Man, don't keep jeering at my armor so!
> D. Man, don't keep peering at my thrushes so!
> . . . .
> L. Surely the moths my crest have eaten up . . .
> D. Sure this hare soup I'll eat before I sup! . .
>
> (1097–1112 *passim*)

The second episode completes the first. Lamachus' aide enters out of breath and, in a parody of tragedy's indispensable messengers, announces that his master has been mortally wounded. "Jumping over a ditch, he broke his ankle on a stake and his skull on a stone! . . ." (1178–80). This so very Chaplinesque description was, unfortunately, a prophetic one. Eleven years after the production of the *Acharnians,* the real Lamachus was killed in the Sicilian expedition, while jumping, Thucydides tells us, over a ditch (VI, 101).

The moaning general is now brought into the orchestra on a stretcher, while Dicaeopolis enters dancing, in the company of two pretty girls. War and Peace have each rewarded their faithful accordingly. The reveling pacifist and the moribund warmonger are once more contrasted in an antiphony that reaches simultaneously the paroxysm of joy and the convulsion of physical pain!

L. My brain is dizzy with the blow of hostile stone!
. . .

D. Mine's dizzy too: to bed I'll go, and not alone!
. . .   (1218–21)

Between the two parallel scenes, an allegorical figure, bearing the name of Reconciliation, makes her appearance. The old men of the chorus, with tears of happiness in their eyes, honor her by singing an ode of Anacreontian flavor: "O dear Reconciliation, we had forgotten how beautiful you were! . . ." (990). Though the figure is mute, her presence is eloquent. Years later, in the *Lysistrata,* the same personification will appear before the spectators, but she will be something quite different: a cockteasing little tart, whom the heroine will use as a decoy for the fighting males. The present Reconciliation has only spiritual charms; the poet is still young.

With the apotheosis of Reconciliation, the catastrophe of Lamachus and the joyful *kordax* of the inebriated Just Citizen, the play comes to its end. Private peace has triumphed and Dicaeopolis is lauded by the Acharnians. The pacific manifesto is over and Aristophanes hopes to win the approbation of all the Athenians—including, of course, the dramatic judges. The comic hero demands a prize for his drinking victory and the comic poet demands a crown of ivy for his dramatic victory. The chorus leaves the orchestra singing the Olympic Hymn of Archilochus (*tenella kallinike!*) as an ovation to both the play's hero and its poet, as if the two were—and they certainly were —one person.[17]

The plays of Cratinus and Eupolis, competing on that day, were defeated by the *Acharnians*—and that is practically all we know about them. By crowning Callistratus, alias Aristophanes, the Athenians showed that they deeply sympathized with his political tribulations and approved of his advocation for peace. After five years of war, most families were lamenting over their dead, heroic slogans had lost their meaning, and the very cause of the war had certainly disappeared in a cloud of uncertainty. After all, those "two whores of Aspasia's" might have been the real cause, as Aristophanes had flippantly suggested. Why not? Stupid causes make wars idiotic.[18]

The Athenians were certain, however, that the young playwright had told them "things disagreeable, but just" (501). And from then on they adopted him as their worthy spokesman. While the Assembly was still searching in the chaos for a leader, the theatre had already found one.

Chapter VI

The *Knights* and Its Enigmatic Hero

*In the end, horror and laughter
may be one.*

T. S. Eliot, *Shakespeare and the
Senecan Tradition*

When he was sitting in the Dionysus Theatre under the hazy winter sun to watch his Acharnians rehearse, Aristophanes was probably already pondering the idea of his next play. It was going to be a comedy forecasting Cleon's downfall. It would present the tanner as a stage character, bearing such likeness with his live model that the public would behold one Cleon being slapped in the orchestra and another witnessing furiously, from the first row, his own degradation.

Aristophanes imparted his idea to Callistratus, no doubt, as he did every year. It seems, however, that for the first time the faithful collaborator shrank. He had so far taken his share of the risk in two of the poet's pacifistic campaigns. Now he chose his own peace. That refusal accounts, perhaps, for the fact that Aristophanes sought a new collaborator in the person of his rival Eupolis. This able dramatist, not much older than he, had been defeated at the Lenaea of the previous year, but two months later he had won first prize at the Great Dionysia, with his comedy the *Golden Race*. We can safely imagine that the

two young playwrights decided to join forces in the making of a political satire. Aristophanes must have been
quite pleased with the project; first, because the attack on
Cleon would become twice as powerful, second, because
he would not have to worry about staging the play, and
third, because the common product could be presented at
the Great Dionysia, since Eupolis, unlike himself, was not
banned there.

The ancient scholiasts saw in Aristophanes' *Knights*
the hand of Eupolis, namely, in the second of the two *parabases*. Eupolis also mentions the event, in his *Baptai* (Fr.
78), saying that "I co-authored those *Knights* with the
Bald One and I let him have them." [1] Why this promising
collaboration did not bear fruit we are unable to say. It is
one of the unsolved mysteries of literature. What we know
is that, after the split, the two playwrights became quite
angry at each other. As for that contemptuous "I let him
have them," it means, of course, that Aristophanes actually pirated the Eupolidean text in the final version of
the *Knights*. The opposite, however, may be true as well;
for Aristophanes will give us his account of the story in
the *Clouds:* "Eupolis dragged his *Marikas* on to the stage,
by turning my *Knights* inside out, as badly as you would
expect him" (553–54).[2] We are meant to understand that
some of their common drafts were used by Eupolis in his
play *Marikas,* produced three years after the *Knights.* The
guess that we can risk, as regards their breach, is that fear
was the cause of Eupolis' retreat, as it had been that of
Callistratus somewhat earlier. He too preferred to play the
part of the prudent Ismene, leaving the "bald" Antigone
to get into trouble alone. Eupolis, as Aristophanes insinuates (*Clouds,* 551), never aimed too high. He was satisfied to attack Hyperbolus and other lesser personalities,
and his invective was never too sharp. When we read his
anti-Periclean lampoons,[3] we cannot make out whether he

besmirches or praises the statesman. Only once, as far as we know, will he attack a strong man openly—Alcibiades. And this unique temerity, the legend says, will cause his death by drowning during a sea-battle commanded by Alcibiades.[4] In this particular case, however, we cannot help wondering why Eupolis first agreed to the collaboration and then recanted. Did he not know from the beginning that the comedy would aim at the notorious demagogue? The answer may be that by the summer of 425 B.C. Cleon, thanks to his victory at Pylos, was ten times more powerful than in the previous winter.

As Thucydides describes the event, the Athenian fleet, commanded by the generals Nicias and Demosthenes, had defeated the Spartans at Pylos, on the southwestern Peloponnesus, and had besieged some of their troops on the small island of Sphacteria. The siege was prolonged and the Athenians seemed incapable of capturing the enemy. The Lacedaemonians, on the other hand, were sending envoys to Athens for peace negotiations. The Athenians on the Pnyx—the same Athenians who five months earlier had applauded Dicaeopolis' peaceful message—were once more mesmerized by Cleon's rhetoric and refused any negotiation. The dynamic tanner, accusing the other generals of being slack with their strategies, undertook the campaign himself, promising to conquer Sphacteria within twenty days. Indeed, in that space of time, he led the army to Pylos, took Sphacteria, and returned victorious, dragging two hundred Spartan prisoners in chains. The people of Athens were greatly impressed by that spectacular success. It was the first time that they had ever beheld an array of so many defeated Spartans marching through the streets of their city. They used to believe that neither starvation nor anything else in the world could ever make the Spartans surrender. Nevertheless, Thucydides does not consider the Sphac-

terian victory as Cleon's achievement. Knowing that Demosthenes was about to capture the island, the shrewd
politician succeeded, by a sudden maneuver, in stealing
the other man's victory. Aristophanes shares this view.
Anyway, the fact remains that in August, 425 B.C., Cleon
was at the apex of his power, while his two rival generals,
Nicias and Demosthenes, had been temporarily eclipsed.
Unchallenged and uncontrolled, Aristophanes' *bête noire*
governed the fates of Athens. Both the rich and the poor
trembled out of fear of him. It was only natural that Eupolis should tremble too.

Cleon's triumph, which made the author of the
Golden Race draw back, had an altogether opposite effect
on Aristophanes. It stimulated him to write the most
ruthless political libel that was ever put on any stage, a
masterpiece of political satire, which among all his works
stands, perhaps, nearest to Cratinus' model of virulent
comedy. This does not imply in the least that the author's
wrath asphyxiated his laughter. The play is a madly hilarious one.[5]

When he first set his mind on the *Knights*, Aristophanes had realized that peace would never be more than
a utopian fancy as long as Cleon dominated the Pnyx. He
knew, therefore, that he could not persuade his audience
to vote for peace, unless he made them see what dangerous sort of a man their leader was. He was determined,
like a courageous knight, to face the terrible enemy in single combat. "Valiantly," as he puts it, he "marched against
the Hurricane and the Tornado" (*Knights,* 511).

Aristophanes and Thucydides are the only writers
who have left us an "after nature" picture of the famous
demagogue. Both have painted a repulsive portrait. In Aristophanes' case, we may conjecture that the poet was
blinded by personal antipathy. And yet, he does not cheat.
The truth which his play projects is, perhaps, a distorted

truth—a truth as fantastically padded as the comic actors —but still the truth. Furthermore, if the playwright becomes in this comedy more vulgar than is theatrically necessary, he does so on purpose. He believes that the best way to fight the demagogue of the Assembly is to become a demagogue of the theatre. After all, only a few minutes' walk separates the one public platform from the other.

Among the eleven surviving plays of Aristophanes, the *Knights* possesses the cleverest prologue, though its comic spirit may be beyond the grasp of the modern spectator. Two slaves emerge from the stage-building, dolefully wailing and rubbing their behinds—a trivial low-comedy scene, inherited from the Dorian farce. When, however, the two slaves stop jumping around and turn to the audience to explain what their trouble is, the public immediately recognize in the actors' masks the generals Demosthenes and Nicias. In fact, the two comedians inform the audience that their old master *Demos* (State) has just bought a new slave, a wild Paphlagonian, who began bullying, beating, and bothering every other servant in the household.[6]

This introductory scene is remarkable for its highly amusing allegory, as well as for another reason: it introduces for the first time the pair of clowns—of the Laurel and Hardy type—which will gloriously survive until our own times.

In a funny sequence of the prologue (117–43), which reminds us of the witches of *Macbeth* prophesying on the succession of the Scottish throne, the two slaves consult some oracles on the succession of the Athenian demagogy. First, there was a rope-seller (Eucrates), ousted by a sheep-seller (Lysicles), ousted in his turn by a leather-seller (Cleon). "Oh god!" exclaims Nicias, "isn't there another 'seller' to oust him too? . . ."

At this very moment (146) as if guided by the hand of a god, a young sausage-seller is seen passing by the theatre, on his way to the market. They call him at once and try to secure his co-operation. "O rich, O blessed one, today nothing, tomorrow a superman! . . ." The butcher-boy looks at them in utter bewilderment and presently answers: "Let me go. I have guts to wash and sausages to sell." The two slave-generals become more persistent. They try to convince him that he is made for a political career. As for his illiteracy it is no obstacle, for vileness, vulgarity, and lack of education are the very virtues of a great politician.

While the sausage-seller is still bewildered by the proposal, two tumultuous events take place. First, the terrifying Paphlagonian makes his entrance, hurling insults and menacing everybody (235). Second, the chorus of the knights gallop in, following at the heels of their mortal enemy (247).

These knights are the only chorus of young men in the surviving Aristophanic plays. They are also among the rare specimen of Athenian youth that the playwright has painted in flattering colors. They are presented as noble and dashing horsemen with idealistic principles. We may imagine that according to fashion, they wear their hair long. We can also presume that they come into the orchestra riding on horseback: not on real horses, of course, but on theatrical ones, symbolized either by two men in a horse disguise, or by a single man wearing a horse's head, or even by toy-horses adjusted around the riders' waists. The last mentioned is a device still in use today during Greek carnivals.

Aristophanes chose the Athenian knights for his chorus, because they were opposed to Cleon's policy. They had revealed that the tanner had been bribed by some of the allied states and they had obliged him to admit his crime before the court. He, on the other hand, had made a counter-accusation against the knights for refusing to fight in the war. So, the comic poet and the Athenian cavalry had, as far as Cleon was concerned, common cause.[7] "His chorus of the *Knights,*" Jaeger writes, "embodied the defensive alliance of nobility and intellect against the growing power of barbarism and political terror. . . . This kind of criticism constituted a revolution in the history of comedy."[8]

As in the *Acharnians,* here, too, the parodos is a violent one, even more so, perhaps, because of the horsemen's youthful verve. Harassed and frightened, the stage-Cleon extends his arms toward the public and appeals for help to the magistrates, reminding them that he had raised their salary to three obols.[9]

One wonders how the real Cleon, sitting among the audience, reacted to all that. This dramatic festival was the first since his military triumph and, according to the custom, he had to occupy the place of honor; therefore, he could not have been absent. Of course, the two spectators who must have enjoyed the anti-Cleonic gags more than anybody else were Demosthenes and Nicias—the real ones.

At this point of the play (275) we have a *coup de théâtre.* The young sausage-seller, who up to that moment had been gaping idly at the goings-on, is suddenly visited by some mysterious spirit and emerges in the first line of action. The farcical idiot is miraculously transformed into the champion of the poet's ideal and takes upon himself the task of exterminating the Paphlagonian tyrant.

What is the real meaning of this change? Are we beholding, as a Marxist would probably say, the awakening of the dormant conscience of the people, or is it something more irrational—a trance, a divine seizure—not much different from that which, centuries later, will en-

able Charlie the Tramp to clear Easy Street of its criminals
or capture single-handedly the Kaiser's army. I prefer either of those two explanations to the criticism often pro-
pounded, that the hero's transformation is a dramatic
lapsus, due to Aristophanes' preoccupation with the political side of his play.[10]

Now the comedy's *agon,* between the sausage-seller
and the Paphlagonian, begins. The two opponents sweat
and strive within the orchestra, in a manner both amazing
and repulsive. Arguments and insults have but one aim:
which of the two will out-Cleon the other. This relentless
battle lasts almost throughout the play; it is the longest
agon, the most breathtaking debate in Greek Comedy, or
in any comedy. It is made up of many rounds, separated
by choral interludes, allowing the fighters to catch their
breaths; the most important is the *parabasis.*

The long flow of the parabatic *anapaests* is a valuable
autobiographical and critical document. Aristophanes reveals his secret publicly for the first time: he confesses that
he is the author of the present comedy, as he was of all
those registered under Callistratus' name. He also explains what has so far prevented him from acknowledging
the plays as his own; not laziness or timidity, but the belief that "staging a comedy is the hardest of all arts" (516).
Among all those, he says, who have flirted with the comic
Muse, only a few really conquered her; and even they
were not for ever happy, because "You," he tells his audience in all earnestness, "are shifting and changeful!"
Thereupon, he recalls the fate of Magnes, Cratinus, and
Crates, yesterday's comic geniuses, who were betrayed and
renounced by their public. The *anapaests* close with the
chorus expressing the wish that Aristophanes' first official
appearance will be hailed by a wonderful "Lenaean noise"
of cheers.

The strophe of the *parabasis* is a hymn to Poseidon,

protector of the knights, and the antistrophe, a hymn to Athena, protectress of the city; the *epirrhema* contains the Aristophanic *leitmotiv* of the glorious forefathers, the heroes of the Marathon epoch. The poet never misses a chance of setting their example before his contemporaries, in the hope that the younger Athenians may decide some day to imitate them. Year after year, however, his faith in his own generation will give way to bitter doubt, until complete disenchantment will make him abandon Athens for the plumed Utopia of Cloudcuckoo City.

During the *parabasis,* the Paphlagonian has gone to the Parliament, to accuse the knights and the sausage-seller of high treason.[11] The butcher-boy now returns, frolicking, and relates how he managed to dissolve the Parliament, while the Paphlagonian spoke, by just telling its members that "very cheap anchovies were on sale at the market." Upon hearing that, he says, the Representatives rose at once and, jumping over their benches, ran to the market.

The stage-Cleon returns, too, shamefaced, but still foaming. He swears that he will be avenged by the State itself, that is, by their master, the old Demos. We cannot help suspecting that this may have been exactly the menace that the real Cleon had pronounced, when he had lost his first round against Aristophanes (710). The old Demos, who is now requested to come out of the house, is a fatuous centenarian, wearing most probably a mask similar to Pollux' frowning *second Pappos,* or his *Hegemon presbytes,* who is raising his brow.[12] The old man symbolizes the Athenian State and, besides being silly, he is clothed in rags, wears town sandals, and has the overall aspect of a fallen lord.

The fiery verbal tournament of the two antagonists before Demos is the strongest part of the *agon.* Repartees are sometimes as politically colored as if they were copied from the minutes of the Pnyx. Occasionally, however, the action becomes pure slapstick. The two opponents, trying to outshadow each other in obsequiousness and flattery toward their master, are an early version of Arlecchino and Capitano competing for Pantalone's daughter or purse. The Paphlagonian speaks about his services to the State: "I had to press, to squeeze, to crash and to mash the taxpayers, O Demos, to make you rich!" The sausage-seller uses a different method. He starts by insulting the old man for his imbecility, and then suddenly switches from insults to endearments—the first being a soft pillow which he offers Demos, so that hereafter he can sit on birds' feathers and not on the hard rock, where the heartless Paphlagonian had left him. The elder is enormously impressed by such generosity. He turns and stares at the butcher-boy, as if he were seeing him for the first time, and exclaims in utter admiration: "Man, who are you? . . . Are you, by any chance, a descendant of our mighty Harmodius, the slayer of tyrants? . . . Because this gesture of yours was, in truth, heroic and philodemic! . . ." (786–87).

The most decisive moment of the combat, however, is the "rabbit." The Paphlagonian brings forth a stewed rabbit, hoping that with this gift he will definitely win the master's favor. The sausage-seller, making use of a Falstaffian or, more literally, Megarian trick, steals the rabbit and offers it on his own behalf. The Paphlagonian is furious. "You stole another man's stuff!" he screams. The sausage-seller promptly answers: "You did the same at Pylos!" And the heretofore frowning Demos now roars with laughter. The Paphlagonian is finally compelled to accept his defeat and falls down in mortal agony.

The mediocre *second parabasis* (1264–1315)—possibly, the Eupolidean one slightly manipulated by Aristophanes—is necessary to permit old Demos to leave the stage for a while and presently return wearing the mask of a young man. He has been rejuvenated, thanks to a miraculous bath prepared by the sausage-seller, who apparently knows all the magic tricks of the Euripidean Medea.

The name of the sausage-seller is now revealed— Agoracritus (the Chosen One of the Market Place)—and his solemn triumph before the Propylaea of the Acropolis will close the play. Was there a change of scenery to indicate the Propylaea? And how did it work? By a large *ekkyklema?* By the *pinakes?* Or were the *periaktoi* in use since Aristophanes' times, contrary to what archaeologists believe? . . . In any similar case, we would contend that nothing really changed, and that poetry alone conveyed a new scenery to the spectators' imagination. Here, however, the word *rhothos* (noise) is used by the hero (1326) which implies that some machinery did actually function to present the Propylaea.

The knights hail their home-city and the rejuvenated Demos with Simonidean rapture, while Agoracritus, the new chancellor, presents his sovereign with a peace-treaty of thirty years. The procession of those *spondai* composes the grand finale of the comedy. In what theatrical aspect did they appear, we wonder? Most probably, as wine-jars. In the *Acharnians* too the *spondai* were visualized as jugs full of wine and, after all, the word itself suggests libations. So the closing procession must have been both a symbolic vow for Peace and a homage to the wine-drinking god of the theatre.

Just before the *exodos* of the chorus, for which no song is provided by the existing manuscripts, the young Demos orders his servants to carry the comatose Cleon out of the theatre, "so that all the foreigners may see him." In other words, the foreigners who did not attend the performance, because Aristophanes was restricted to the local Lenaea, will now have a chance of beholding the fallen Cleon and of rejoicing thereof. On the other hand, Agoracritus, the Savior of the State, is invited to a princely banquet at the Prytaneum, where he is to occupy Cleon's former chair.[13]

As we watch the sausage-seller's prodigious rise from the marketplace to the Prytaneum, we cannot avoid repeating to ourselves the bewildered old Demos' question: "Man, who are you? . . ." That question had been, in fact, in our minds since Agoracritus' first appearance in the play. Who is he? Where did Aristophanes discover him? What did he mean by him? . . .

To say that the sausage-seller is merely a clever representative of the lower classes, a cunning slave, like those of the Dorian Drama or the future Sosiases, Xanthiases or Carions is not the answer to our question. The author of the *Knights* had set the tone from the beginning for an allegorical satire. The two whimpering slaves were Nicias and Demosthenes, the Paphlagonian was Cleon, Demos was the Athenian People. Agoracritus could not, therefore, deviate from the general scheme. He could not be *any* sausage-seller, a fortuitous personage introduced for the sake of the plot. We are not yet in the domain of New Comedy or even the later Aristophanic plays. Here, the comic rascal is also a hero, a militant ideologist who wins the *agon* and ultimately triumphs as the savior of the City.

The popularity of comedy in Athens relied much on the easy riddles, which it proposed to its public. Taking, therefore, this particular case as a riddle, we may attempt some guesses as to its meaning.

1. *First guess:* Agoracritus is the average Athenian, representing the whole population of the city.

Objection: Sausage-selling was not an average Athenian trade. Besides, the average Athenian could not be typified by a common, uneducated loafer.

2. *Second guess:* The comic poet chose on purpose a common, uneducated specimen of mankind for his hero, in order to emphasize Cleon's lowliness and vulgarity. He matched, that is to say, the famous scoundrel of the Pnyx with an infamous scoundrel of the market-place, sarcastically theorizing that no respectable or virtuous citizen was destined to beat Cleon.

Objection: Agoracritus may be vulgar and illiterate, but he is also an ingenious and patriotic young man, with a real concern for his country's prosperity.

3. *Third guess:* The sausage-seller is the theatrical disguise of a real political personality, who embodies the hopes of all anti-Cleonic Athenians. As this conforms to the play's concrete allegory, it is probable that the mask worn by the sausage-seller represented some definite person.

Objection: If it were so, the ancient scholiasts, who tell us who the "rope-seller" and the "sheep-seller" were, would have deciphered the sausage-seller's identity as well. Furthermore, no political personality mentioned by history could in those days be considered as an outstanding figure in the People's Assembly, or even in Attic Comedy. Alcibiades had, of course, begun his career; but this up-and-coming politician, so typical of the depraved youth that Aristophanes loathed, could by no means typify the comic poet's vision of the State's savior. Besides, nothing alluding to Alcibiades' precious personality can be traced in the role.[14]

4. *Fourth guess:* Agoracritus is a thoroughly fictitious dramatis persona: the incarnation of a hope, the vaguely anticipated political messiah. Let Athens be saved, Aris-

tophanes seems to pray, even if its savior is a butcher-boy! The slave of Alcestis was none other than Apollo and the one-sandaled tramp none other than Jason. Likewise, that butcher-boy may be the reincarnation of Cecrops or Theseus.[15]

There is *no objection* to this guess, because fantasy knows no boundaries.

5. *Fifth guess:* Agoracritus is Aristophanes himself. Of course, the identification of a playwright with his hero is a general rule in drama. More particularly, Aristophanes' heroes always project his views and fight for his ideals. What we suspect in the *Knights* is a more definite similarity between the creator and his creation. Aristophanes created a mirror-image of himself, destined to appear on the stage in his own clothes and manners, speaking with his own voice, and wearing a mask with his own features.

The comedy deals with the efforts of a young Athenian—a funny man at the beginning, who later takes his purpose seriously—to exterminate Cleon. It is the chronicle of a long fight between the two rivals, one being the *pharmakós,* the evil influence on the People, the other emerging as *alexíkakos,* the People's honest protector. By revealing the Paphlagonian's crimes and fallacies (as Aristophanes was doing), Agoracritus becomes (as Aristophanes desires to become) the City's spiritual guide and savior. Rejuvenating the State is the sausage-seller's achievement and the comic poet's ambition.

The fifth guess is the one we vote for; and here are some arguments for this preference:

a) The name and the profession of the hero both begin with the same letter and both have the same number of syllables as the poet's name (*Agoracritus-Allantopoles-Aristophanes*).

b) The hero is mentioned as "very young" (611) with no other obvious reason than of being Aristophanes' own age: about twenty-five.

c) The Paphlagonian says to his young opponent: "Go ahead, talk! Words you have plenty! . . . In a little trial once you spoke about immigrants . . ." (344–46). The famous law-suit between Cleon and the poet is insinuated more than once.

d) The knights praise Agoracritus, more than choruses usually praise the comic hero, by exclamations such as: "O excellent speaker!" (617) or "I envy your eloquence!" (837). In fact, there is a phrase of the chorus wonderfully suggestive of the comic poet's art: "So, there are things which burn more than fire! And words more impudent than impudent discourses of politicians! . . ." (382–84), which may refer to Aristophanes' flaming attacks on the demagogue. It should be noted that no other Aristophanic character is ever so much lauded on his skill in speaking, not even Praxagora, the suffragette, and certainly not Socrates, the sophist.

e) The rejuvenation and beatification of the old Demos is also a parable of the poet's ambition to make his city young and healthy again, with his admonitions and with his entertaining art.

f) As the playwright had remained anonymous in the past years, only now producing a comedy under his own name, in the same way his hero remains anonymous throughout the play and reveals his identity only at the end.

g) Agoracritus' final gift to Demos is Peace: in other words, the very same beneficial gift that Aristophanes hopes to offer the Athenian State through his wise persuasion.

h) The hero's profession is also relevant to the play's allegory. A satirist deals, much like a sausage-trader, with

the bowels of the animal called Public Life. At the end of
the play the defeated Paphlagonian is condemned to become a sausage-seller, and to mix hereafter "dog and donkey meat." Is not that exactly the comic poet's job: to deal
with the canine and asinine phenomena of social life? . . .
Having overthrown Cleon and having taken his place as
spiritual leader of the people, Aristophanes condemns his
fallen foe, with a sense of generous humor, to the playwright's unrewarding profession!

   i) One last argument, derived not from the play itself,
but from the literature written around it. A rumor had
reached the grammarians of Alexandria that Aristophanes
himself had acted in the *Knights,* having painted his face
with vermillion pigment. Both the ancient biographer
and the second argument to the *Knights* state that Aristophanes was obliged to incarnate the Paphlagonian, because no actor risked appearing in the part. Most probably, the information has its root in the playwright's own
joke: that mask-makers were so scared of Cleon, that they
would not dare reproduce his features on the Paphlagonian's mask (230–33). It is possible, however, that the
rumor was not completely fallacious and that Aristophanes had actually acted in his play. But in that case would
he have chosen the part of Cleon, instead of that of Anti-
cleon? I doubt it. I would rather imagine that the comic
poet not only presented himself, symbolically, under
the stage personality of the sausage-seller, but also that he
performed the part in the theatre. He appeared in person
in the orchestra, as if he were on the Pnyx, to face his political enemy.

   As for the passage on the frightened mask-makers, I
don't think it should be taken seriously. Athenian mask-
makers, who so often had shaped Pericles' long head for
comedy purposes, would not have been afraid to do the
same for the tanner's. After all, democracy was still a fact,

and the perils involved in the freedom of individual expression were part of the system.

Abandoned both by Callistratus and by Eupolis, Aristophanes was obliged to stage the *Knights* himself. This new venture, superimposed on the intensity of the play's political outcry, makes the year 424 a crucial one for the poet. By now he had acquired, no doubt, the necessary knowledge about stage techniques. By watching Callistratus rehearse, he must have learned how to move a performance, how to coach the actors, how to arrange and teach his own musical score. He would know to what extent the *melos* (song) and the *parakataloge* (chant or recitative) should be used to achieve aesthetic symmetry, what was the right contribution of the flute and the lyre to the performance, when was the *endosimon* or signal given by the leader of the chorus for collective movement, and so forth. He knew, of course, all about the *kordax,* comedy's vivid and obscene dancing-solo; about the various *harmonies*—Lydian for passion, Dorian for grandeur, Phrygian for realism, and so forth—and about the traditional theatrical *attitudes, gestures,* and *moves* of the chorus, that Pollux, half a millennium later, will describe. And, of course, he knew more than well what to do with the *anapaestic tetrameter,* his favorite verse rhythm.[16]

As for scenery and machinery, his special interest in Euripides must have been reason enough for making him familiar with every technical trick known to the stage-hands of those days. His plays attest, on the other hand, that he was well aware of every type of theatrical costume: what dress befitted a master, a slave, a god, a scullery-maid, or a free-citizen's wife; who should wear a long and who a short *chiton,* an *exomis,* a *krokotos,* an *amphimaschalos,* and so forth.[17]

Masks were not yet as strictly classified as they will be during the era of New Comedy, when stock characters will dominate the stage. Old Comedy did not, as a rule, deal so much with types as with real persons and allegorical figures. Consequently, Aristophanic masks must have enjoyed a certain freedom, depending primarily on their designer's imagination.[18]

There is abundant information about tragic actors and very little about comic ones. We are free to accept or reject Tzetzes' testimony that Cratinus was the first to establish the number of three actors in comedy, as Sophocles had done in tragedy. Aristophanes, however, does not seem handcuffed by that rule, using occasionally as many as five actors.[19] Most of the comic poets had so far been the protagonists of their own plays; but this was no longer the rule in Aristophanes' day. The names of Myllos and Maison are vaguely mentioned as early Athenian actors, possibly poets too. It is also suspected that a certain Hermon had existed. The only actor's name to be found in the official *didaskaliai* is that of Apollodorus, the interpreter of Trygaeus (in the *Peace*).[20] He may have appeared in other plays as well, for many Aristophanic protagonists belong to the Trygaeus species. And we know from Shakespeare, Molière, Chekhov, and others that great dramatists usually put their trust in certain actors, to whom they remain loyal.

The best proof that Aristophanes was by now well trained in play-production is the fact that the Lenaean judges of 424 B.C. gave him first prize. It was the third first prize that he received within his four years in the theatrical profession. We may, therefore, say that the rise of Aristophanes coincided with that of Cleon; for they reached together the summit of professional success. As for the Athenians, those astonishing specimens of "inconstancy and irresoluteness," they applauded with equal enthusiasm the former's comedies and the latter's speeches. No sooner would they embrace the opinion of the first than they would be persuaded in the opposite sense by the second. During four consecutive years, by acclaiming the comic poet, they expressed their disapproval of the demagogue. And yet, during the same years, they themselves created the monster of Cleon's omnipotence.

These Athenians, who had raised the twenty-six-year-old dramatist to the zenith of glory, would also very soon let him fall.

Chapter VII

The *Clouds* and Socrates

The Tanners Shoemakers and Seam-
stresses of Athens applauded a farce where
Socrates appeared in the air and said
that there is no God.
                    Voltaire, *Philosophic Dictionary* [1]

In the spring of 424 B.C., there lived in Athens an unhappy old poet and a happy young one. The old poet was
at the end of his life; he felt tired and looked back with
bitterness at his whole life's work which had now fallen
into ruins. A number of years ago he was the king of
laughter in Athens, but now he inspires nothing but pity
from those he encounters in the streets or from those who
attend his comedies in the theatre. For two consecutive
years he has been defeated at the Lenaea and the second
prize he did receive was perhaps given to him as a mere
consolation. The once audacious old poet who made even
Pericles tremble has now no other company than his
wine jug, which has been his great love as well as the
cause of his decline. Late at night he returns home from
the tavern and there, "on a filthy sheepskin," Cratinus
goes on snoring.[2]

The young poet is not yet twenty-six and already all
Greece has cheered him. He is the man who, more than
anybody else, makes the soldiers relax from the miseries of

war with his god-sent laughter. He is, moreover, the idealist who fights for peace, often endangering his personal
freedom. In the small towns where the Greeks build walls,
demolish walls, moan and groan, one of his quips comes
every now and then by word of mouth to bring the balm
of gaiety. Cleon, of course, is always after him, trying to
trap him; on the other hand, Eupolis, Ameipsias, and
Phrynichus, even the old Cratinus, are dangerous rivals.
But the glory of dramatic creation and the love of his
fellow Athenians have made our young poet spiritually
immune. Therefore, he is no longer afraid to declare
publicly his name—Aristophanes, son of Philip, of the
Cydathenaeon deme and the Pandionis tribe—an immense ego.

   With his next play, Aristophanes is resolved to compete in the Great Dionysia. And to avoid being disquali-
fied in advance, he will submit a harmless literary satire,
which will by no means damage Cleon's authority. His
anti-Cleonic attacks will be heard again, as in the two previous years, in the Lenaea. He will thus expand his theatrical campaign on both Dionysiac fronts. He plans the
Merchant Ships for January and the *Clouds* for March.

   From the *Merchant Ships* (*Holcades*) we possess
about fifty lines, but we are ignorant of its fate in the competition. According to the grammarians, peace was the
main subject of this comedy, in which Aristophanes assaulted "the bellicose Lamachus and the reactionary
Cleon." [3] In other words, the politician and the military
man, who had begun their stage careers in the *Babylonians* and the *Acharnians,* reappeared in new adventures.
They had become by now stock characters, and the public
looked forward to laughing at them. Scholars even go so
far as to surmise the plot: the Athenians and the Spartans,
wishing to exchange their complaints, ship them to each
other. The cargoes of complaints, however, are so enor-

mous that by looking at them the two rivals decide to make peace.[4]

The *Clouds,* on the other hand, is one of the best known plays of Aristophanes and, without doubt, the one that has given us more trouble than any of the others. It contains the most puzzling riddle in the poet's entire production and one of the major question marks in the history of literature. Why did Aristophanes attack Socrates? Why did the young and intelligent playwright present the wisest and most virtuous man of his time as a ridiculous and improbable buffoon—an exaggerated combination of the Homeric Thersites and the Sileni offered in abundance by the satyr drama? This question, especially in connection with the condemnation of Socrates twenty-four years later, transcends the narrow limits of literary criticism to become a historical enigma.

Numberless pages have been written to explain the Aristophanic Socrates, as well as Plato's subsequent attitude toward the man who ridiculed his beloved teacher. In our opinion, the position taken by Aristophanes in the *Clouds* is in full accord with the policy he has so far maintained. His target here is the prevailing educational system which he considers the cause of the overall degeneration of Athenian thought. Under its influence, the citizens vote for Cleon and carry on a disastrous civil war. The subject is not unsimilar to that of the *Banqueters,* though more passionately treated. In the former play, the problem of youth was simpler: their shortcomings were laziness, illiteracy, and sophisticated blabber. The *Clouds* aims at a more dangerous evil: the inclination of youth to the new philosophic theories which shake the foundation of religion, family, democracy, and morality.

In those days, many schools of higher education had been opened in Athens, most of them directed by foreign sophists. From the picture that Plato will give us in his

Protagoras—where three famous sophists meet in the house of the rich Athenian Callias—we get an idea of how important and how eccentric these teachers were.[5] Aristophanes could very well have chosen one of these three sophists as his hero. Why didn't he do so? Someone has said that Attic comedy tactfully limited itself to attacking none but Athenian monsters.[6] On the other hand, our playwright may have been unwilling to slander any actual school; he didn't hold responsible this system or that, but modern education in general. This is, perhaps, one of the reasons why he chose Socrates, who was a native Athenian, did not have a school of his own, and in the public eye was not so very different from the teachers of revolutionary and preposterous ideas.

We must not forget that the Socrates we know today is mostly the Socrates that Plato has created. The ideal personality, immortalized by the faithful pupil, will first appear nearly thirty or forty years after the *Clouds,* when the early dialogues will be published.[7] Only then will the enormous difference between Socrates and the sophists become obvious, as well as the deeper significance of the former's teachings. For the average Athenian of Aristophanes' time Socrates is nothing more than a peculiar type of the agora, a barefooted and impecunious tramp who frequents the gymnasium, lectures on new and never-heard-of-before ideas and is always amusing because he makes fun first of all of himself. Although he never has enough money to pay for a meal, he is invited to dinners as a special attraction, because he is able to deliberate until dawn and drink without getting tipsy.[8] It is not very likely that he has, as yet, created his famous method or fathomed the mystery of the human mind. His present theories may be identical to a certain extent with all the strange things that the sophists are telling their students about astronomy, geology, geometry, or even, as Aristophanes mocks, about whether gnats hum from their mouths or their behinds (*Clouds,* 157–58). In the classic Greek century the sophists were generally regarded like the surrealists or the existentialists in our own era; and very probably every person of daring ideas, unshaven and unkempt, would be deemed a sophist. So the pre-Platonic Socrates may have been a victim of such a misunderstanding; because even in his days of posthumous glory the orator Aeschines will refer in one of his speeches to "Socrates the sophist." [9]

The Platonic Socrates that we are more familiar with, therefore, is not the original Socrates. Aristophanes, responsible for the oldest portraits of Cleon and Euripides, was also the first to give a picture of the forty-seven-year-old philosopher. This practice was eagerly exploited by some of his fellow playwrights and, henceforward, Socrates became a fashionable attraction on the comic stage. We discover many invectives referring to the philosopher, about his dirty and shabby cloak, his absurd chatter, his poverty, and so on. "I too hate Socrates, the impecunious," Eupolis says, "who thinks about everything and only forgets to think how to eat" (Fr. 352). Aristophanes was the first to accuse Socrates—arousing Voltaire's wrath many centuries later—of stealing the athletes' clothes in the palaestra for the sake of his students (*Clouds,* 179). Similar thefts were exploited by Ameipsias (Fr. 9) and Eupolis (Fr. 361). After all, Attic Comedy had license for even worse charges. An unwritten theatrical privilege made comedy the executioner of all the great figures, from Aeschylus to Pericles and from Homer even to its own god Dionysus.

At any rate, the Socrates of the comic poets was the first Socrates to appear in history. It was, furthermore, the only depiction of himself that Socrates lived to know. On the contrary, the Platonic dialogues are posthumous appraisals, in which one might discern more of Plato's own way of thinking than of his quasi-legendary master's. It may not, therefore, be too daring or sacrilegious to surmise that, between the caricature made by Aristophanes and the hagiography made by Plato, the first bears more likeness to the human original. In fact, the Aristophanic view finds its advocates to a considerable degree in Xenophon, not to mention Plutarch, Diogenes Laertius, and ancient anecdotology.[10] No matter how biased our playwright was in his social sermon, it is unlikely that he distorted the real Socrates more than he had done the real Cleon or the real Euripides; and we know well (from Thucydides' descriptions of the former as well as from the tragedies of the latter) that whatever Aristophanes wrote about them remains within the bounds of probability. Notwithstanding the laughable exaggeration that ancient comedy could make use of, the Athenian spectators would never accept a false theatrical semblance. Thus, we may blame Aristophanes for his lack of understanding of the Socratic mind, but we can by no means reject altogether the plausibility of his Socrates.

Many things have been written both by ancients and moderns, with the purpose of justifying or of analyzing the comic poet's attitude toward the philosopher. Some, for instance, said that Anytus and Meletus instigated the Aristophanic attack; yet the two accusers of Socrates could not have been more than children when the *Clouds* was produced. Others have maintained that Aristophanes was jealous of Socrates, because Archelaus, the art-patron king of Macedonia, had invited the philosopher to his court and not him. And the old *Life* vaguely states that the comic poets had "some controversy" with the philosophers.[11]

Perhaps the following speculations may cast some light on Aristophanes' choice of his comic hero:

1. He chose this free-lance philosopher who never

had a school of his own, in order to avoid libeling any of the particular sophistic academies.

2. It is a well-known truth that our comic poet, although he hits *en passant* many petty nuisances, never condescends to fight seriously except with those standing high. "Having the temper of Heracles, I fight with the greatest," he himself will comment on his audacity (*Wasps*, 1030). His heroes, when they are real characters, will always be the most prominent Athenian statesmen, generals, or tragic poets. So the fact alone that he dedicates a whole play to Socrates signifies that he picks him out as the most important, and for that reason the most dangerous, teacher of the young.

3. Attic Comedy was supposed to present familiar faces; the likeness of the mask would guarantee half of the success. Quite naturally, the wandering Socrates was, for the man-in-the-street, a more familiar face than the various sophists known to academic circles alone. Therefore, just by his appearance on the stage, he could create mirth, for even such a favorite disciple as Alciabiades admitted that to meet Socrates was, at first, a funny experience. With his Silenean features, his bald head, his belly, his bare feet, and shabby clothes, Socrates offered the comic poet a ready-made figure of Megarian farce.[12] So the mere external appearance of the philosopher must have been a great temptation to Aristophanes.

4. Socrates was himself a man with an acute sense of humor, always ready to laugh when people teased him. Aristophanes, therefore, feared no reprisals. He knew that the starving sage responded good humoredly to every joke made at his expense. There is a story, mentioned by Diogenes Laertius, that once a man kicked Socrates, and when the latter's friends asked him why he did not sue the offender, Socrates replied "What for? If a donkey kicked me, would I sue him?"

The deeper reason, however, which compelled Aristophanes to write the *Clouds* was not a matter of joking. He wanted to attack collectively all the imposters of education, all the philosophic quacks by whose influence, he thought, young Athenians were being led astray and old ideals were being forsaken. If he became the moral instigator of Socrates' later condemnation, it was beyond his intention. Socrates was destined to serve as the scapegoat for the sins of the sophists; no one among them drank the hemlock and none even became so famous a comedy character as he. What argues for Aristophanes' innocence of purpose is Plato's complaisance toward him. If the playwright had been seriously responsible for the philosopher's condemnation, Plato would not have included him, as friend among friends, in the famous *Symposium,* written fifteen years or so after Socrates' death. About Plato's attitude toward Aristophanes we shall speak in due time. Now the future author of the *Dialogues* is not more than four or five years old and not, as yet, acquainted either with the Socrates wandering in the agora or the Socrates wandering among the Aristophanic clouds.[13]

A chronological detail, however, seems to be anything but flattering to the playwright. During the summer of 424 B.C., while Aristophanes was sitting comfortably in his home worrying about peace, Socrates, as a plain soldier, was fighting for his country at Delion. The noncombatant Aristophanes, in the *Clouds,* shoots the recruited philosopher for leading young people away from the patriotic ideals of Aeschylus and the Marathon warriors. He attacks at a moment when the poor defendant is much more Aeschylean and much more Marathonian than his heartless prosecutor.[14]

The two comedies of Aristophanes are approved by the respective archons in charge of the two festivals and are performed in the same year. The *Clouds,* attended by the

Athenians in the City Dionysia of 423 B.C., is not, at least
in its entirety, the *Clouds* that we know. Ancient grammarians inform us that "two *Clouds* are mentioned";
moreover, taking their information from Eratosthenes,
they distinguish between what the playwright wrote in
"the performed *Clouds*" and what he writes in "the modified" version.[15] The modified version is the one which has
come down to us, and philologists date it three or four
years after the original one. In the next chapter we shall
try to discover the reasons which compelled Aristophanes
to rewrite this play, as well as the reasons which made posterity retain the second version of the comedy, leaving the
first to oblivion.

According to the valuable Argument VI of the
Clouds, the second play "is similar to the first and has
been revised in various parts . . . generally it has been reworked throughout; some elements have been taken out
and new ones have been added and many changes have
been made in the structure and the characters. The parts
transformed altogether are the *parabasis* of the chorus, the
scene where Just Reason speaks to Unjust, and finally the
burning of the house of Socrates." The elements given by
this Argument help us to reconstruct, *mutatis mutandis,*
the performance of 423 B.C.

The comedy opens in the house of Strepsiades, where
the old father and his son are sleeping. Actually, the son is
snoring profoundly, whereas the father cannot find peace.
Strepsiades is a typical Aristophanic elder, whose *moira*
had him born in the country but married in the city. Contrary to Sheridan's Sir Peter Teazle who had to suffer a
country wife, Aristophanes' hero has had a hell of a time
with his city wife. "When at night we went to bed together, I smelled of wine, figs and sheep and she of per-
fumes" (49–51).

The fruit of that incongruous coupling was a single

son Pheidippides, named so because the aristocratic
mother insisted that in the boy's name the word *hippos*
(horse) be incorporated as a sign of knighthood. When
the son grew up, he was caught in the cross-fire between
his parents, who had conflicting ideas about his education.
The maternal influence being more drastic, the son took
the road to laziness, snobbishness, and flattery, a perfect
example of the depraved younger generation. The result
was that he learned nothing and is currently caught up in
debts.

Utterly nonchalant, the young Pheidippides sleeps
and "farts," wrapped in five blankets, while the poor sire
keeps ruminating about his son's expenses, debts, and
horses. The last cock has already crowed when Strepsiades
makes his decision. He wakes up the young man and implores him to follow him. (They will not go far: if their
house was indicated by the left door of the proskenion,
they only walk to the right door, where we must imagine
the sophists' school.) Along the way the old man tells the
sleepy youngster that he must enroll as a student of those
wise teachers. Thus, he says, "if you study the Unjust Reason, taught by them, we will not have to pay a penny of
your debts" (117–19).

The urgings of the old man are all in vain, for the
son is adamant in his refusal to obey. "How shall I be able
to face my fellow knights, if I become one of those pale
and miserable students?" he exclaims (119–20). Furious,
Strepsiades sends him to hell and decides, as the last resort, to enroll himself. So he knocks at the door, while the
son returns to his bed.

The scene that follows (126–275) is the second part
of the prologue, for the chorus entrance has not yet taken
place. Still it has the character of an episode, because two
new characters, the student and Socrates, make their appearance. This student who opens the door, scowling be-

cause the knocking has made him miscarry a philosophic idea, agrees to let Strepsiades have a glimpse of the school's interior; and this is technically realized by the *ek-kyklema*, which presently reveals the sanctum with all the unshaven and pale-faced scholars, who, like nuns in ecstasy, are prostrated. The old man asks, quite astonished, what they are doing in that position. "They are doing research on the Underworld," the student replies. "And why do their behinds point at the sky?" "Because they study astronomy" (192–94).

The student, however, orders his fellows to disappear because they must not "stay too long in the open air." And then, all of a sudden, Strepsiades sees, high above their heads, an incongruous spectacle: over the central door of the proskenion there hangs a basket in which a man is sitting. "Who is that fellow hanging in the air?" he asks. And the student replies with monosyllabic veneration: "He!" (219).

With the help of the *mechane,* the teacher descends to earth like a Euripidean god. In fact, the first words he utters, when Strepsiades interrupts his lofty brooding, bears a divine grandeur:

> SOCR.: Why do you call me, O mortal?
> STREP.: Tell me first, what are you doing up there?
> SOCR.: Air-borne, I examine the sun. (223–25)

And when the ignorant visitor inquires why it is necessary to get into a basket to study the sun, the sage explains that "If from below I should look up I would not discover anything: the earth attracts and absorbs the fluids of thought, like the sap of the cress." And the poor retarded old man whispers: "No kidding, so the cress also thinks! . . ." displaying the same astonished admiration as, centuries later, Molière's would-be-gentleman before the new horizons of philosophy.

In the meantime, the space-surveying Socrates has landed, though he will remain "in the clouds" throughout the play. He is the antipode of common sense: an eccentric and highbrow mastermind; an intellectual snob. As such, he belongs to the comic tradition of all the pedantic professors of the universal stage. As Lamachus is the ancestor of all braggart soldiers (*Acharnians*) and the Aristophanic elders the originals of all pantaloons and gerontions, so this Socrates is the first pedant or doctor of the theatre.[16] Nevertheless, although lizards excrete on his skull while he is contemplating the stars, he is a person of enormous authority. He impresses with his eloquence and profundity. The explanations he offers about natural phenomena are even scientifically convincing. In creating his sage's theories, Aristophanes borrowed indiscriminately from the sophists and the natural philosophers, maybe also from genuine Socratic pronouncements of the early period. It is quite illuminating for the history of Greek thought that the first instruction that Socrates gives to the amazed Strepsiades concerns the substitution of new gods for the old ones. Thus, after praying to Air, to Ether, and to the Clouds, he invokes those last-mentioned powers to appear before the elderly novice.[17]

The *parodos* of the chorus does not take place at once, as in the previous comedies. The Clouds' song is heard from afar (275 ff.) answering Socrates' call. Thunder is heard at the same time, frightening Strepsiades, who is trying to discern the strange goddesses arriving over the top of Mt. Parnes.

The teacher tells him why these Clouds are the most precious of all the new divinities and why they protect the philosophers; in so doing he also explains to us why Aristophanes chose them for the chorus of this play: "These Clouds, great and heavenly, are the goddesses of the idle: they offer knowledge and shrewdness, discussion and excessive talk, skill in lying and the art to attack and to get away with it" (316–18). In other words, the dialectic expertise of the sophists is no more than cloudy masses, dull and empty, thundering and made of thin air.

The Clouds appear (probably at line 358) still singing; it is a strange and rare chorus, not only in its symbolism but also in its physical appearance. Comedy choruses usually were human beings, men or women, having in common either a geographical origin, a profession, or a vice. In other cases, they belonged to the kingdom of animals or semihuman beings. We can easily visualize most of them in their costumes, masks, plumes, horns, or tails. Even Cratinus' *Androgynes* can, with a little effort, be imagined. Yet, what could possibly have been the aspect of other choruses, personifying abstract ideas, such as the *Laws* or the *Riches,* the *Islands* or the *Cities?* [18] We possess no description of them and the vase-paintings do not help us in any way. One such case is the misty and mystic chorus of this comedy. The only thing that we are told is that they look like "mortal women" and that they have "noses" (341, 344). As for the way they move and for their general comportment, we cannot help recalling Brecht's admiring description of Mei Lan-fang's art: "He could imitate a passing cloud." [19]

Now, with the Clouds sitting around, like priestesses of the New Thought, the systematic conversion of the old man begins (364). The first thing that he learns is that what causes rain and thunder is the Clouds and not Zeus, whom he had always imagined "pissing through a sieve." Socrates explains those facts with a popularizing method that could be envied by all our school texts; as, for instance, the simile of the thunder: "In the Panathenaean festival, when your belly is full of soup, you suddenly begin to thunder" (386–87).

Strepsiades, however, has no time to waste; he only

wants to learn what is necessary for him to do in order to slip "like an eel" out of his creditors' hands. He is ready even to masquerade as a sophist. In a passionate song, he swears allegiance to the Clouds and follows Socrates inside the mystic halls, after having stripped naked, in accordance with the rules of the school (509).

At this point, we have the *parabasis,* only 152 lines after the *parodos,* something quite unusual in Aristophanic comedy. The *parabasis* is one of the three parts of the play which, according to our information mentioned above, were revised some years later in the second version. So, the extant *parabasis* is inspired primarily by the failure of the 423 B.C. performance of the play. It is a vigorous apology by the poet and a bitter retrospection of his career. It is the only instance of an Attic comedy narrating the chronicle of its own performance and also the unique case of a play writing its own autobiography. Aristophanes' chief point is that the 423 B.C. *Clouds* was the best play the Athenians had ever seen and that they—public and judges—were unable to appreciate it (518–25). Aside from being an interesting literary document, however, this *parabasis* does not tell us anything about the topic discussed in the original one. Perhaps only the *epirrhemas* (575–94 and 607–26), which mention persons and events of 423 B.C., belong to it.

In the subsequent episode (627 ff.) Socrates comes out of his school swearing. He never before has had such a helplessly idiotic student. Nonetheless, he makes a final effort to educate the naked Strepsiades. Of this course, which is extended on grammatical, etymological, and rhetorical subjects, we should like to emphasize one particular episode not only because it brings to our minds the well-known introspective method of Plato's *Dialogues,* but also because it foreshadows in a funny way the psychoanalytic methods of our own century. The sage orders his stu-

dent to lie down on a couch and try to concentrate: "Now
think as deeply as you can and get together your
thoughts" (700–701). He adds that if he is unable to continue one thought, he must jump quickly to another. Accordingly, Strepsiades remains for a while alone with his
subconscious, and yet he is unable to concentrate. "What
have you been thinking?" Socrates asks. "Whether the
bed-bugs will spare any part of me," the old man answers.
A second concentration follows, with no better results.
This time Socrates has had enough, and therefore sends
away the helpless sophist-to-be. The Clouds, pitying the
old man, suggest to him a compromise—to send his son in
his place (812).

Up to this point, we have had a parody of the sophist's teaching. The following episode is a parody of the
parody. Proudly imitating the airs of the great teacher,
Strepsiades instructs his son. He swears by the Goddess
Fog and laughs at the young man's obsolete ideas, to believe "at his age" in Zeus and other such things. The
young man shakes his head in despair and wonders what
is the best thing to do, to appeal to the court for guardian-
ship of his father or order him a coffin. He has no time to
decide, however, because the old man has already called
for Socrates.

Here the *agon* of the comedy takes place (889–1104).
It is the second of the parts modified by Aristophanes, and
so we must again make the distinction clear. The surviving *agon* is a duel between two opposed mentalities, two
different ways of life, personified as the Just and the Unjust Reason. The Just, who advocates the old manner of
living, is senile and ugly; he has endowed the past with
good morals and has brought up the victors of Marathon,
but he stinks of mold and outdatedness. The Unjust is
young and handsome, bisexual, verbose, impertinent, and
rich, because he earns a lot from his sophistries. Their

dialogue is not only a battle for supremacy but also a combat to gain the young Pheidippides. It resembles, in its wild fanaticism, the battles to be fought one day between angels and demons for the souls of the dead.

Just Reason enumerates in a lyrical sermon the virtues of ancient education, when youthful beauty was admired and sons respected their fathers. He advises Pheidippides to choose a simple and natural life which is better for health, physical appearance, and character, as well as a pleasure in itself. In spite of this nostalgia for the past, Aristophanes, as Jaeger has noted, does not preach a return to bygone days. "He was not a rigidly dogmatic reactionary. But he was living in an age of transition when thoughtful men shrank from being whirled along in a constant stream of innovations, seeing good old things destroyed before they were replaced by something equally good" (p. 375).

Unjust Reason has nothing else to boast about except his ability to make the crooked straight and the unjust just. Yet this ability is all he needs in order to demolish with sophistries the honest arguments of his antagonist. Unlike the sausage-seller (*Knights*) or Aeschylus (*Frogs*), who won their *agons* because they deserved to win, the Unjust Reason wins because he ought *not* to. With this ironic conclusion, Aristophanes makes his satire more piercing.

The outcome of the duel is unexpected and droll; not only does Pheidippides join at once with the Unjust Reason, but also the Just Reason himself, throwing away his investments, declares: "I come with you to become a fairy!" Such is the magic attraction of philosophic deception and moral depravity that, Aristophanes postulates, whatever wise and honest was left in our country was swept away by deceit.

A conventional lapse of time allows Pheidippides to enroll in the school and attend the courses. Meanwhile

(1114–30) the chorus tells the audience about the services offered by the Clouds, not so much to sophists, as to vegetation. Then (1145 ff.) Strepsiades and Socrates meet in the street and kiss each other fondly. Our old buffoon is still in agony about how to pay his creditors. The professor calms him down by telling him that his son has graduated from the school with honors and is now a master in deceit. The proud father calls his son, and as soon as he sees him he notices with joy the results of sophistic education in his physiognomy, namely, that "Attic look," the familiar facial expression of the Athenian wise-guy who knows how to find his right by wronging others. Saying good-bye to Socrates, the old man takes the graduate home to celebrate (1212).

The comedy, however, has a tragic conclusion. No sooner have we witnessed how happy Strepsiades is in dispelling his creditors with his sophistic counterattacks, than we see him running out of his house screaming, while his son pursues him with a whip (1321 ff.). The new education has surpassed the old man's expectations. The whole trouble started, he tells us, when he asked his son to sing with the lyre some patriotic melodies of Simonides, whereupon the young man answered, quite cynically, that those were old stuff and, instead, began to sing from Euripides about how a brother and a sister had committed incest. Strepsiades could not prevent himself from swearing at Euripides, and at once Pheidippides started to beat him. The old man now tries to move his son with reminiscences of his childhood—in a parody, we might say, of Clytaemnestra begging Orestes for her life. Yet the well-educated son remains unmoved. Bringing forth solid sophistic arguments, he proves to his father that he has *justly* punished him:

PH.: When I was a child, didn't you beat me?
ST.: Yes, for your own good, because I loved you.

PH.: Isn't it right then for me to love you and beat
you, since beating means loving? (1409–12)

Exhausted from the *stichomythia,* and from the beating too, the poor Strepsiades raises his arms to heaven and
curses his offspring: "May you fall into abysmal Hell
along with Socrates and Unjust Reason!" And, like the re-
penting King David, he asks the true gods to help him
punish the school-master.

Here, in the final episode of the play and in the *exodos* of the chorus, we encounter the third modified passage (1493–1510). The surviving version presents the old
man ordering his servants to set fire to the school. Socrates
and the students appear amid the flames and smoke
coughing. "What are you doing up there on the roof?" the
philosopher shouts to the demented old man. And he
with savage satisfaction answers, "Airborne, I examine the
sun!" The 423 B.C. version, undoubtedly, displayed a
more extended final episode. There was a dialogue between Strepsiades and the god Hermes, who came to advise him about the burning.[20] One can also suspect that
Socrates' humiliation and downfall were not restricted to
a single suffocated cue, and that the exodus of the chorus
did not consist of a single line: "Let us go now, we have
danced enough for today." The burning of the Socratic
precincts must have been one of the basic ingenious ideas
of the comic poet. He might even have borrowed it from
a real happening: the fire which, according to a legend,
destroyed the school of Pythagoras.[21]

Around this performance many anecdotes have grown up.
Aelian tells us that Socrates himself was sitting in the theatre and when his "double" appeared in the orchestra, he
stood up so that everybody could see at whom the satire
was aimed. Plutarch, on the other hand, records a conver-

sation which supposedly took place when the play was over: "Aren't you angry, Socrates?" somebody asked him. To which the philosopher answered: "No, by Zeus; as they tease me at banquets, so they tease me at the theatre." [22]

At that City Dionysia—the first in which Aristophanes appeared after a two-year expulsion—the *Clouds* met with disaster. It was the most terrible defeat that our playwright had so far experienced, a trauma that he will not easily overcome. Not only had he been spoiled with three victories in four consecutive years, but he also thought of the *Clouds* as his wisest play to date and the best comedy that the Athenians had ever watched.

All the same, the judgment was not favorable. We gather from the *parabasis* of the *Wasps* and of the second *Clouds* that the judges and the public were not yet ready for that kind of intellectual message and so they misunderstood it. Theatre art is like a chariot race; the man who runs faster than all the others has the greatest chance to break his neck (cf. *Wasps,* 1050). What the true cause of the unfavorable verdict was we shall never know; it will remain a question open to conjectures of all kinds, just as the other two unanswerable questions related to the *Clouds:* why did the poet attack Socrates and why did he re-write and then apparently not finish the comedy? [23]

Winner of the competition was old Cratinus' *Wine Jug (Pytine)*. This play did not oblige the spectators to worry about the dangers of unorthodox philosophy or meditate on the sophists' good or bad faith. It was an innocent comic allegory on drunkards, easy as wine to swallow. It had the additional interest that the comic hero was the playwright himself in a ruthless self-derisive confession. A few fragments which have survived enable us to restore the plot, supplying plaster where the marble is missing.[24] A middle-aged Athenian, married to Dame Po-

etry, falls in love with a glamorous prostitute Intoxication; and for her sake he abandons his home. His legal
wife goes to court. Her complaint is that "in days gone by
he cared only for me and didn't have an eye for tarts; but
now in his old age Intoxication has made him a different
man." Up to this point the comedy refers to well-known
events: it is the old Cratinus, pub-crawler and derelict,
twice beaten by Aristophanes, and, as his young rival has
said, "wandering around with his laurel crown withered, a
prey to his thirst for wine" (*Knights,* 533–34). The
comedy, however, proceeds to future miracles. The friends
of the comic hero break all his jugs and pitchers and
oblige him to return to a dry and virtuous life. The poor
man protests: "When you drink water, you think of nothing wise" (Fr. 199). Nevertheless, much against his will,
he returns to his lawful wife Poetry.

The dramatic denouement is repeated in real life.
The comedy's victory revived the ancient Cratinus and his
withered laurels blossomed again. We might note that,
contrary to Euripides, who, in his last tragedy, will return
to the worship of Bacchus, Cratinus, in his last comedy,
becomes a renegade to the wine-god. The paradoxical conclusion of this play is that only water brings real inspiration.

The *Wine Jug* must have been Cratinus' last comedy,
for there is some vague information that the old playwright left this world soon after his artistic restoration.
Let us add that one of the fragments (307) contains the
well-known invective on Aristophanes:

"Who are you?" a smart spectator might have asked.
"A subtle word-mincer, epigram-chaser, Euripidaris-
tophanizer!"

It seems that the judges, acclaiming the old poet at
the expense of a younger one, did no more than put into

practice Aristophanes' own preaching. Had he not always, in fact, stressed the Just Reason of the old and the Unjust Reason of the young? Now his own whip was turned against him and slashed him. We might also say that, in the event of the *Clouds'* failure, there was mutual benefit to both Cratinus and Socrates. Unknown to them, each one brought about the rightful rehabilitation of the other.

Thus, among the crowds leaving the Dionysus theatre on that spring evening, there walked a happy old man and an unhappy young one. And, somewhere in the distance, a barefoot philosopher strode blithely toward the river Ilissus.

Chapter VIII

The Wasps Go to Court

*The Athenians knew very well what the
Attic wit was; and when they had
laughed they were sure that they had
not laughed at something silly.*

Racine, Intro. to *Les Plaideurs*

In the spring of 423 B.C., Athenians and Spartans decided
upon a one-year truce. History does not tell us whether
Aristophanes' fellow citizens were influenced at all in this
decision by the *Merchant Ships,* which three months earlier had appealed to them for peace. What history tells us
is about the tragic war events of the previous year—the
failures of the Athenian army at the Hellespont, at Delium, and at Amphipolis, and about the mounting
triumphs of the Spartan general Brasidas.

Now the war clangor ceases temporarily and the
streets of Athens are crowded with soldiers on leave. At
the Lenaea of the following winter (422 B.C.), the theatre
is packed with all those who for the past ten years had
been fighting in Macedonia, Thrace, and the islands. Aristophanes, through his chorus of the *Wasps,* will hail his
spectators with the words "O, you countless myriads!"
(1100–1101). This year he once more competes with two
comedies; but both are offered at the Lenaea—something
quite original, as far as we know. He signs only the *Wasps,*

however. The other one, called the *Proagon,* is produced under the name of Philonides, who had been his collaborator in the *Clouds* as well. Aristophanes always calls for his assistance for the staging of his literary plays, while he turns to Callistratus whenever his comedy has a political plot.[1] As its title suggests, the *Proagon* is connected with the first day of the City Dionysia, when the dramatic poets and their choruses used to appear before the public and speak about their forthcoming productions. We have no more information about this play than a scholium stating that Euripides was one of the characters. We easily deduce, therefore, that it had to do with backstage life and literary criticism.[2] We can go so far as to suspect that he chose this subject in order to protest against the bad reception of last year's *Clouds.* In any case, Aristophanes will be still protesting and making comments upon this misadventure in many plays to come.

The *Wasps* is a social satire, aiming at the abuses of the judicial system. In spite of its courtroom subject, however, the play's overall theme is political. Aristophanes continues his crusade against Cleon, who in his opinion is leading Athens to disaster. In his five preceding comedies, he had urged the Athenians to change their way of thinking, revitalize their ideals, and, above all, disinfect themselves from the tanner's unhealthy influence. This time he condemns the official system of jurisdiction, because the notorious demagogue is drawing therefrom most of his political power. Through various devices of graft he has the legal authorities in his power and can use them as a weapon against any undesirable opponent.[3]

This comedy does not attack either the laws in their essence or any judge in person. It exposes the corruption and degradation of justice, due to Cleon's autocratic rule. It scourges, furthermore, the foolishness of Athenians, whose vanity delights in holding court offices and whose greed for money is stirred by the easily available jury-man's fees. Aristophanes does not insinuate that all his fel-low citizens prefer the Unjust Reason to the Just Reason, but simply that they are incapable of distinguishing be-tween the two.

Many times, so far, the playwright had touched upon the subject of justice and had exposed the court system as calamitous. From the little we know of his personal life, we can surmise that it had not been devoid of legal tribu-lations.[4] It goes without saying, therefore, that Aristoph-anes' resentment against courts and judges was not merely theoretical, but sprang from a personal wound as yet unhealed.

Justice administered by the people was one of Peri-cles' major innovations. Every citizen who was over thirty and not indebted to the State could become a judge, or, in the modern sense, a juror. Pericles had established the judge's daily wage, which was later raised by Cleon to three obols, a sum very attractive to all.[5] The courts were divided both by colors and by the letters of the alphabet. Colored rods were distributed to the judges, bearing the color of the courtroom to which they had to report. In the trials the accuser was called the *pursuer* and the defendant the *pursued*. They delivered speeches which were some-times composed by professional orators. The first stage of the trial aimed at determining whether the pursued was innocent or guilty; the judges cast their ballots into either of two urns, one for guilt, the other for innocence. If the defendant was found guilty, the second stage of the trial decided upon his punishment. Frequently—and this is relevant to the *Wasps*—cases were settled by arbitration before reaching the courtroom.[6]

No critic has ever called the plays of Aristophanes "comedies of manners," because theatrical "manners" usually refer to private rather than public life. If there existed, however, a kind of drama by the name of "comedy of public manners," Aristophanes' plays would be the ideal examples. In the *Acharnians* he offers us a miniature Assembly of the People, as well as a parody of the Dionysiac Festivals; in the *Knights* a session of the Parliament is described; in the *Clouds* we get a free pass into the secret world of the sophists. Now, in the *Wasps,* we shall witness a burlesqued arbitration and a mock-heroic trial. And the language of the comedy will seem in places as if it were taken from the proceedings of a real court. What is, furthermore, notably amusing is that, thanks to the plot, the legal *agon* and the theatrical *agon* become one.

The play presents a father-and-son team as did both the *Banqueters* and the *Clouds*. The father is Philocleon (or Cleon-lover), an old judge crazy about litigation and an adherent of Cleon's. The son is Bdelycleon (or Cleon-hater), a reasonable young man, who disapproves of Cleon's policies and despairs over his father's mania. In the prologue, two slaves, Xanthias and Sosias, explain the plot: their young master has locked his father in the house to prevent him from going to court. (These two slaves do not stand for real persons, as was the case in the *Knights;* they are pure farcical types, the precursors of all the servants who will populate the comic theatre in the centuries to come; even their names will become traditional.) The old man, who cannot resign himself to legal inactivity, uses every imaginable way to get out of the house; he pretends to be a swallow flying away, or smoke escaping from the chimney, or even, in a take-off on the famous Cyclops sequence of the *Odyssey,* he tries to escape ingeniously hidden under the belly of a donkey and calling himself Nobody. But all his attempts are frustrated by his son's prompt intervention.

The chorus of the play, making its entrance at line 230, is composed of twenty-four old judges bearing the as-

pect of wasps. Chronologically, this is the first animal chorus of Aristophanes. (He will create, in all, four such.)
These senile wasps are dressed, we may suppose, in black-
and-yellow uniforms, wear small wings, and brandish
pointed sticks of various colors. These sticks stand both
for the dicasts' rods and for the wasps' stings: they are, besides, the comic emblems of Aristophanes' judges, as sy-
ringes will be those of Molière's physicians.

The *parodos* of the chorus is rhythmically slow and
tired; these men of law are so old that they need little
children to help them march. They are chanting nostalgic
melodies of Phrynichus, the early tragic poet,[7] and, like
all Aristophanic elders, long for the good old days. The
reason that brings them here before daybreak is that they
missed their friend Philocleon, who normally used to be
the first to arrive at the court. They call him and the prisoner appears at his window, moaning like a Euripidean
heroine (316).

A farcical scene ensues (395–525) in which the old
man tries to escape by means of a rope, and there follows
a battle between the Wasps and the young Bdelycleon,
who finally defeats them by means of fumigation. Then,
father and son agree to settle their differences by arbitration: the one will speak for, the other against, the judge's
office, the chorus serving as arbiter. In this *agon*
(548–724) the old man's discourse is a panegyric of court
life, something, in fact, that all law students should be
taught in order to gain confidence in their chosen voca-
tion. "What other kind of life is happier or loftier than
that of judges?" he asks. A judge's bliss begins the moment
he leaves his home in the morning. All those he meets
will bow and offer him their hands still moist from being
dipped in the public trough. He generously distributes
promises and verdicts; yet, when he gets within the court,
he forgets them. He spends a highly pleasant day, because

the defendants are usually amusing; and when he returns home in the evening with the three obols in his pocket, his wife caresses him and serves him a frugal dinner, while his daughter washes his feet with ointments and, whispering affectionate "daddies," grabs the money.

When Philocleon's arguments are over, his son rises to propound opposing views. His speech is not as lyrical as the old man's was; it is based, more realistically, on numbers and statistics and intends to prove that a judge's profession, when seen through a financial prism, is not so much a public honor as it is hard labor. Numerous city-states, he says, from Sardinia to the Black Sea, pay tribute to Athens; nevertheless, from her annual revenue a trifle is budgeted for judges while the big money goes into the pockets of political impostors, those who only pretend to sweat and strive for the people.

This solidly argumented peroration wins the case for the son; at the same time, it has a great psychological effect upon the chorus and upon the old comic hero. Philocleon remains mute, having suddenly discovered, like Lear, that his whole life has been a mistake. The first words that he is able to utter are against Cleon: "O, let me catch him once again stealing and I shall expose him" (756–59). The old maniac has recovered from his political fanaticism but has not yet been cured of his passion for jurisdiction. Life without suits and trials is something that he is totally unable to conceive of. However, the affectionate son has a solution for that, too. He proposes a compromise: to turn their own courtyard into a Court, where the old man will leisurely administer private justice. As we remember, it is not the first time that Aristophanes chooses the solution of a private remedy for a public evil: let each man save himself as best he can. In the *Acharnians* his hero enjoyed a private peace with Sparta; here the old judge plays justice for his own benefit. The comic poet

appears, in a way, as the inventor of a therapy much proclaimed by modern psychiatry. Behind this gag, however,
his message is one of total despair. If we don't see reason,
he seems to tell the Athenians, if we don't become sane
and wise, there is only one thing left for us—to abolish
any idea of state or community and to return to primitive
individual existence.

Now the charming Trial-play begins, which accounts
for the comedy's notoriety (805 ff.). It is the oldest parody
of court procedure, foreshadowing similar ones in *Maître
Pathelin,* the *Merchant of Venice,* the *Marriage of Figaro,*
and many other comedies. As for Racine's *Les Plaideurs,*
it is, admittedly, an imitation of the Aristophanic original.[8]

Bdelycleon and the two slaves transform the courtyard into a courtroom and two litigants are presently
brought in, announcing their arrival by barking: they are
two dogs fighting over a piece of cheese. The court procedure begins with the necessary prayers to Apollo. One of
the slaves acts as prosecutor against the dog accused of
stealing the cheese, while Bdelycleon defends the canine
criminal with heart-breaking speeches.

The old judge, however, having known no other verdict in his long career but condemnation, is ready to vote
the defendant guilty. And it is thanks only to a farcical
trick, played on him by his son, that he finally casts his
vote for acquittal. When he realizes his mistake, he almost
suffers a fatal stroke. "I have acquitted a defendant!"
he screams. "Oh, gods, what shall become of me?"
(1000–1001). Bdelycleon cuddles his father into the house
and promises him to find some other kind of occupation
that will help the fallen judge forget his passion. As they
leave the orchestra, the chorus takes its place for the *parabasis* (1009 ff.).

This *parabasis* is Aristophanes' professional *de pro-*

fundis. He expresses his bitter resentment against the public and the critics who, a year ago, committed an act of injustice by condemning his *Clouds.* He proceeds to an anything-but-modest appraisal of his services to the State, of the originality of his ideas, as well as of his courage to fight, like another Heracles, with none but the mighty of this world. Later in the play, in a brief *second parabasis* (1265 ff.) he will compare himself to the vine and the Athenians to the wooden supports which, although meant to uphold the vine, deceitfully let it fall.

The second part of the comedy (1122 ff.) is devoted to the son's efforts in the bringing-up of his father. He had promised the old man a pleasant cure for his malady. He educates him, therefore, to luxury and leisure; he teaches him how to dress, to behave socially, to tell jokes at dinners, to sing, to be nice to ladies. In the dinner scene (1208–64), we find another Athenian public custom reenacted: the singing of the *skolia,* a unique document on the way this special genre of lyric poetry was delivered. Needless to say that the symposium, which calls for a greater number of actors than that allotted to comedy, is pure theatre and that Bdelycleon, with a remarkable protean ability, incarnates each of the invisible guests in turn. Thanks to all those lessons in savoir-vivre, the old man is completely transformed. It is not long before we see him well groomed and well drunk, making his dancing entrance with a sexy flute-player whom he calls "Golden apple of my eye!" And when a multitude of irate citizens, who had suffered various physical or moral injuries from the old man, menace him with a lawsuit, the reformed judge answers them with a fit of sarcastic laughter. That is, perhaps, the best proof that Dionysus has defeated Themis and that his magic potion has cured Philocleon's court-mania.

Now the old man, completely possessed by the god of

wine and dramatic poetry, almost as if he were a second Cratinus, twists his body, kicks his legs, jumps and whirls, pretending that he is a dancer in tragedy (1482–1537). Some of the dancing steps and attitudes that he specifically mentions, as inherited from Thespis and Phrynichus, may have belonged, indeed, to the *emmeleia,* the dance of tragedy. And, very possibly, the comic *kordax* may have been, as a rule, a broad parody of its sublime tragic counterpart.[9]

The old buffoon's dance is contagious, and shortly the heretofore grumpy chorus joins him in a turbulent and exhilarating *exodos.* As they dance out, to the vivid accompaniment of the flute, the wasps shout in admiration: "No actor has ever before led a comic chorus out of the theatre!" [10]

This is the comedy's conclusion. The judges have become dancers; the stings have become drumsticks; and grumbling has turned to carousing. Our poet has proved his theory by a charming reduction to the absurd.

The *Wasps* was presented in January, 422 B.C., competing with the *Proagon,* also by Aristophanes, and a third comedy, the *Ambassadors* by Leucon. From the text of the existing Argument, some contrive that the *Wasps* was also signed by Philonides; this, however, seems hardly probable.

It is also a matter of controversy which of the two Aristophanic entries won first victory, as the Argument has survived in a rather mutilated condition. What is certain, anyway, is that Leucon got third place.[11]

About the value of this juridical comedy, opinions vary; some see in it the poet's weakest play, others one of his most successful.[12] The first view can be considered only as the response of a modern audience; for his own times, Aristophanes' libel of the courts had a social significance equal to Zola's "I accuse" or Daumier's courtroom caricatures, and a much greater import than our contemporary efforts in courtroom documentary drama. The poet's comic art is at its best. In Philocleon and Bdelycleon he has created two of his most vigorous personalities, genuine both as social symbols and as human beings. In the case of the second, especially, we have a character most rare in Attic Comedy: a serious, tender, practical, ingenious, dashing, and enduring young man. Besides, the part demands an incomparable *mime*-actor. He has to personify convincingly many well-known Athenians of the day; and we can be sure that this *mime*-recital was among the chief attributes of the original performance. By presenting this character, Aristophanes restores the virtue of Athenian youth, which he had maltreated in the *Banqueters* and the *Clouds*. In fact, we are immediately struck by the difference in approach between this and last year's comedy. In the *Clouds* a father tried to educate his son; in the *Wasps* a son tries to educate his father. And where old Strepsiades had failed, young Bdelycleon succeeds. Hence, a question rises quite spontaneously: was there some specific reason that compelled the playwright to idealize in this comedy the young Athenians whom he had reviled? Can we assume that the disapprobation of the *Clouds* came mostly from the younger members of the public, who admired the progressive Socrates—even the sophists, perhaps—and were appalled by Aristophanes' too conservative ideas?

The *Wasps* may also boast a great many merits of *pure* theatre: the old juryman's efforts to flee from his house, the arbitration, the trial of the dogs, the imaginary banquet with its songs, the hero's eloquent drunkenness, his take-off of the tragic dance, and, of course, the picturesque ensemble of the dancing wasps with their wings and stings. It is true, perhaps, that the play's political side and unfamiliar allusions often escape our present-day sense of humor. Unknown personalities of Cleonic Athens crowd like a buzzing swarm, not of wasps but rather of drones, in the comedy's air; hastily counting, we shall find not less than sixty contemporary Athenians mentioned in this play.

A short speech delivered by one of the slaves at the beginning of the comedy (54–66) refers to the comic poet's art and its character is clearly parabatic. One wonders why Aristophanes took it out of the *parabasis* to put it in the mouth of a comic slave. He did so, we can only say, to make the irony of it all more evident. He never makes his self-criticism with complete seriousness. All those little things that he pretends to abhor, as examples of an inferior dramatic art, compose the main body of his farcical inspiration. What we may call his sense of aesthetic proportion is expressed in two lines, belonging to the passage quoted above, which we ought to retain perhaps as an index of the playwright's mentality and as a measure of his *vis comica*. The play that we are going to present, the slave says, is "a meaningful little tale, not exceeding your intelligence, but superior to low farce." [13]

This proportion, as we have called it, will always be Aristophanes' aim. His plays must stand higher than the cheap comedies of his colleagues, and still not be too high-brow for the understanding of the common people.

Chapter IX

The Peace of Nicias and the *Peace*

O Panhellenes! Let us help, now if ever,
to get rid of armies!

Aristophanes, *Peace*, 302–3

After his double success at the Lenaea, Aristophanes must have spent a few weeks of relaxation consulting his notes and planning two new plays. One of them might have been the mythological parody the *Centaur* (also called *Dramas*), and the other one his first "feminine" comedy, the *Women Getting Hold of Tents*. Their dates, of course, are conjectural, because we possess neither *didaskaliai* nor any precise information about them.

The first of these deals with a famous centaur of Greek mythology, Pholos, who, in the play, most probably was Heracles' host. The latter, besides eating, drinking, and shouting—traditional characteristics of that ancient hero of the Dorian farce—is involved in some trial or arbitration (obviously, the "wasps" were still buzzing in the poet's ears). One also suspects that the eternal Cleon might have been hidden behind the mask of the centaur.[1]

The *Women Getting Hold of Tents* most likely displays a feminine chorus, one composed of real women and not allegories like the Clouds. The action takes place either on the Pnyx, where tents had to be erected during the Assemblies (*Thesmophoria*, 658), or at one of the national festivals, possibly the Isthmian, where the first to arrive secured the best seats under the canvas. In his *Peace,* Aristophanes has one of his characters say "At the Isthmia, I got hold of a tent for my penis" (880). He is alluding, perhaps, to this comedy. We also find in it the playwright's answer to Cratinus' famous invective against him: that, although he lampoons Euripides, he nonetheless imitates the tragic poet's arty-crafty style. Knowing Aristophanes' preference for immediate counterattack and up-to-date issues, we can be certain that he would not leave more than a year go by before responding to his rival's challenge. So, in the *Women Getting Hold of Tents* his answer is: "I use his [Euripides'] well-shaped words, but I offer ideas less vulgar than his" (Fr. 471). It is a rather clumsy answer, which sounds more like guilty apology than witty repartee. In the *Peace* he will strike his old antagonist somewhat more violently!

> HERM. Is the wise Cratinus still alive?
> TRYG. He died when the Spartans invaded Attica.
> HERM. How come?
> TRYG. He shrivelled in despair on seeing a beautiful
>   jug broken in pieces. (700–704)

Of course, this is not evidence for Cratinus' real death, as in recent years there had been no Spartan invasion; Aristophanes refers, no doubt, to the invasions during the first war years, insinuating thus that Cratinus was artistically dead ever since he, Aristophanes, first appeared in the theatrical field. And the broken "wine jug" was nothing else but Cratinus' comedy, that was smashed by the *Acharnians* in 425 B.C.[2]

The truce of 423 B.C. had for almost a year sweetened life in both camps. Soldiers were able to visit their farms and embrace their families. Perhaps, the much-desired peace would have settled in for good had the two leaders, Cleon of Athens and Brasidas of Sparta, not been against it. They resented peace, Plutarch says, for war covered up the former's wickedness and adorned the latter's virtues. Thucydides is even more explicit when he states that "Brasidas refused to accept peace, because of the honors he had gained from war, and Cleon, because he knew that in peaceful times his political crimes would be exposed." [3] In the spring of the same year, while at Delphi the Pythian Games—the feast of friendship and concord—were being celebrated, the truce expired and enemy actions began again.

One of the great mysteries related to the days and works of Aristophanes is his military status. What was the activity of the author of the *Peace* during the war? Was he deferred for reasons of health, family obligations, his profession, or his dangerous ideas? It is more or less a fact that Aristophanes did not fight. It would have been impossible to follow the Athenian army on land or sea and at the same time write and produce, approximately, two plays a year. Furthermore, his comedies, so full of references to himself never linger on any personal military impression or reminiscence. Nor does any other ancient author seem to recall Aristophanes with spear and shield, as Aeschylus, Thucydides, and Socrates are often remembered.[4] Where, then, does his tremendous peace obsession really have its source? In patriotic ideology or, more prosaically, in lack of heroism? When the war broke out, our playwright was somewhere in his late teens; he belonged to the unlucky generation who had to bear arms throughout the ten years of the civil strife. It would be easy to infer that Aristophanes was a coward; after all, his cowardice would fit marvelously with the legend of Archilochus and Alcaeus, both of whom had thrown away their shields in battle; it would even fit with the legend of the theatrical god himself, who once jumped into the sea to escape

Lycurgus' anger.[5] Unfortunately, such a conjecture does not necessarily hold. I say unfortunately, because it is always agreeable to find little weaknesses in great men. If Aristophanes were a coward, he wouldn't have carried on so heroic a campaign against authority and public opinion, exposing himself to continuous danger. Also, in his plays, even in those that aim at peace, he always praises human heroism; he advises the citizens to vote for a truce, but does not advise the warriors to throw down their weapons. In his *Knights* (368, 444) he accuses Cleon of having escaped twenty condemnations for desertion and makes mincemeat of all cowardly Athenians. If he, himself, had been a coward or a deserter, his audience would never have accepted such invectives and, instead of laughing, would have asked for the author's head. Had the *Babylonians* or some other of his early plays survived, we might have had perhaps a key to this mystery.

In the summer of 422 B.C., the two enemy armies reluctantly took up arms to meet at Amphipolis. This battle, in which Socrates took part, has remained in history as one of the greatest Athenian debacles. The ambitious Cleon, who had merged in his person both the political and military leadership of Athens, was proved unable to repeat his miraculous success of Pylos. In the battle of Amphipolis the leaders of both armies were killed. And their corpses had the fate of those of Oedipus' sons, Eteocles and Polynices. Brasidas was buried ceremoniously in the center of the city, with all the army of Sparta and her allies paying him due honor; while Cleon remained unburied where he fell until they shipped him, along with other dead, back to Athens.[6] This double death brought the first period of the Peloponnesian War to an end. Nicias took over in Athens and Pleistoanax in Sparta, and they called all the allies together to discuss terms for a permanent peace.

In the general joy caused by the anticipation of this armistice, Aristophanes begins to write his own welcome to peace. As it was too late to complete it before the Lenaea, he will present it at the Great Dionysia, which innumerable foreigners will be able to attend again, now that the war is over.

Aristophanes' *Peace* was written in evident haste. Compared to his other comedies, it displays a naïve plot, a weak dramatic structure, and only a few genuine jokes. The poet is obviously going through a crisis of spiritual exultation which, naturally, does not help the satirist's job. Furthermore, Cleon, the red cloth that used to excite the comic bull, is no more, and this emasculates his assaults. In these days of beatitude, he no doubt spends on life itself all the vigor that he used to put into his art.

The fanciful initial idea of the *Peace*—the enormous beetle flying to heaven—must have already been in his mind a year before, when the drunken Philocleon had recited the Aesopic myth about the eagle and the beetle.[7] Since the beetle was the only animal ever to reach the Olympian gods, the hero of the present play chooses a big beetle to carry him, like another Pegasus, to the heavenly prison where Peace has been incarcerated.

The trip to outer space (82–728) takes up the whole first part of the comedy and is conveniently forgotten in the second, thanks to a program of agrarian festivities without any plot. A sign of the author's hastiness is the *parabasis:* the *epirrhema* and the *antepirrhema* are completely missing and so is the usual lyric fugue of the strophes. As for the anapaests where Aristophanes proclaims his virtues as a dramatist, they are more or less a repetition of the *parabasis* of the *Wasps* in the same way that the joyful song on the pleasures of peaceful life imitates a similar one of the *Acharnians,* and Hermes' description of the causes of the war paraphrases Dicaeopolis's analogous speech. It looks as if Aristophanes found all those passages in his files and, to avoid delay, jumbled them together in his new comedy, notwithstanding his boasting that never has he twice presented on the stage the same thing (*Clouds,* 546).

For the above reasons, the *Peace* might be called an inferior play; yet, for other reasons, it holds a unique place in Attic Comedy; and we should by no means snub the grammarian's Pepys-like comment that "the play is one of the most successful." [8] Primarily, it is a hymn to rural happiness. The county fair, which makes up the second part, ends like a perfect specimen of Aristophanic comedy, with a reconciliation, a marriage, and a *komos;* and everywhere the warm joy of the meadows and the fields predominate. After ten years of fighting abroad or depending on the walls of their cities, all the people of Greece join hands in this mirthful return to nature. Such a sight makes even the god Hermes exclaim: "How wonderful it is to see this crowd, so vast and swift!" (564–65). The *Peace,* in spite of its dramatic shortcomings, brings fresh air and sunshine, the smell of earth and thyme, the murmur of the leaves, the buzzing of the bees, and the sweet taste of the ripe fig into a theatrical area so far devoted to civic worries, political turmoil, and the miseries of the *lumpenproletariat.*

Another virtue of the play lies in its wide sense of patriotism. Here, more than in any other of his comedies, Aristophanes appears less an Athenian than a pan-Hellenist. His chorus is a mosaic of laborers from every corner of the Hellenic earth. When his hero, Trygaeus from Maroussi, sets forth on his Quixotic mission—which he will carry out successfully only because he has the common sense of a Sancho Panza—he is not thinking of the salvation of Athens or Attica only, but of the entire land. Even the chorus address themselves as: "O Panhellenes!" a word rather rare in ancient literature (302).

It is possible that Aristophanes "was not the only one who advocated peace, but other poets too," as the second Argument states. We possess, in fact, fragments of Cratinus and Eupolis which praise that ideal; also one by the old Teleclides (Fr. 1), who recalls "the golden times when peace was as available as water." Aristophanes, of course, had not invented peace, as Pindar had not invented athletic games. He became, however, the golden-mouthed priest of its religion; and, no less, an unabashed scatologist for its sake. Therefore, the playwright would have every reason to believe that the peace, celebrated a few days after the City Dionysia, was officially the Peace of Nicias, but essentially his own.

The plot of the play is a very simple one. A single phrase of the Argument can sufficiently express it: "Trygaeus, an old peasant from Athens, mounted on a beetle, flies to heaven for the sake of Greece."

In the prologue, the two traditional slaves feed a huge beetle from Aetna, which their master keeps in the stable for his forthcoming trip to heaven, where he shall discover Peace and bring her back to earth. This gigantic coleopteron (which would have, no doubt, fascinated Hieronymus Bosch) is not yet in sight. We shall behold it only when it will eventually rise in a din of peculiar noises and amid a multitude of astonished people for its interplanetary journey, carrying on its back the peace-loving astronaut (82).

This sudden ascent over the proskenion combined with the staccato rhythm of the flight make of this eccentric scene a rare gem of Aristophanic ingenuity. Naturally, in such theatrical cases, the actor's competence to improvise is of primal importance. Therefore, the success of Apollodorus, who interpreted Trygaeus and who is the only Aristophanic actor who has escaped anonymity, must be attributed, to a great extent, to his ad-lib histrionics during the space trip.[9]

How was this trip realized, technically? . . . Among the comedies of Aristophanes, the *Peace* and the *Frogs*— in other words, the ascent to heaven and the descent to hell—present the most excruciating stage problems. The Scholiast on *Peace* 80 provides the information that the insect "is raised by the machine; and this is called a crane (*eorema*)." In trying to visualize the beetle's flight, we sometimes resort to a fantastic conglomeration of practicables, double levels, double walls, and other scenic paraphernalia, next to which the magic settings of Torelli or Vigarani would seem quite elementary.[10] All this is not only superfluous but also foreign to the austerity of the Greek stage and to the spirit of Aristophanes, who makes use of machinery merely to mock Euripides. Especially in the *Peace* it seems impossible that he abused this device, for in this same comedy he scoffs at young tragic poets as "machine-makers" (790); this remark, had the *Peace* been too mechanistic, would have turned his arrow back upon him. It is much simpler and more plausible to imagine the crane picking up the hero near the proskenion, stage right, suspending him in the air, and finally depositing him stage left, in front of the entrance to Zeus's abode. During this short and symbolic flight and between stops and bumps, Trygaeus has time to shout: "I fly for the sake of all the Greeks!" or, fear-stricken, beg the spectators "not to excrete for three days," lest the beetle, attracted by the smell, should throw him off with a sudden landing. His last, trembling words bid the stagehands to be very careful in handling the crane. Thus, very simply, like the acrobatics of clowns in circuses and without any attempt at illusion, the celestial journey is accomplished (172).

Hermes, whom Trygaeus meets at the gates of heaven, is an ambiguous character, made up of antitheses —tempestuous and good-natured, autocratic and humane, a god and also a common man, a cunning scoundrel and a conscientious idiot. First and foremost, he is the model of the perfect porter. He is easily bribed by Trygaeus and sells him the information that the gods have gone to a higher region of the heavenly dome, not able to bear any longer the sight of belligerent Greeks. In their place they have left Polemos (War) with full powers; he keeps Peace imprisoned in a deep cave (or well), having amassed stones at the entrance, so that men can never recover her.

Presently War makes his entrance (236), a roaring stock-character of the Heracles or the Cyclops or even the Cleon type. He is holding an enormous mortar into which he throws all the Greek cities, as if they were varieties of food. He lacks, however, a pestle to mash them. He sends his assistant Tumult to bring him a pestle either from Athens or from Sparta. In both instances, Tumult returns with news nefarious to War: the pestles, which used to mash the two cities, namely Cleon and Brasidas, exist no more.

On hearing this, Trygaeus thanks the gods and, turning to the audience, he speaks with passion:

> Now is the time, O Greeks,
> free as we are from wars and quarrels,
> to liberate our beloved Peace
> before a new pestle appears . . . (292–95)

Then, raising his voice, he shouts to all the corners of Hellas for his fellow countrymen to come and help him. His call is immediately answered and the chorus (301) dashes into the orchestra. It is composed of peasants and laborers, not only from Attica but from the whole Greek territory. (And we are inclined to imagine that this chorus, as the one in the *Birds,* is not uniformly costumed, but that each dancer wears a tunic different in color and design, and typical of his city of origin.) [11] These laborers are not senile men as the Acharnian coal-dealers; they are men of the Peloponnesian War, still in their prime, fathers, husbands, fighters, who have suffered more than anyone else, for the absence of peace. They arrive with keen eagerness, brandishing ropes, sticks, and shovels, to lend a hand in the rescue of "the vine-protecting goddess." They optimistically believe—and this is, alas, Aristophanes' chimeric faith too—that "no one will ever take peace from us, once we rescue her!" (316–17). They dance their enthusiasm in the merriest *parodos* that our playwright has so far written or will ever write. In vain does Trygaeus try to stop them for reasons of precaution. "We don't want to dance," they say, "but our feet dance by their own will!" (324–25). Dance, Plato will write some day, is the form of inner delight put into motion (*Laws,* II, 654–56).

The first episode following the *parodos* (361 ff.) consists of the preparations for the rescue of Peace and of the hero's efforts to convince Hermes about the just nature of their mission. In this scene, the comic hero utters a phrase which should have been inscribed on a marble stele as an epigram of courage and perseverance. "Zeus," Hermes says, "has ordained death for whoever liberates Peace." And the old peasant answers with comic fear: "Is it then absolutely necessary that I should die?" (371–73). The stubborn determination of all men who struggled and suffered for an ideal is contained in this humble phrase. Trygaeus, though trembling, does not consider even for a moment shrinking before danger. His answer is of a kind with Luther's: "Ich kann nicht anders." The little man's comic phrase has in it, perhaps, as much heroism as a whole Aeschylean tragedy.

Hermes, when he is promised that he will be the first god to drink at the libations, is finally convinced. At once the laborers begin to remove the stones from the pit and prepare ropes to pull Peace out of her prison. The pulling of the rope, or of the many ropes or, even better of no rope at all (the scene being acted in pure mime) follows a rhythmical vocal pattern, as though the rescuers of Peace were fishermen pulling their nets. It seems, however, that among the spectators, there are some evil spirits, some bellicose demons, who wish to prevent Peace from getting out of her prison. Trygaeus turns suddenly toward the audience and shouts: "Lamachus, your presence is an obstacle to our job!"

Finally, when the poor peasants are at the point of collapsing from exhaustion, Peace is liberated. We should note that the playwright does not present her as a real person in the way tragedy presents its gods. In Attic Comedy the gods have been irremediably ridiculed and Aristophanes wishes to spare his divine Peace the comic fate of the other immortals. He produces her, therefore, in the form of an idol, a "colossal" statue, as his contemporaries have said.[12] Her two attendants, on the other hand, Theoria and Opora—or Festivity and Fruitfulness—are live beings. They emerge along with her from the dark pit, as they always return to mankind in days of peace.

Where the celestial prison—cave or pit—was placed, and how exactly the sudden apparition of the enormous idol took place we cannot imagine. Considering that the device was unfavorably criticized by Eupolis and the comic Plato, we deduce that it must have been an unusual and quite radical theatrical innovation. Perhaps the goddess' statue was brought out through the central door of the stage-building with the help of a special *ekkyklema* or *exostra,* as is suggested by the chorus line: "Bring the greatest of all goddesses to the light with machines and levers" (307).[13]

Breaking the sacred silence which hailed the apparition of the goddess, Trygaeus solemnly welcomes her. He says that her perfume has already made the war's stench disappear, and the whole country smell of fruits, feasts, Dionysiac celebrations, flutes, songs, melodies of Sophocles, twisted phrases of Euripides, ivy, tender lambs, women's breasts, drunken maids, spilled wine . . . "Look," Hermes marvels, "how the cities, reconciled, laugh and talk with each other!" (530–40).

And in the next episode the god narrates, as Dicaeopolis had done four years earlier, how peace was originally lost thanks to Pheidias' mischief and to Pericles, who set "all the world ablaze" (603–48). The satirical verve, however, is soon replaced by patriotic exultation: the burlesquing Hermes disappears, replaced by the passionate Aristophanes himself. He speaks in vivid colors about the misery and abuse which reigned side by side during the war, the fig trees that were uprooted, the storehouses that were emptied, and the farmers who had not even a raisin to eat, but were fed words in abundance. Naturally, the ultimate moral of this discourse is—what else? —Cleon's disastrous influence. At the mention of that hateful name, Trygaeus stops Hermes: "Say no more about him, conductor of souls, because he no longer belongs to us, but to you!" The demagogue is dead and the dramatist does not want to offend the dead, yet he cannot avoid a few more delayed insults.

After a charming conversation between Trygaeus and Peace, who, having no voice, suggests her questions to Hermes who promptly translates them, the first part of the play is over and with it the hero's celestial trip. Trygaeus returns to earth not on the flying beetle's back, but on foot. Why does our Bellerophon not ride his Pegasus this time? Aristophanes explains jokingly that the beetle has gone to eat Ganymede's "ambrosia"; but technical reasons, more probably, prevented a second flight: Trygaeus' co-travelers, Theoria and Opora, would make the air-borne ride rather problematic and the stage-hands had their objections. So, while the hero is marching back to earth and the *exostra* takes the statue away, the chorus advances toward the audience to deliver the *parabasis* (729–817).

As in the *Knights,* the *Wasps,* and the surviving *Clouds,* its main part is devoted to literary criticism. We shall examine it, therefore, in the next chapter, where we shall endeavor to analyze all the dramatic precepts of the younger Aristophanes.

An atmosphere of a village *fiesta* [14] dominates the second part of the comedy, when the hero returns to Athens with his triumphant but chimeric "peace in our time!" All he has to do now to complete his mission is to offer Theoria to the Assembly and to marry Opora. The two glamorous girls leave to take a bath and comb their hair, and a solemn sacrifice to Peace takes place. This is interrupted by the entrance of various tradesmen, all of whom had been profiting by war and are now desperate—a soothsayer, a helmet-maker, an armourer, a spear-polisher, a trumpet-seller, etc. Trygaeus finds an honorable rehabilitation for each: "the helmet-maker will sell his crests for brooms, the spear-polisher will sell his spears for vine-poles, the trumpet-seller will make scales of his trumpets, and the armourer will barter his breastplates for pissing-pots" (1039–1264).

Finally, the moment of the wedding arrives (1316). Opora appears in a bride's attire, many people are gathered, tables are laid, torches are lighted, and Trygaeus invites everyone to dance, voicing at the same time the people's great wish:

> May we produce much corn
> plenty of wine
> eat figs
> see our wives fecund

get all the goods we lost
back again
and from the murderous iron
have no more troubles. (1320–28)

With the wedding of Trygaeus and Opora the
comedy ends. This is of course a symbolic wedding, sug-
gesting the reunion of the farmer with rich vegetation or,
in a wider sense, of every Greek with a peaceful life. The
peasants of the chorus, carrying the bride and the groom
in their arms, march out to the fields singing in joy.

Argument II of the *Peace* [15] states that Apollodorus was
the protagonist of the comedy. It is probable that this
comic actor had also incarnated other Aristophanic old
men—Strepsiades, for instance, Philocleon, and especially
Dicaeopolis, who was not only a funny elder but also a
fighter for peace, like Trygaeus. In the composition of
comic characters there must have existed a mutual influence between Aristophanes and his actors, as it will exist
between Shakespeare and the various Kemps or Armins
who interpreted his clowns.

Aristophanes was defeated in the competition, in
spite of his comedy's exhilarating message. The *Peace* received second prize, leaving the ivy to Eupolis for his *Flatterers*. So the author of the *Cities* and of the *Golden Race,*
and almost of the *Knights,* revenged himself on Aristophanes, exactly as Cratinus had two years earlier. The
Flatterers was a bitter satire on the social parasites who
flatter the great and the mighty, in order to survive in
their shadows; and its main target was the wealthy Callias,
Alcibiades' brother-in-law, who attracted impecunious
poets and philosophers, as honey attracts flies. The same
subject and hero will be later taken up by Aristophanes in
his comedy the *Fryers*.

The dramatic *Peace* preceded by a few days the real one. The armistice began, Thucydides tells us (V, 20), in the early spring, just after the City Dionysia. The truce proposed was not for five years, nor for fifteen, not even for thirty, as the hero of the *Acharnians* had hoped, but for fifty: something that exceeded even Aristophanes' most daring dreams. We may be sure, therefore, that, in the arms of his much anticipated peace, nothing, not even the triumph of Eupolis, prevented our poet from sleeping blissfully thereafter.

Chapter X

Intermission

Jests that are true and natural seldom raise laughter with the beast, the multitude.

Ben Jonson, *Timber; or, Discoveries*

The Peace of Nicias brings the first period of the Peloponnesian War to an end and, with it, Aristophanes' youth.

His work had been, so far, a ruthless invective, and his mission, like that of Heracles, to fight undaunted against the monsters. In his case, the role of Eurystheus was played by the Athenian public, who, fickle and ungrateful, incessantly forced him to set off on new feats. As the legend of Heracles, however, could not have been created without his feats, Aristophanes, too, would not have existed if things in Athens had been as he wished them to be. The comic poet's purpose is indignation; and discontent is his breath of life.

Now, in his thirties, he will stop for a brief relaxation. The Greeks have at last recovered peace. His attitude, negative to war, cannot be negative to peace as well. It appears as a fact that, between the Peace of Nicias (421 B.C.) and the Sicilian Expedition (415 B.C.) Aristophanes produced very few plays. Perhaps he devoted those years to the creation of a family. The presumption that he married in this period accords, after all, with the age that his younger son must have in 388 B.C., when he is to appear as his father's collaborator.[1]

Two comedies, possibly written in those years, are the *Old Age* and the *Anagyros,* both lost. The first of these exploits an idea lingering perhaps in the dramatist's mind since, in the *Knights,* he had rejuvenated the old Demos. Here rejuvenation does not affect one man only but the entire chorus: twenty-four old men change masks and re-appear as twenty-four young Fausts! If the conjecture is valid, then the *Old Age* presents a novelty; because a chorus undergoing a transformation within a single play is a rare phenomenon in the Aristophanic canon; more generally, in the ancient Greek drama we know there is but one analogous case: the Erinyes who become Eumenides in the *Oresteia.*

Anagyros, the hero of the second comedy, belongs to Athenian folklore, and the play bearing his name may have been a parody on the *Hippolytus* or the *Phoenix* of Euripides. The fragments betray some common points with the *Banqueters* and the *Clouds:* debates between a father and a son, and mention of horses and races.[2]

The first surviving play that Aristophanes will write during these days of peace is the *second Clouds.* As likely as not, it was never performed. The Arguments inform us that the poet was willing to produce the play again but "for some reason" he did not do it. As we see, the reason was unknown even to the Alexandrian scholars. We also read in the Arguments that Aristophanes "was much more unlucky in the *second Clouds"*; this "unlucky" may mean either that the play was rejected by the archon or that the author himself did not consider his revision successful.[3] If, however, our playwright had been "unlucky" in his *second Clouds,* how can we explain the fact that this play and *not* the first version, the one produced, was preserved in the grammarians' files? The answer is not unrelated, perhaps, to the Socratic worship which had its heyday in the Alexandrian age. Having to choose between the two *Clouds*, erudites decided on the one less damaging to the great philosopher's memory. If the supposition is valid, then we have to accept that the *first Clouds* was much more bilious in its attack on Socrates than the version we know. And this accounts, in a way, for the great significance that Plato gives to it in the *Apology* (18b, 19c) and the *Phaedo* (69d).

Now, why did our poet rewrite the *Clouds?* One answer might be that his first *Clouds* had been a ludicrous failure and that he wished to repair the injury to his pride; another answer, that he was impressed by Socrates' magnanimous attitude toward the first attack or that, in the years between the two plays, he had a chance to know Socrates better and to realize that he had been unfair to him. Anyway, we ought to assume that the second rendering is the milder of the two. An argument in favor of this view is also the fact that not one single mention of Socrates is made throughout the whole *parabasis*.[4]

We have spoken already of this *parabasis* and said that it offers the poet's self-criticism. The same applies to the *parabases* of the *Knights*, the *Wasps*, and the *Peace*. Besides his views on himself, which are laudatory, we learn those on his fellow dramatists, which are destructive, as well as those on the theatre public, which are both. His critical flare will mature as he approaches the *Women at the Thesmophoria* and the *Frogs*. Never again, however, will he share with his spectators his intimate thoughts and opinions in such auto-analytical confessions.

Let us list first his serious axioms, those concerning the moral and artistic virtues that the superior dramatist must possess, or, to put it somewhat differently, the vir-

tues that make him, Aristophanes, superior to other playwrights:

A. *To fight for the people's rights*
   a) He [Aristophanes] is a worthy poet because he
   hates those you hate. (*Knights*, 509–10)
   b) He is again fighting for your sake. (*Wasps*, 1037)
   c) Fighting for your benefit. (*Peace*, 759)

Also, in the *Wasps* (1043) we find the two words which
express the Attic playwright's purpose: *alexíkakos* (protector) and *kathartes* (purifier) of his country.

B. *To side with his enlightened public*
   a) The wise will think highly of the poet. (*Wasps*,
   1049)
   b) I believe that you are intelligent spectators.
   (*Clouds*, 521)
   c) I will never betray, by my own will, the intelligent among you. (*Clouds*, 527)

C. *To be fearless*
   a) He dares proclaim what is right and marches cou-
   rageously against the tornado. (*Knights*, 510–11)
   b) With Heracles' valiancy he attacks the most
   mighty. (*Wasps*, 1030)
   c) He, who, when Cleon stood high, punched him in
   the belly. (*Clouds*, 549)

On the contrary, Hermippus, Eupolis, and Phrynichus,
being scared of Cleon, attacked only the less dangerous
Hyperbolus and his mother (*Clouds*, 551 f.).

D. *To be modest*
   a) Neither did he put on airs nor did he start going
   around the gymnasiums boasting. (*Wasps*,
   1024–25)

This, the scholiast tells us, is a barb at Eupolis. In the
same play (1028) Aristophanes assures us that he never
"turned his muses into pimps." In the *Clouds* (545) we

find the most singular expression of modesty: "I do not exhibit pretentious hairdos!" Naturally, for he was already bald. An exception to this rule is his philippic in the *parabasis* of the *Clouds,* a passionate outcry of indignation about the inferior art of other playwrights, still popular with the naïve Athenian public: "I don't want the admiration of people who laugh at such-like jokes; those, however, who enjoy me and my inventions, will always be men of good judgment" (560–62).

   E. *To be an innovator*
   - *a*) He has sown novel ideas. (*Wasps,* 1044)
   - *b*) Bringing always new ideas, I invent nothing which is not original. (*Clouds,* 547–48)
   - *c*) To offer witticisms and invent gags. (Fr. 892, Blaydes)

In the *Knights,* his dancers say that they would not address the public if one of the "outdated" comic poets asked them to (507–9), while they do so heartily for modern-minded Aristophanes.

   F. *To maintain the purity of his art*
   - *a*) He [Aristophanes] created great art for us and fortified it with lofty words and thoughts. (*Peace,* 749–50)
   - *b*) He put a stop to the vulgarities of his rivals. (*Peace,* 739)
   - *c*) Defeated by inferior comic poets. (*Clouds,* 524–25)

In the last play he also criticizes Eupolis for presenting a tipsy old woman dancing the *kordax* (555).

   The six virtues mentioned above constitute the code of honor of the comic poet. Aristophanes believes in them and proclaims them without laughing. He is also very serious when he chaffs his audience who raise him to Olympus or thrust him to Hades with equal eagerness. This audience he had at first avoided facing in his own name, remembering how ungrateful and inhuman they had been in the case of Magnes, Crates, and Cratinus (*Wasps,* 1023, 1044; *Knights,* 518 f.). He compares his own public to a vine-pole which let the vine—*viz.* himself—fall (*Wasps,* 1291).

In the playwright's parabatic manifestoes the serious and the droll always come together, like swans and ducks swimming side by side in a lake. Being a comic poet, Aristophanes must never let his audience assume that he takes his art too seriously. So, every climax of self-adulation will be promptly followed by an anticlimax of self-derision.

Let us look at some examples of what we might call the Aristophanic bathos. He proudly declares that:

1. He has never asked his actors to dance the *kordax* (*Clouds,* 540). [Yet Dicaeopolis in the *Acharnians* as well as Philocleon in the *Wasps* dance it, for, after all, the *kordax* was comedy's official dance.]

2. He never displayed a "red-leather phallus" to make the children laugh (*Clouds,* 538–39). [Very possibly; however, his male choruses had leather phalluses tied around their waists; furthermore, two future characters, Mnesilochus in the *Women at the Thesmophoria* and Cinesias in the *Lysistrata* will elaborate on that symbol quite extensively.]

3. He didn't present old men chasing others with a stick or people being beaten (*Clouds,* 541–42; *Peace,* 742). [The coal-traders of the *Acharnians* and the judges in the *Wasps* fight with sticks; and characters in almost all his plays run about the stage to escape somebody's blows.]

4. He didn't present sniveling slaves or other people whimpering *"iou, iou!"* (*Clouds,* 543; *Peace,* 743–45). [Nevertheless, all the Aristophanic slaves snivel at some time or another and the *"iou, iou"* is uttered on numberless occasions.]

5. He didn't present people struggling to get rid of

their lice (*Peace,* 740). [Yet, Strepsiades fights against an army of bed-bugs.]

6. He did not mock the starving nor the bald (*Clouds,* 540; *Peace,* 741). [Socrates and his students are starving; so is the Megarian who sells his daughters to buy salt and garlic. As for baldness, in the *Peace* (767 f.) he makes fun of himself and of all bald spectators.]

7. He did not use lighted torches in his plays (*Clouds,* 543). [At the end of every comedy, however, the actors enter in torchlight; in the *Clouds,* even the school of Socrates became an enormous torch.]

8. He never showed slaves throwing nuts at the audience (*Wasps,* 58–59). [Still, corn is thrown at the spectators by the slaves in the *Peace.*]

9. He saved comedy from vulgarity and indecency (*Peace,* 739). [If we take this braggadocio for granted, then it is difficult to imagine what his fellow poets must have been like in that respect.]

10. He never made fun of women or little men (*Peace,* 751). [We can almost be sure that he has already ridiculed the fair sex in the *Women Getting Hold of Tents;* and he is to do so extensively in the *Lysistrata* and his other feminine comedies. As for the little men, we have the Megarian of the *Acharnians* and all the parasites in the *Peace* to contradict his statement.]

11. He never presented Heracles chewing and swallowing food (*Peace,* 741). [Heracles must have noisily chewed in the *Centaur* (Fr. 266, Blaydes) and his gluttony will be featured again in the *Birds.*]

12. He didn't produce rags to get laughs (*Peace,* 740). [Euripides in the *Acharnians* was a rag-tag poet; Old Demos, Socrates, and Philocleon are also shabbily dressed.]

13. He did not lampoon Euripides (*Wasps,* 61). [Well, he had done so heretofore in the *Acharnians,* the

Proagon, and possibly in the *Anagyros.* The *Women at Thesmophoria* and the *Frogs* are still to come.]

14. He didn't "mince" Cleon when he stood high (*Wasps,* 62–63) nor did he attack him after his death (*Clouds,* 550). [The mincing of Cleon in the *Knights* took place immediately after his triumph at Delos; in the *Peace,* written after the demagogue's death, Aristophanes labels him "impostor, braggart, informer, provocator."]

15. He never checked the public, writing the same thing twice (*Clouds,* 546). [This is true, of course, for his basic ideas, which were always new, but not for his jokes. Every other comedy offers us more or less the same mockeries about the effeminacy of Cleisthenes, the cowardice of Cleonymus, the tragedies of Euripides, Melanthius, Morsimus, and Carcinus, and the overall viciousness of Cleon.] What is surprising is that the above statement is found in the *second Clouds,* a play written twice! . . .

16. He didn't make use of jokes "stolen from Megara" (*Wasps,* 57). [We could, nevertheless, fill a whole book with such Aristophanic jokes imitated from low farce.]

17. In the *Peace* (734–35) he risks a rather dangerous aphorism: "If a playwright praises himself in the parabasis, he must be beaten at once by the theatre guards." [Yet, two lines later, he apostrophizes himself as "a superb and illustrious comic poet."]

In all the examples stated above, Aristophanes' euphemistic intentions are more than evident. Neither was he so absent-minded nor his public so idiotic as to take the exaggerated lies seriously. As a rule, the playwright's self-appraisal is sarcastic, and this is the greatest example of his inner modesty; every self-laudatory attempt is in no time turned by him into an enormous absurdity. Otherwise, as he himself has said, the theatre guards would beat him.

We should always, therefore, try to use an imaginative approach to the Aristophanic *parabases*. The Attic poet addressed his audience on various extremely serious matters, pertaining to both private and public life; this does not mean, however, that the play ceased to be comic and that it put on the frowning aspect of a political assembly. In his *parabases,* Aristophanes succeeds in achieving a wonderful harmony between the sublime and the ridiculous—what one day will be proclaimed by Victor Hugo as the basic contrasting elements of good drama. The Aristophanic method of anticlimax, aims, we might say, at the Kantian definition of laughter: the abrupt reduction to zero of an intense expectation.[5]

While in the first six years of his career (427–421 B.C.) Aristophanes produced, approximately, ten or eleven plays, it is doubtful whether in the six years that followed (421–415 B.C.) he wrote more than four, including two of his old subjects revised: the *second Clouds* and the *second Peace*.

About the *second Clouds* we have already spoken. The purpose of the *second Peace* may have been to invigorate the peaceful feelings of the Athenians, when rumors about a new war were again in the air. In the revision of his old comedy, he probably theorized *si vis bellum, pacem para,* to blame his fellow citizens for their inability to preserve peace.

A charming allegorical figure, Agriculture, appeared in this play and perhaps she was a substitute for the Opora (fruitfulness) of the original one, or even of Peace herself, as Norwood supposes.[6] The *second Peace* has been identified by some scholars with another play mentioned in the list of Aristophanic comedies, namely the *Farmers*. Indeed, many fragments of this lost play refer to peace, in the same way as many of the *second Peace* refer to farmers.[7] In this play we find, also, the poet's famous eulogy of his native land:

> O beloved city of Cecrops, bud of Attica
> Hail glowing soil! (Fr. 110)

as well as an infamous mention of his fellow countrymen:

> Don't remind me of the Athenians!
> They are greedy pots. (Fr. 865, Blaydes)

The tantalizing question, however, is how should we interpret this temporary sterility of the bald playwright, still in his thrities? As a prevailing bitterness over his recent failures? As a disenchantment caused by the failure of peace? Or as the spiritual fatigue which every creative artist is subject to, when like a ship's mainmast he is continuously resisting the tempest?

When we read Aristophanes' comedies or enjoy his choruses dancing in the orchestra, we often forget all the backstage troubles of the poet. We sometimes take it for granted that his life began and ended in the gaiety which animates his plays. Behind that, however, there was the natural depression which the comic author felt as a highly conscientious citizen; there was also his unsteady private life, his days without inspiration, his sweat during rehearsals, his agony before the performance, the resentment and hatred that surrounded him, the huge army of enemies that his invective had created, the intrigues and conspiracies organized against him, the calumnies, menaces, implorations, yesterday's friends who turned away, the claques who were paid to hiss his plays, the judges who were predisposed to annihilate him, and even those of his countrymen who might have gone so far as to spit in his face. "Producing comedies," Aristophanes admitted "is an extremely difficult job" (*Knights,* 516). In reality, it consists of a few hours of theatrical merriment in a whole year of labor and anxiety.

There is the other side of the coin too, however. What appears as a dark and unexplained silence may have been for the poet a luminous interlude of Attic sunshine spent by the Saronic Sea or in the Dionysiac exhilaration of all-day banquets. Incidentally, it is in this barren period of his career that historians date the famous symposium at Agathon's house. The wonderful parable on the *androgyna,* with Plato places in the mouth of Aristophanes, was very possibly inspired by an actual dissertation of the comic poet at a banquet. We have also surmised that in those years his wife gave birth to their three sons: Philip, Araros, and Nicostratos (by others called Philetairos).[8] Following our imagination still further, we can see them being brought up in Aegina, on the family farm, where our poet trims his vines, tastes his figs and, occasionally, pinches the buttocks of his Thracian maid, exactly as his beloved characters had the habit of doing. Aegina is as necessary in the life of Aristophanes as Stratford and Shottery are in the life of Shakespeare. On the rocky slopes and grubby forests of Aegina, Aristophanes falls in love with the world of birds, and tapes in his memory the various *"kikkabau"* and *"torotorotorix,"* which will soon resound in a chirruping comedy of his.

The year 415 B.C. marks the end of Aristophanes' creative silence. After all, the war that he hated was the fountainhead of his inspiration.

Chapter XI

Sicily and Cloudcuckoo City

*We approached the Clouds where we
saw and admired Cloudcuckoocity . . .
and we recalled the poet Aristophanes, a
wise man who always spoke the truth.*
        Lucian, *True History*

In those few years of peace, Athens still holds its old place of supremacy among the Greek cities. But she no longer enjoys her former wealth and well-being; there are no stored goods left, the fields have been devastated, the new plantings have not had time to give fruit; and within the city, the soldiers of yesterday wander jobless. What is worse, fear has never ceased that the Spartans will once more blow the martial trumpets and that they, the Athenians, will have no resources for waging war anew.

Thus an old dream begins to take shape again: colonization. Not a departure to the old colonies of the Ionian shores or to the poor Aegean islands so many times shared by lot, but an escape to a new and rich land, able to feed many families and ship quantities of goods to the metropolis. This land is Sicily. Even in Pericles' days, the Athenians looked upon this island as a land of promise. It had always been a magnet for potential immigrants and for political adventurers. Now, in this uncertain recess of war, the ancient dream reappears more tormenting than ever.

Besides, the conquest of the big, mostly Doric island would automatically separate her from Doric Greece and would thus blockade the Peloponnesus from all sides. Moreover, Sicily would serve as a bridge for Athens to expand further, to Italy, Carthage, even, perhaps, to the Pillars of Hercules—today's straits of Gibraltar.

The idea is introduced to the Assembly with new vigor by Alcibiades. The prodigal dandy, the perfect representative of the new generation, and a blood-brother of the Aristophanic Pheidippides, is now a grown-up man. He spends his nights carousing, but knows how to be on the Pnyx early in the morning. He is at this time the most notorious political figure of Athens. Handsome and intelligent, a breath-taking orator and fervent "democrat," he drugs the people with the opium of the Sicilian paradise. And the Athenian citizens, gathered on their democratic hill, begin to be tempted by the advantages of an offensive war, for which they finally vote. From this crucial moment, perhaps, the downfall of Athens begins. Giving faith to the promises of the deceitful new demagogue, the city agrees to sacrifice not only blood and money, but also her most precious ideal, her democratic conscience.

At the beginnings of 415 B.C. the expedition is prepared. The most optimistic among the citizens already divide up the Sicilian land by drawing maps of the island. The only person to stand up against the plans is the scrupulous Nicias, but nobody will listen to him. And so, on a summer day of that year, the whole city marches to Pireaus to watch the sailing of the famous fleet: 134 triremes with 5,000 Athenian, Chian, Cretan, and Argive soldiers, 30 cargo ships with provisions and besieging machines, and 150 smaller ships with various traders and idlers. A few days later, however, the Assembly sends the *Salaminia,* the government ship, to catch the fleet and bring the commander-in-chief back to Athens on a criminal charge. A day before the departure, the "Hermes" columns adorning the city had been found mutilated, and rumors were spreading that Alcibiades and his companions were responsible for this sacrilegious act.[1]

If Alcibiades had not been recalled, would the course of history have changed? Maybe no. Or maybe the Greece of Alexander the Great would have been created a century earlier by an Athenian leader. What is certain is that with the recalling of Alcibiades, the Athenians deprived their military machine of its originating spark. They left army, ships, money, and hopes in the hands of a dangerous humanitarian, Nicias, and of a narrow-minded soldier, Lamachus. The expedition being an enormous act of madness, only a great lunatic, like Alcibiades, might have been successful with it.

Knowing what was in store for him at home, Alcibiades decides to take refuge in Sparta, where he opens a new chapter in his life: the elegant patron of the turf and charmer of the Assembly now enters his second phase, that of an expatriate and eventually a traitor. In the meantime, Athens has taken on the aspect of a giant tribunal. A committee has been formed and receives indiscriminately every accusation about the Hermes columns, submitting all suspects to torture (Thucydides, VI, 60). The Aristophanic wasps have been let loose and sting everywhere.

In this grim climate our comic poet writes the *Birds*. We should probably assume that he had started it sometime earlier, for it is a long play, with a great number of characters, rich in ornithological detail and literary reference and poetically more elaborate than most of his other comedies. At about the same time, he completes another play, the *Amphiaraos*. It will be presented by Philonides at the Lenaea, while Callistratus will produce the *Birds* at the City Dionysia.[2] The poet, making his return to the

Athenian stage after a long interval, appeals once more to his two former collaborators. "Producing a comedy" is still for him "a difficult task."

In the *Amphiaraos,* Aristophanes presents a sick and god-fearing old man who goes with his wife to the curative temple of Oropos, to recover his youth. The rejuvenation theme, as we remember, brought about the denouement in the *Knights* and constituted most likely the plot of the *Old Age.* Scholars believe that the old man symbolized, as in the *Knights,* the State. The fragments describe a noisy campsite of pilgrims with tents, pots and pans, prayers and quarrels; a very odd throng of sick people, similar to those who still gather nowadays in the international shrines of miraculous cures. Carion's description of the miraculous night at the Asclepieion (*Plutus,* 653–747) may give us an idea of the *Amphiaraos'* overall atmosphere.[3]

When this play was produced, in late January, Alcibiades had already convinced the Spartans to send an army to Sicily to fight his fellow countrymen. Things look still favorable for the Athenians, however, and the western wind brings no dark cloud from the Sicilian front. In the March festival the revelers forget all about Alcibiades and attend the performance of the *Birds.* To say that they forget is an absurdity, for Greek Drama keeps the conscience of its spectators constantly awakened to contemporary events, even when it deals with the most fanciful fiction.

In this comedy, Aristophanes inaugurates a novelty, as far as we can judge. For his traditional duo of slaves to introduce a play, he substitutes two travelers, thus entering directly into the comedy's action. The first characters that we see are the comic heroes themselves—Evelpides and Peithetaerus—two Athenians, not naïve villagers this time but sophisticated bourgeois from the city itself, who are in search of a propitious place to recommence their lives more successfully. Their names are symbolic: the first signifies the hopeful man, the second, the persuasive one.[4] In these two characters we meet for the first time, conjoined in a comic pair, the two species of Aristophanic heroes: Peithetaerus is the militant ideologist (Dicaeopolis, Trygaeus) and Evelpides, the irresponsible buffoon (Strepsiades, Philocleon).

In the vague and certainly abstract landscape of birdland, our two travelers wander, guided by a crow and a magpie which they hold in their hands, like two primitive Geiger counters. They hope that the wise Hoopoe, who in his human life had been the legendary king Tereus [5]— will help them find a better world to live in. This Hoopoe makes a majestic and at the same time ludicrous (92) entrance. Having once been a king, he retains, beneath his crestfallen aspect, his royal airs; he is something like a gentleman farmer of the remote British countryside; he is also an amateur singer, and the duets he practices with his wife—the beauteous Procne, alias Nightingale— make the whole feathered population rejoice.

After rejecting various countries proposed by their plumed host, the two disenchanted Athenians inquire about life among the birds. Tereus answers that it is not bad at all, money is valueless and living is poetically assured by seeds, myrtle, and thyme. This immediately generates in Peithetaerus' brain a great idea: "You should build your own city-state in the clouds!" he says (172, 178). And, thanks to this inspiration the astute Athenian emerges from this moment as the basic protagonist, elbowing aside Evelpides, less prolific in ideas. "You should surround it," he continues enthusiastically, "with huge walls and starve the gods by preventing men's sacrifices from reaching heaven."

"By traps and nets and decoys!" exclaims the Hoopoe, who, like all primitives, swears by the powers of destruction, "I've never heard of a better idea!" He will awaken his Nightingale and both together will sing a melodious call to all the birds. In the manuscripts we read the stage direction: *aulei* (plays the flute), which according to the ancient scholiast signifies that the flutist of the performance imitated the nightingale's trills. This scene gives us the best example of a device (apparently called *mesaulion*) where the flute is underscoring an ode or a choral song. As for the several *io, io, ito, ito, tio, tio, trioto, trioto, toto brix,* etc., they may connote either the singing voice of the nightingale or the flute imitating it.[6] This is the call of the Hoopoe (and Nightingale?) to the birds.

Calling first to the landbirds:

      O Birds of fellow feather come!
      Come, you Birds who graze, who feed
      over the farmers' fresh-sown fields!
      Barley-eating tribes, in thousands come!

      O peckers after seeds, hungry nations,
      swift of wing! Come, O chirrupers!
      All you who flitter in the furrows,
      who throng, who flock the new-turned sod,
      who sing your chirrup, chirrup-song,
        tio tio tio tio tio tio tio!

      All you who in the gardens nest,
      who perch beneath the ivy's leaves!
      O rangers on the mountain, come,
      arbutus-stealers, olive-thieves!
      Flock, fly to my call! Come, O come!
        trio trio trio totobrix!

To the birds of marsh and meadow:

      O Birds of swamp and river, come!
      You whose beaks snap up the whining gnats,

who splash in water where the earth is wet
or skim the meadows over Marathon!
O Birds of blazoned feather, come!

To the seabirds:

Come, Birds who soar upon the sea
where the kingfisher swoops!
O Birds with delicate necks,
O taper-throated, come!
Come and see the world remade!
Come and see the Birds reborn!

Lo, a MAN has come, of skill and craft,
    whose wit cuts like a knife,
and to the Birds he brings the Word
    of more abundant life.

Hear ye, hear ye, hear ye!
Come to council, come!
Hither, hither, hither! [7]

A chorus of twenty-four birds enters violently with
feathers wide open and great din and fray (327). The two
strangers enumerate twenty-four different kinds; and this
variety is a proof, perhaps, that the chorus members were
not costumed homogeneously, that feathers, masks, crests,
and beaks created a counterpoint of color and design. It
should be taken for granted, however, that beneath their
ornithologic accoutrements the dancers wore their usual
body-tights. The Greek theatre, being unrealistic, kept reminding its spectators that they did not behold real birds
or wasps or clouds, but actors disguised as such.[8]

At first the birds do not regard the foreigners too favorably. They come from the hateful race of men that has
always been their enemy. Like many irascible Aristophanic choruses, they get immediately into battle forma-

tion and begin a fluttering Pyrrhic dance, during which the word "wing" (bird-wing, army-wing) occasions many puns which, later, Plutarch will condemn.

The two earthly visitors see their lives at stake. A solid argument of the serene Hoopoe, however, brings the battle to an end. "Wise people learn from their enemies," he tells the birds. "Wasn't it from their enemies that all the states learned to build fortresses and to arm ships?" (375–80). So the chorus leaders order at ease, and the birds wait in silence for Peithetaerus' explanation. The Athenian idealist—idealist, truly, but not less of an impostor than most idealists—climbs upon a rock and delivers his speech (462–538). His first argument: that the birds, had they read their Aesop, would know that they had been the original masters of mankind—the cock was ruler of Persia before Darius, the cuckoo reigned in Egypt and Phoenicia, and the kite in prehistoric Greece. While Peithetaerus is developing his cosmogonic theories, extemporizing with an amazing eloquence both plausible and implausible data, Evelpides sees to the spectators' laughs by his comic interjections.

The excellence of this comedy lies fundamentally in its chorus: the colorful aspect it offers and its natural gift for poetry, music, and dance. Beyond these, our birds are presented as stubborn, superstitious, ignorant, and afflicted with a great amount of *sklavenmoral;* they don't differ much, in fact, from the Athenian people gathering on the Pnyx to decide on monumental issues. At the end of the *agon* (538), conquered by man's wisdom and practical sense, they beg him to help them recover their lost supremacy.

"I advise you," he expostulates from his pedestal, "to create a city of birds!" He tells them, furthermore, to compel Zeus to recognize their revolution officially, and, if he does not, to declare a holy war against him and never let any god pass through their territorial air on his way to a mortal mistress. At the same time, the birds should send a herald to men, decreeing that, from now on, whenever they sacrifice to the gods they must first sacrifice to the birds; and, if they do not comply, then a squadron of swallows will eat their crops and a battalion of crows will peck out the eyes of their cattle. "O reverent elder," the fickle people of birdland exclaim, "instead of our worst enemy you have become our dearest friend!" And they accept blindfolded his leadership in the realization of the great project.

The *parabasis* of the *Birds* presents a charming originality; it has an individual actor or singer, namely the Nightingale, participate in the choral songs:

O suffering mankind,
        lives of twilight,
                race feeble and fleeting,
like the leaves scattered!
        Pale generations,
                creatures of clay,
the wingless, the fading!
        Unhappy mortals,
                shadows in time,
flickering dreams!
        Hear us now,
                the ever-living Birds,
the undying,
        the ageless ones,
                scholars of eternity,
Hear and learn from us
        the truth
                of all there is to know—
what we are,
        and how the gods began,
                of Chaos and Dark.

(And when you know
                    tell Prodikos to go
                                        hang: he's had it!)
There was Chaos at first
                    and Night and Space
                                        and Tartaros.
There was no Earth.
                    No Heaven was.
                                        But sable-winged Night
laid her wind-egg there
                    in the boundless lap
                                        of infinite Dark.
And from that egg,
                    in the seasons' revolving,
                                        Love was born,
the graceful, the golden,
                    the whirlwind Love
                                        on gleaming wings.
And there in the waste
                    of Tartaros,
                                        Love with Chaos lay
and hatched the Birds.
                    We come from Love.
                                        Love brought us to the light.
There were no gods
                    till Love had married
                                        all the world in love.
Then the world was made.
                    Blue Heaven stirred,
                                        and Ocean,
the Earth and ageless gods,
                    the blessed ones
                                        who do not die.
But we came first.
                    We Birds were born
                                        the first-born sons of Love,

in proof whereof
>
> we wear Love's wings,
>
> > we help his lovers.
> >
> > (676–704)

The *anapaests* (685 f.) of the *parabasis* are also original, compared to those of other plays. The poet ignores his own self, the traditional hero of the parabasis, and leaves the floor to the birds. There is no professional apology here, no artistic theory or political attack breaks the continuity of the plot. (In this way, the style is akin perhaps to that of Crates, Pherecrates, or even Eupolis, who favored parables more than direct political sermons.) The dancers, addressing the audience, deliver a Hesiodic narrative of how the world was made.[9] In the *pnigos* (723–36) they name the services which they render to mankind, pleading to the gods proclaimed by all mortals. "If you elect us your gods, we shall not slumber on the clouds like Zeus but we shall always give to you and your children Wealth, Health, Happiness, Longevity, Youth, Peace, Laughter, Dances, and the Milk of the Birds." These promised favors could be taken, equally well, as a pledge of the actors and the playwright to their public. Is it not, after all, comedy's privilege to bestow on men health, happiness, peace, laughter, youth, and all those rare treats? It is Aristophanes' way of saying to his audience: "We, theatre artists, should be your real gods, and not the conceited politicians who sit on the clouds indifferent to the fate of ordinary people!"

It is utterly futile to try to convey this comedy's charm without quoting abundantly from its poetry; yet, as Heine says, these ethereal choral songs are untranslatable.[10] Here are the two strophes of the *parabasis:*

> O woodland Muse
> with lovely throat,
> *tio tio tio tinx!*

who with me sing
whenas in glade or mountain, I,
perched upon the ashtree cry,
tio tio tio tinx!
my tawny-throated song of praise,
to call the Mother to the dance,
a song of joy for blessed Pan,
totototototinx!
whence, like a bee,
the poet stole his honied song,
my ravished cry,
tio tio tio tinx! (737–52)

And so the swans
their clamor cry,
tio tio tio tinx!
and beating wings
and bursting throats
lord Apollo sing,
tio tio tio tinx!
by Hebros' waters, swarming, crying,
tio tio tio tinx!
And every living thing is still.
On bird, on beast, the hush of awe.
The windless sea lies stunned when—
totototototinx!
All Olympos rings,
and wonder breaks upon the gods,
and echoing, the Graces sing,
and lovely Muses raise the cry,
tio tio tio tinx! (769–84)

When the *parabasis* is over (800) the two heroes re-enter disguised grotesquely as birds. The Hoopoe does not
reappear with them, because the actor has to change mask
and costume to interpret some more parts. For the same

reason, Aristophanes will make Evelpides disappear, too, after a while. This play, incidentally, is his most abundant in number of characters.

The building of the city of birds proceeds with dispatch. The inventive Peithetaerus proposes a name for it, which is unanimously approved: Cloudcuckoo City (819). A whole sequence of short episodes, each one introducing an obnoxious visitor, constitutes the second part of the comedy. All the unemployed, good-for-nothing, lazy, and profiteering parasites of Athens will swarm one after the other to the plumed state. And all the evils which our two heroes tried to escape by leaving their country will follow them as far as the clouds. Needless to say, Peithetaerus sends all the intruders away with a salutory beating. Finally, a messenger comes and announces, in an amazingly Disney-like description, that the walls of the city have been erected (1122–63).

The foundation of the new state and the emergence of a new political power—that of the birds—creates a double response, to the immortal gods and to mortal men. Humans hurriedly pledge submission. Meanwhile, Cloudcuckoo City has become very fashionable among Athenians and everybody dreams of feathers and a winged way of life. Iris, the gods' messenger, comes flying to the birds' country, by means of the stage-crane, her veils blowing in the wind (1199). Later, a more impressive Olympian delegation arrives: Poseidon, Heracles, and Triballus. Aristophanes chooses these particular gods because, possibly in the Peloponnesian War days, they were considered as enemy gods; Poseidon was worshipped at the Isthmus, Heracles was an ancient hero of the Dorian drama, and Triballus was somehow connected with a Thracian tribe who had fought against the Athenians. Besides, there are some purely theatrical reasons for this choice: Triballus offers the opportunity for an extravagant dialect, Heracles is a popular glutton and, finally, Poseidon is known as a frowning Homeric god, who befits a grotesque political delegation, as its serious master mind. The episode of the starving gods has the integrity of an accomplished mime drama (1565–1693). It gives us to a certain degree an idea of the lost mythical parodies of Epicharmus. The bombastic Poseidon, the vulgar Heracles, and the idiotic Triballus discuss the conditions of peace, while Peithetaerus turns a barbecue on a spit to tickle their noses.

A little while earlier, the illustrious tragic hero and enemy of the gods, Prometheus, had made a secret trip to Cloudcuckoo City to advise Peithetaerus that his victory over men and gods would not be complete unless he succeeded in obtaining from Zeus his royal mate, not the undesirable Hera, of course, but Basileia, a beauteous maiden who symbolizes Zeus' supreme Sovereignty (1494–1552). The debates between Peithetaerus and the gods end with his victory, and the comedy comes to its conclusion with our hero's triumphal wedding to Sovereignty. While the birds are singing and praising their leader, the great "idealist" departs ceremoniously for heaven, where the throne of Zeus awaits him. As most revolutions end sooner or later in the dictatorship of a Cromwell, Robespierre, Stalin, or Hitler, so the birds' revolution against the gods has created a new god. The sovereignty they had dreamt of recovering is finally realized, as the domination of an individual over their masses.

The symbolic wedding with which the play ends is reminiscent of the one concluding the *Peace*. There, the wedding was a popular feast, here it is an allegorical glorification. We admire this phantasmagoric finale, exalting the triumph of the human mind over nature. But the conclusion of the former comedy, the more earthy one, revealed a more optimistic playwright who spoke more warmly to the people's hearts. The Aristophanes of 421

B.C. saw peace still as a tangible reality and his theatrical symbolism conveyed a holiday of fig trees, vineyards, birth, and wine. The *Birds,* on the contrary, conceived in a period of doubt, leaves an ambiguous taste of joy and anxiety; it celebrates a chimeric prosperity. Cloudcuckoo City was founded, grew powerful, subdued the gods, and won celestial supremacy; yet its name will never cease to signify something essentially unrealizable.

As had happened with the *Peace,* seven years before, the *Birds* secured only second prize. Ameipsias with his *Revellers* was the victor, and Phrynichus with the *Solitary* came in last.[11]

It seems surprising that this fascinating comedy did not win the dramatic contest, though it is possible that to ancient Greek judgment it presented some shortcomings which escape us. First of all, the subject was not an original one: Magnes and Crates had written *Birds;* also Cratinus' *Vengeance* (*Nemesis*) may have had a bird chorus. Notwithstanding Michelangelo's dictum that only a real inventor can use other people's inventions, the Athenian judges had to choose there and then between three plays. Perhaps this comedy lacked, in their estimation, the satirical exuberance and the burning contemporaneity usually displayed by the professedly bellicose pacifist, Aristophanes. Another reason, though rather doubtful, may have been the poet's irreverence toward the gods. "I am immortal!" Iris tells Peithetaerus; and he answers: "All the same, you should have died. We are now the masters of the universe and it is preposterous for you gods to put on airs and not bow to your betters . . ." (1224 f.). The problem of Aristophanes' religious beliefs, however, is insoluble and his own contradictions are perplexing. In the *Clouds,* for instance, he attacks the sophists as atheists, while in the *Birds* he, himself, objects to the necessity of gods. In the *Women at the Thesmophoria* he will praise the Olympians with ardent respect, while in the *Plutus* he will ridicule Zeus and his priests. (Plato, in the *Symposium,* will have his Aristophanes begin a speech by saying "with due respect to the gods . . ." What does the phrase hint at? Was the comic poet, in the philosopher's conception, a bigot? Or was he an infidel who would sarcastically invoke the divinities that he had excessively mocked?)

The *Birds* has created two opposed responses among modern scholars. The idealists see in this comedy a play of escape, a fascinating fairy-tale whose purpose is to take us far from grim reality. The materialists perceive between the lines a coded description of the Sicilian Expedition and of the political events surrounding it. Here are two contrasting opinions expressed by modern specialists: Allardyce Nicoll writes: "Aristophanes endeavoured to find expression for his disgust at the real in the building for himself of an imaginative, fantastic world." And N. B. Kliatchko: "The comedy describes the preparation of a plan for the military expansion of 415 and its perfect success, as anticipated and desired by the Athenians." [12]

The materialist's view is based on the conviction that Aristophanes—that theatrical sponge of political life— could have never remained indifferent to such an enormous contemporary event as the expedition to Sicily. They believe that the whole comedy, simply because it was written in 414 B.C., must have been a camouflaged parody of Alcibiades' utopia. They go so far as to suggest a code for deciphering the play's meaning: Peithetaerus conceals the dynamic Alcibiades, Evelpides, the outshadowed Nicias, and Cloudcuckoo City, the utopian kingdom of Sicily. Furthermore, the birds, who, by building a new state, recover their lost power, are the Athenians; the gods, who finally surrender, are the Spartans; and so on and so forth.

The idealistic view, on the other hand, accepts actuality only to a certain degree. The colonization theme was in the air and there Aristophanes found it. The expedition had the character of piracy, highway robbery, and adventure. All the poor and the unadjusted, all speculators and opportunists looked upon this new land as an Eldorado, not unlike Australia or the Golden West millenniums later. From that multiform crowd of potential colonists the poet borrowed his characters. And as Sicily was everyman's Utopia, he wrote a utopian comedy. Unable though he was to predict the tragic enormity of the Sicilian disaster, he, nonetheless, did not believe in the success of the enterprise. So, what he seems to tell his fellow Athenians is that it is as impossible to succeed in such a mad project as to build a bird-city in the clouds.

That may have been his political message, if any. Apart from it, the comedy follows its own way as a pure work of art. With beautiful poetry, exotic sounds and melodies, spectacular dances, and the colorful presence of the birds, the playwright builds on the Dionysiac orchestra a winged paradise, utterly crazy, Greek, and nonexistent. I am sure that Coleridge had that particular play in mind when he said that Aristophanes rose "to a great distance above the ludicrous of real life" and that, "in this one point of absolute ideality," Attic Comedy and that of Shakespeare coincide.[13]

We have already spoken of an implicit melancholy casting its shadow on this luminous fantasy. In this period of his life, Aristophanes must have become painfully aware that his dangerous lifelong enemy was not so much the warmongering Cleon as War itself. For if the old demagogues and warmongers were gone, others had taken their places and quite recently Alcibiades, who could prove more destructive, perhaps, then any of the former ones. Aristophanes silently admitted that War had defeated him for good.

Was he defeated, though, only by War? It did not

look so. All the evils which he had tried, since his tender years, to uproot from his native earth were still there reveling over his failure—informers, bad poets, impudent youths, false preachers, perverse intellectuals. The "unwashed Socrates" still influenced young men, and trials still enraptured the Athenians; on the Pnyx the demagogues prevailed and Euripides was quoted by the people. Every disease he had tried to fight appeared more incurable and more fatal than ever.

Therefore, the only remedy for him was to set off on a trip, as everybody else was intending to do. Instead of sailing on a ship for Sicily, however, he chose to sail on his imagination for a land of birds. And he wrote this comedy.

Chapter XII

The *Lysistrata*, Last War Play

I am a woman, yet I have brains.
Euripides, *Melanippe the Wise*

The celebrated Peace of Nicias (421 B.C.) was nothing more than a wolf in sheep's clothing. In the summer of 413 B.C. the Spartans, enticed by Alcibiades, invaded Attica and established their fortifications at Decelea. It was their answer to the Sicilian Expedition. About the same time, messengers arrived from Sicily itself bringing dire news to the astonished people of Athens: failure of their army on the ramparts of Syracuse, disastrous defeat at the battle of Epipolae, numerous consecutive losses on land and sea (Thucydides, VII, 43).

The last Athenian blood was spilled at the Assinarus River. As the hoplites, dead-thirsty from many days' wandering in the wilderness, threw themselves down to drink, the Sicilians and the Spartans attacked them from all sides, until the river's waters ran red. Those Athenians who escaped death on that blazing summer day were sold as slaves in the various towns of Sicily, and thousands were put to labor in the quarries, where most died of hunger or sickness. In the long months of slavery they found consolation in Euripides and recited lines from his plays. Many of them, Plutarch tells us, thanks to these verses touched the enemy's heart and won their freedom.[1]

The two Athenian generals, Nicias and Demosthenes, were disgracefully slaughtered, paying with their lives for Alcibiades' audacity. In other words, the two sniveling slaves of the *Knights* now faced death heroically and without tears, victims of a new Paphlagonian.

Ten years have already elapsed since the *Knights.* Aristophanes is nearing his forties and the war its twenties. Did our poet produce any plays in the uneasy spring of 413 B.C. or in the desperate one of 412 B.C.? Scholarship conjectures that three at least were written in the period between the *Birds* (414 B.C.) and *Lysistrata* (411 B.C.). One of them may have been the *Storks,* an ornithological allegory resembling the *Birds,* and dramatizing, perhaps, the controversy between the old and the young generation, a subject always dear to Aristophanes. Possibly, he may have also produced in those years his *Heroes,* a social satire on the personality-cult of the Athenians and their mania for creating new public idols. It is not improbable, on the other hand, that the policy of Alcibiades, the national hero turned traitor, had something to do with the play's main theme.[2]

In the mournful Dionysia of 413 B.C. Aristophanes may have presented his *Polyïdos.* Thucydides writes that the Athenians cursed the orators who had pushed them into the disastrous expedition and the soothsayers who had given them hopes for the acquisition of a Sicilian paradise (VIII, 1). Polyïdos was a seer of Minoan times, mentioned by Homer and dramatized by Euripides. Possibly, taking this mythical person as a pretext, Aristophanes, in this comedy, attacked all the professional prophets and fake seers.[3]

The first post-Sicilian comedy that has survived is the *Lysistrata.* It was produced at the Lenaea of 411 B.C. under the name of Callistratus. In this year, the Athenians, who had not yet recovered from the shock of the Sicilian plight, were faced with new calamities: all their allies, with the exception of the Samians, had abandoned them; the Spartans were encamped fifteen miles from the city; and Alcibiades had secured an alliance between Sparta and the King of Persia. The primal scheme of the political adventurer was to bring his fellow countrymen into utter despair and thus oblige them to call him back as their savior.

What is amazing about the *Lysistrata* is Aristophanes' intention to amuse the Athenians with a grim subject— their lost peace. In this crazy comedy he will dissolve the last drops of his peace-loving anguish in the pure wine of Dionysiac art. With an overpowering skill he will bring his message from darkness to light, from yesterday's death to tomorrow's life. Most peace-loving dramatists of all epochs, from the authors of the *Persians* and the *Trojan Women* to those of *Wallenstein* or *Journey's End,* have composed in the tragic key. Even the most sarcastic antimilitarists, almost Aristophanic in their bitter satire, like Jarry, Chaplin, Hasek, or Brecht,[4] depict nothing besides war miseries; by accusing war, they forget peace. Conversely, Aristophanes follows the constructive and not the catalytic method. He doesn't paint for his spectators the nightmare of war to make them hate it; he reminds them of the blessings of peace to make them love it. He had done so in the *Acharnians* and in the *Peace,* perhaps also in the *Merchant Ships* and the *Farmers.* He repeats his effort in the *Lysistrata,* this time focusing his message on one single advantage of peaceful life—sexual bliss. We can fairly well live, he tells his audience, without grapes or olives, without eels or rural Dionysia; but without sexual love, impossible.

In his comedy this idea is cooked in the pot of the feminine mind and is served as a military stratagem. The women of Athens had been suffering from war for many long years. Now one of them, Lysistrata, decides that the only way to compel the male citizens to vote for peace is to blackmail them by a cunning device, to confront them with a dilemma—love or war. She summons a congregation of women from all the towns of Greece, both enemy and allied, and convinces them to raise a love strike—not to let their husbands or lovers touch them unless they stop the war. The oath is taken, although many women are reluctant, and they barricade themselves on the Acropolis to wait until the men of all Greece accept their terms.

In this comedy, the women are Aristophanes' agents of peace; they are the wise, the brave, the patriotic. So far, in his plays, the welfare of Athens or Hellas has been a masculine concern. Now he offers it to the women. If we are to give faith to his words, i.e., to Lysistrata's words, the Athenians walked in the streets asking "Is there no man in our city?" and answering "None!" (524). The comic poet, exasperated with his fellow Greeks who had proved incapable of exterminating war, turns to the women, not only those of Athens, but also the Boeotian and the Corinthian, even the Spartan. After many long years of reclusive life in their private quarters, the women of Greece run loose into the theatre orchestra and the playwright leaves the field to them. Where the men have failed, the women may succeed. As they possess the art of persuading husbands and lovers, they may persuade the audience as well.

We soon discover that they are well organized in their campaign and animated with an excellent spirit of teamwork. Compared to them, most Aristophanic male heroes seem incurably egocentric. After all, Trygaeus was ambitious to become an astronaut, and Dicaeopolis enjoyed his private peace in spite of public opinion. Lysistrata, on the contrary, strives uniquely for a common cause. As she is the only one *not* to be mated at the end of the play, her only gain from the whole struggle is a moral one: to be named the war's annihilator, or, as her name signifies, the disbander of the armies.[5] She and her comrades are more socially minded than men are. With zest and intelligence they coordinate a perfect plan. They are a huge beehive in action: a queen with twenty-four workers, buzzing incessantly about the orchestra and having their sting always ready to function. Hereafter, in Aristophanes' feminist comedies, men will always be brainless and strengthless drones and will exist only to the extent that women allow them to.

The *Lysistrata,* with the separation and reunion of its two choruses (the male and the female) reminds us somewhat of the androgyna, who in the Platonic *Symposium* (189c) are purported as Aristophanes' invention. In this comedy, too, the separated sexes seek each other continuously, either out of hatred or desire, and finally unite into what we might call a hermaphroditic group.[6]

The *Lysistrata* is, chronologically, the seventh or eighth manifesto for peace produced by Aristophanes, and also his last. How different it is, though, in tone and technique from all the previous ones. In the *Babylonians* and the *Acharnians,* the passionate young poet could not yet forget himself to become an objective observer; he was like the Byron of *Childe Harold* or the Goethe of *Werther*. Later, in the *Peace* and the *Farmers* he was fascinated by folklore and the spirit of public festivity to the detriment of drama. In the *Lysistrata,* however, he appears as a mature and experienced playwright; he knows how to restrain his personal feelings and to subdue every element of entertainment to the overall theatrical pattern; his own personality disappears behind the plot and the characters; he avoids even the sermon of the *parabasis,* having no hope of convincing the Athenians through direct admonition; his message is embodied in the play's action.

At this point, he has learned to perfection how to coordinate creatively the true fundamental and always rival dramatic forces, which he might well have called: the Laughing and the Unlaughing Reason.

With the *Lysistrata,* Aristophanes takes an important step toward comedy in the modern meaning of the term. The most striking novelty is the discarding of the *parabasis,* reduced to no more than a few chats with the spectators (614–705 and 1043–71). Among the four surviving comedies still to come, two will have short *parabases* and two none at all. This should be seen as a syndrome of the evolution of Attic Comedy in general; the theatre leaves the Pnyx and approaches the Odeum. Henceforward, Aristophanes will be less of a social reformer and more of a popular entertainer. He will restrain his personal bias and indulge his theatrical fancies. His plays will move farther from actuality to come closer to dramatic fable. Having realized, after nearly twenty years of pacifistic campaign, that he is shouting at the deaf, he abandons direct intervention and makes his presence felt indirectly, by sheer farce.

The atrophic *parabasis* is not the *Lysistrata*'s only novelty. Another one is the breaking of the chorus into two different semichoruses, a male and a female. Yet another is the so-called *metastasis,* or second *parodos,* which, as far as we know, is here used by him for the first time. The chorus which was supposed never to leave the orchestra, here goes out and returns, perhaps more than once. Furthermore, in one of its entrances, it is no longer divided between men and women, but between Athenians and Spartans.[7] Another important innovation is that the leaders of the chorus escape from the abstract ensemble to create individual types—an old man and an old woman are featured in three quick, short dialogues which humorously record the progress of the relations between the sexes. Their duels culminate in the whimsical little *agon* (1014–41) where the old woman removes a tiny insect from the old man's eye, a proof that, even when physical attraction has waned, woman is always indispensable to man.

In this comedy we find the most accomplished comic episode so far displayed in Aristophanic drama: the scene where 'the young Myrrhine, sworn to sexual abstention, excites her husband only to let him finally go whistling down the wind (870–958). It is a scene with admirable structure and density of dialogue and, undoubtedly, the best comic skit ever written.

There is evident progress, also, in the technique of character drawing. Cleonice is an accomplished caricature of an aging coquette, one of those who will flourish abundantly in seventeenth- and eighteenth-century comedy. Equally successful are Myrrhine, with her provocative innocence, and her bourgeois husband Cinesias who climbs the Acropolis (pushing their baby in a carriage) in the hope of making love with his wife in secret. In the center, however, of all the comic satellites shines the heroine herself, whose imposing personality brings the whole play to life just by herself.

What is Lysistrata? She is an idealistic revolutionary, like Dicaeopolis, and a political messiah, like the Sausage-seller. She is a born leader who awakens the women's conscience from its slumber, as Peithetaerus had awakened that of the birds, and who establishes a perfect cloudcuckoo-woman-city. She is a pacifist, like Trygaeus, but one who seeks peace on earth and not in heaven. Last of all, she is a solid Athenian woman with awakened conscience and strong will. And that conveys the playwright's belief that the soil of Athens doesn't breed only "gaping idiots" but that there is still hope for the glorious city of Cranaus. Even in these days of complete disenchantment, Lysistrata is a token of Aristophanes' unquenchable optimism.

Let us add that this comic heroine is the most three-dimensional personality that the playwright has so far produced. The chorus implores her at one moment of the play to be "wicked, kind, naughty, serious, and resourceful." But those are exactly the contrasts which give volume and depth to her person. Let us examine her more closely. The author tells us nothing about her appearance or amorous life. We can, nevertheless, deduce that she is neither ugly nor inexperienced; she knows more than well the mating game and has, no doubt, made many a male sigh. Her age and social position are not explicitly stated, yet her good education is evident and she stands out socially from "the bakers' wives" or the "vegetable-sellers" who surround her. As for her age, she must have passed spring and is now at the beginning of the summer of life; the experience of maturity and the liveliness of youth meet in her, in the same way as the spirit of the crusade and that of the practical joke meet in her policy. Her family life is a mystery; we never see her husband; and when the other women mention their husbands, she speaks about lovers, vaguely, of course, but with spontaneous passion; on the other hand, she appears to know about married life and also displays strong feelings of motherhood. At any rate, whatever her family status may be, she does not allow any marital or sexual tie to interfere with her purposes. In that respect she is ruthless, as any perfect suffragette ought to be. Whether she has a husband or not, she willingly condemns him to be a nonentity.

Her character being composed of so many antitheses, sometimes critics as well as interpreting actresses go to extremes. Some visualize her as a belligerent amazon; others, as a frivolous and intriguing courtesan; still others, as a tempestuous and impudent Hyde Park orator. The real Lysistrata is all these things combined but not one of them alone. She is the many-faced Hecate of Attic Comedy. Perhaps the most significant thing about her, all contrasts included, is that she is the first feminist in history. She strives not only to bestow upon women the happiness of peace but to awaken them also from their apathy toward the problems of life by giving them the right to an opinion. She is an ardent feminist without ignoring feminine weaknesses: "I am painfully ashamed of our sex," she says. "They are right, those poets who make tragedies out of us. Our minds are always on the affairs of the bed" (137–39). This is, I believe, "the indecency of the Athenian women which shocked ancient Greece," as Rousseau wrote to D'Alembert. It is astonishing that the French philosopher saw this comedy as an expression of feminine indecency and not, on the contrary, as one of wisdom and sense.[8]

Seriousness and frivolity cohabiting in Lysistrata constitute what we may call the contrast *par excellence* of her character. Her seriousness nourishes the comedy's message, her frivolity the comedy's intrigue. In that respect she is a genuine offspring of the dramatist—an Athena who emerged fully armed from his head. She herself admits her importance with the same lack of modesty that Aristophanes usually displays in his personal confessions:

> I am a woman, yet I have brains.
> Besides my inborn sense of judgment,
> I was educated by listening to my father
> and to many other old people. (1124–26)

The first line is borrowed from a fragment of Euripides' *Melanippe the Wise.* This Aristophanic comedy might well have been titled *Lysistrata the Wise.*[9] The difference, however, between the two heroines is that the comic one knows that through wisdom alone nothing can be achieved. Her trump card, therefore, will be frivolous intrigue. Good reasoning and persuasion have not been able to reconcile the two enemy camps. Lysistrata now brings before them reconciliation in person, not a celestial apparition as the one in the *Acharnians* but a much more palpable and earthly symbol, an attractive scantily clad flute-girl. Without suspecting in the least that she is acting as a national benefactor, the pretty teaser shows off her charms to both the male semichoruses, standing for the Athenian and the Spartan delegates. The men on both sides make their final dispute over the natural map offered by the young pin-up's figure and finally reach a friendly agreement as to the partition of Greece—and the girl—between them. Not unlike the gods in the *Birds* who had capitulated because of physical hunger, Athenians and Spartans make peace because of sexual hunger. Thus the comedy comes to a happy ending by proving that in good democracies, strikes always succeed.

In the beautiful *stasimon* of this play (781–820), Aristophanes sings of two legendary men: Melanion who hated all women, and Timon who hated all men.[10] The poet himself seems to side with the latter. He may mock women and repeatedly call them vain, false, and promiscuous, but fundamentally he admires their sense and respects their willpower more than men's. Besides, if he often makes fun of their dipsomania (example: the oath in this comedy, sanctified by red Thasos wine), he does not do it maliciously. Being himself a genuine servant of Dionysus, he knows that his god often had more women than men among his drunken companions.[11]

Chapter XIII

The Trial of Euripides
at the *Thesmophoria*

A subtle word-mincer, epigram-chaser,
Euripidaristo-phanizer!

Cratinus, Fr. 307

The ten years (414–404 B.C.) embracing the *Birds,* the
Lysistrata, the *Women at the Thesmophoria,* and the
Frogs—one of the most turbulent periods in Athenian history—seem to have been extremely creative for Aristophanes. During these years he most probably wrote, besides the plays mentioned above, another twelve of his lost
ones.[1]

    Characteristic of all his dramatic output of this pe-
riod is his turn from political satire to mythological
parable and parody. That was the spirit in the *Birds,* the
Amphiaraos, the *Polyidos,* and the *Storks.* The present
Aristophanes is a professional man of letters; he draws humorous allusions from ancient myths; studies his contemporary poets and makes masterful satires of their works;
composes with great poetic fecundity his own stasima and
especially elaborates his religious odes. He returns, as Euripides will do at about the same time, to the source of
the dramatic river, to "the Dionysus who nurtured me."
He glorifies him with marvelous strophes in the *Women*

at the Thesmophoria, he mentions him in the *Seasons,* and makes him the hero of the *Frogs.* If there is still polemic in the plays of the passionate dissenter, its aim is uniquely the artistic and social degradation of the country; politics are left to politicians.

There is only one political comedy after the *Lysistrata:* the *Triphales,* probably produced in 410 B.C. Before we say anything about it, however, let us remember some of the historical events which preceded it.

A month and a half after the performance of the *Lysistrata,* democracy was disbanded by a successful coup and the oligarchs took control. Four hundred Athenians "bearing daggers under their cloaks," invaded the Parliament, paid off its members and sent them home. According to the new regime, the people would have no more power, and no salaries would be paid hereafter for judges, generals, or other public functionaries, because all those offices would be filled by the Four Hundred. The invisible political force behind this junta is more likely than not Alcibiades, who believed that this reform would make it easier for him to return to Athens as national savior. Simultaneously, he was preparing the ground in Persia, by persuading the Persian ruler Tissaphernes that the Athenian alliance would be more useful to his country than that of Sparta. "He had the double advantage," Thucydides tells us, "to scare the Athenians with Tissaphernes and Tissaphernes with the Athenians" (VIII, 82).

Oligarchy, however, will die only a few months old. In no time the democrats climb on the Pnyx and overthrow the Four Hundred, giving back to the people their supreme authority. Alcibiades appears now on the Democrats' side, because with a swift manoeuver he managed to discredit the Oligarchs: any political conviction is good for him, provided that Athens reclaims him in triumph. Indeed, the newly established democracy will soon vote for his return and will name him general-in-chief of its armed forces.

In what mood does Aristophanes watch this political seesaw? Maurice Croiset thinks that our playwright received temporary political influence, sought useful friendships, also perhaps participated in various political projects, but essentially "did not belong to any party." He cared only for his Athens and its old traditions. In spite of his conservative ideas, "nowhere does he reveal any belief in the oligarchical system," says André Bellessort. A fragment of the lost *Farmers,* as a matter of fact, shows him as a fiery adherent of democracy and an enemy of tyranny.[2]

In the autumn of 411 B.C. good luck begins to smile on the Athenians: in some successful naval battles they defeat the Peloponnesian enemies, and Alcibiades, one of the commanders, shares a great part of the glory.[3] Contemporary with the above events is, probably, the *Triphales,* a comedy which had Alcibiades as its hero. Phales (cf. *Acharnians*) was a phallic demon. Triphales is a Phales to the third degree. We cannot be sure what specific qualities merged in this triple identity of the orgiastic demon; it is obvious though that the real Alcibiades had acquired in the people's fancy a three-fold personality: before the Sicilian Expedition, he was the Idealist; after his flight to Sparta, he was the Traitor; now he is the Savior. These were, perhaps, the three faces of the political demon who is also a friend of Bacchus, "night-wanderer, adulterer, paederast." Plutarch calls Alcibiades "chameleon" (probably taking a hint from Aristophanes): "He was in Sparta sportive and brooding; in Ionia, idle and voluptuous; in Thrace, wine-loving; in Thessaly, horse-loving." [4]

The *Women at the Thesmophoria* (*Thesmophoriazusae*) was produced in the same year perhaps as the *Triphales* (410 B.C.).[5] It is an inoffensive literary satire, to the degree that an Aristophanic play can be called inoffensive. It brings to the stage two tragic poets, Euripides and Agathon, and the majority of its lines are nothing but a travesty of their own tragic verses. Along with the *Frogs,* the play is the most important "Euripidean" lampoon that we possess. In the following chapter, we shall sum up Aristophanes' basic opinions on his tragic fellow poets, for his views constitute the only criticism written in the fifth century B.C. on Greek tragedy.

The Euripides of 410 B.C. is a septuagenarian who has written about seventy tragedies and has so far won not more than four or five victories. He has been twice married and twice unlucky in his marital ventures. He lives a reclusive life, has few friends, and is not interested in politics. His many innovations—such as excessive realism, characters imitated from life, morbid passion, long prologues, and arbitrary denouements—have earned him much adversity, although many intellectuals, like Socrates, think highly of him.[6] The next century, incidentally, will idolize him above all the other tragic poets, and the grammarians will retain eighteen of his plays to the seven each of Aeschylus and Sophocles. His postmortem glory, however, is ambiguous and gives rise to some questions: (*a*) Was Euripides born before his time or was he an inferior poet whom only an inferior epoch could appreciate? Among his contemporaries, Thucydides praises him, Aristophanes deplores him. (*b*) Was he popular with the masses in his own time or not? Schiller believes that he was, Nietzsche, that he was not. (*c*) Did Aristophanes, by mocking him, go against the current of public opinion or did he echo the feelings of the theatre audience? Euripides had won very few victories, yet the Athenian prisoners in Sicily knew his verses by heart.[7] So, the thing speaks for itself. A poet who is quoted by his fellow countrymen in their days of misery does not need to be crowned by the dramatic judges. He lives in every Greek heart, and when he dies, as the epigram puts it, "all Hellas is his tomb."

The opening scene in the *Women at the Thesmophoria* shows Euripides and his cousin, Mnesilochus, walking toward the house of Agathon. Euripides has been informed that the Athenian women, during their annual celebration of the Thesmophoria, will put him on trial for having smirched their reputation in his tragedies. This festival, being an exclusively feminine one, forbids any man to set foot within its sanctuary. What woman will therefore speak in the poet's defense? Naturally, none, unless it is . . . Agathon. This fellow dramatist is not a woman, but cleanshaven and graceful as he is, he may easily pass for one. Besides, there is a rich collection of feminine costumes and wigs in his wardrobe which can create for him an appropriate disguise.

As in the *Acharnians,* here, too, the useful *ekkyklema* reveals the interior of the poet's house. Agathon is sitting at his tablets, composing verses (95). He is not dressed in rags, as Euripides was in the older play, but in woman's garments, because he is actually writing a feminine chorus. He sings his strophes in antiphony; and the scholiast (on 101) explains that he does not recite "as actors did in the theatre, but as poets composed" at home. Mnesilochus' question, "What does he murmur in this fashion, walking to and fro like an ant?" gives us a picture of the dramatist enunciating the same line many times and in different ways to achieve the most melodious result. The intention of Aristophanes is not to satirize Agathon's style in particular but the exaggerations of the tragic art in general. And, what for his audience was just a funny take-off, for us is also a valuable document. Agathon's scene illuminates the theatrical customs of the classic fifth century B.C., as similar scenes in *A Midsummer Night's Dream, The Critic,*

or *The Impromptu de Versailles* reveal those of their respective times.

Notwithstanding his professional esteem for Euripides, Agathon refuses to comply with the former's re-
quest; he is afraid that he may meet trouble with the
Athenian women: "They may think," he says, "that I want
to rival them in the affairs of the night" (204–5). Euripides is desperate. Pitying him, his old cousin, Mnesilochus agrees to undertake the mission, dressed as a woman.
He has not as yet realized the real nature of his self-sacri-
fice, however. His respectable beard is shaven by Euripides
with a razor borrowed from Agathon; he is stripped
naked, and the two tragic poets burn with a candle all the
hairs off his body; a brassiere is put on him, then a yellow
dress and a bonnet. Forthwith the cousin starts to scream
and run around the orchestra to escape from this disgrace.
All the same, he has to drink the cup to the lees and to set
off as a perfect matron. Euripides swears to his cousin that
if he gets into trouble, he will immediately come to save
him, using every device and ingenuity that has ever
helped his heroes out of their tragic impasses (270–76).

Aristophanes has not written an entrance song for his
chorus. The women who march into the orchestra, filling
the air with their chants and the smoke of their torches,
do not come with any particular dramatic aim, chasing the
hero or answering his call, as in other comedies. They
congregate for a real-life event, the Thesmophoria; and
we can conjecture that the hymn which they sing is the
customary one, including the traditional refrain *"Io
paean!"* (311–30).

The Thesmophoria were regional festivities dedicated to Demeter and Persephone. Those celebrated in
Athens took place in late October and lasted four days.[8]
Many different interpretations have been given to those
mysteries, which we need not go through in order to fol-

low the play's action. What we derive from this comedy is
that in the Thesmophoria, as in women's clubs today,
many serious topics concerning the fair sex were discussed
and decisions were taken about them. Here the first item
on the agenda is the trial of Euripides.

After some prayers to the gods, curses are pronounced
against every traitor, every politician who aspires to become a tyrant, every serving-maid who tells husbands of
their wives' mischief, every old woman who keeps a young
lover, every publican who cheats his customers and, above
all, Euripides (331–71).

Three women take the floor. The first is a dynamic
matron who violently sermonizes against the tragic poet:
"He calls us drunkards, deceivers, blabber-mouths, and
man-crazy, real plagues, and has taught our husbands so
many things about us that we are unable to do any longer
what we used to." The second to speak is a mild and de-
mure flower-seller. She used to earn her living making garlands for the statues of the gods; but since Euripides
began preaching his new ideas, people have learned not to
believe in the gods and hence no longer buy garlands.

The chorus responds to both discourses with approv-
ing acclamations. The third speaker is a rather odd-look-
ing crone who wears a funny bonnet and whose high-
pitched voice sometimes falls into bass tones. Her sermon
echoes in a way Dicaeopolis' "long speech" in the *Acharnians:* it is wrought in the same rhetorical mold (467–519).
"I, too, hate Euripides," she starts by saying ("I, too, hate
the Spartans," Dicaeopolis had said). Eventually, what had
begun as an attack turns into defense and the women get
angry. "His tragedies," they protest, "are about shameful
Phaedras and Melanippes: he never wrote a play about
Penelope who was good and virtuous." "The reason is obvious," the hag retorts, "for Penelopes exist no more;
while we see Phaedras everywhere." And she proceeds to

more arguments proving Euripides' innocence. As we notice, the tragic poet's inculpation has disappeared under the mass of feminine crimes brought forth by Aristophanes, and Euripides' trial has turned into the trial of womankind.

In this comedy we observe an evolution contrary to that of the *Lysistrata:* there, a cluster of supercilious females is finally disciplined by one woman's superior will; here, a well-organized sisterhood disbands into a hysterical crowd of shrews who, with wild screams, demand the intruder's head.

The scene that follows the debates is a bold little parody of the tragic *recognition;* Mnesilochus' sex is *recognized* by the frantic women in a way that leaves no doubt whatsoever (639–48). Whereupon they unanimously decide to burn him at the stake.

At this point of the action the essential parody of Euripidean drama begins. As we remember, the tragic poet has promised his cousin to come to his help in an hour of need. Accordingly, the devices by which Euripides intervenes to liberate the prisoner are all inspired by three of his tragedies, the recollection of which was still fresh to the Athenian spectators. The *Helen* and the *Andromeda* had been performed two years earlier and the *Palamedes* five or so.[9]

The *Women at the Thesmophoria* is the only surviving Aristophanic play which offers us evidence of dramatic parody as practiced in the classic Greek Theatre. In certain other cases Aristophanes satirizes lines or incidents from the tragic plays, yet nowhere else does he produce a complete tragic episode in travesty. We should add that, in spite of the liberty enjoyed by Attic Comedy, these take-offs are not arbitrary but strictly pertinent to the plot.

Let us examine each of the three parodies that the play offers:

1. The *Palamedes* (756–84): Mnesilochus remembers that, in that tragedy, Palamedes' brother had informed their father of the hero's death by inscribing the message on the oars of his ship.[10] Not being actually at sea, Mnesilochus writes his message on the tablets hanging in the Thesmophorion and throws them to the four winds. The trick having no issue, Mnesilochus explains that "his *Palamides* is so dull that Euripides is ashamed to appear."

2. The *Helen* (850–919): this parody is embroidered on the prologue of the Euripidean play of that name. Mnesilochus, acting as the heroine, laments: "My Menelaus does not come. Why, then, do I live?"[11] (The tone anticipates that of the "most lamentable comedy" of Pyramus and Thisbe in *A Midsummer Night's Dream*.) Euripides, hearing at last his cousin's piercing cries, appears in the guise of Menelaus. Their comic *recognition* is an exact, word-by-word replica of the Menelaus and Helen recognition in Euripides' tragedy.

Aristophanes' wit does not aim to distort the Euripidean text but rather to create a hilarious contrast between the verses and the persons who utter them. This contrast is the nucleus of Aristophanic parody: contrast between the dirty beetle and the divine Pegasus (*Peace*), between the illiterate sausage-seller and the office of the chief of the state (*Knights*), between the trembling Dionysus wearing the lion's skin and the real Heracles (*Frogs*), between tone and content in Lysistrata's oath, and so forth. (It is the same contrast that will be immortalized in future generations by the gaunt Don Quixote and his heavy armor, the tramp Charlie and his respectable derby-hat, or the uncouth Ubu and his royal throne.) It is the basic contrast implicit in the protoplasmatic form of comic theatre, when children put on their parents' clothes and play at being grown-ups.

The *Helen* device is crowned with no more success than the *Palamedes* one. When Euripides-Menelaus is about to flee with Mnesilochus-Helen in his arms, the chorus stops him, and the prisoner is put in the pillory with a Scythian policeman guarding him. Euripides is obliged to leave alone, assuring his cousin, though, that he shall not fail him, because his tragic tricks are numberless.

3. The *Andromeda* (1015–1135): Mnesilochus is now shedding bitter tears, just as the princess Andromeda used to cry on her rock waiting for the sea-monster. All of a sudden, he hears (as, probably, Andromeda herself heard in the lost Euripidean tragedy) his lamentations repeated by Echo.[12] He understands, thereby, that Euripides is already near and that he will soon appear as a rescuing Perseus.

There is no evidence as to how this echo was presented theatrically: whether she was played by an actor or whether Euripides, hidden in a corner, imitated her voice. The fact remains that Mnesilochus, who at first was glad to hear this familiar voice, is finally exasperated by her insistent repetitions, as Aristophanes was by Euripides' similar vice.

The climax of this incident is the intervention of the Scythian policeman who hears the echo and thinks that Mnesilochus is talking to himself. When he asks what it is all about, the echo, unabashed, imitates him with a perfect Scythian accent. The policeman, thinking that the prisoner is making fun of him, rushes for his whip, when, accompanied by the thundering music of the stage machine, Euripides appears air-borne. He is disguised as Perseus and holds the petrifying Medusa's head in his hand. The conscientious Scythian does not let the rescuer approach the old man. So the tragic plot is modified and the sea-monster (alias the policeman) wins Andromeda, while the suspended Perseus departs on his crane. As he leaves, he insults the barbarian cop who, like all ignorant men, is unable to appreciate the ideas of a great poet.

In this confrontation between the Scythian guard and the flying Perseus, Aristophanes contrasts primitive man and machine. He foresees, one might say, all the tragi-comic after-effects of the expansion of Western Civilization. The corruption of the "noble savage" has already started. But was not that also the main theme of the *Birds?*

Disappointed by the failure of his imaginative ideas, Euripides comes down to earth, both literally and figuratively: he abandons his great dramatic inspirations, proven inept, and descends to a more pedestrian and practical trick; he disguises himself as an old pimp and brings in a pretty half-naked flute player, answering to the name Elaphion, who with a dance routine mesmerizes the Scythian cop. Forgetting all about Mnesilochus and duty, the barbarian has eyes and hands only for the girl's behind, and very soon disappears with her backstage. Euripides is now free to release his cousin and run away with him (1209). Where tragic inspiration had failed, Megarian farce has triumphed. As the beguiling Reconciliation had brought peace in the *Lysistrata,* an attractive strip-teaser becomes the sole valid argument of the tragic mastermind.

Obviously, Aristophanes enjoyed his invention of the amorous Scythian so much as to disregard somehow his main plot. The reconciliation between Euripides and the women is rather naïvely achieved by the former's threat that unless the latter make a truce with him he will tell their husbands all about their secret misdoings.

We should make special mention of two *stasima,* which serve as intervals between the three tragic parodies. The first of these—the *parabasis* (785–845)—is the praise

of Woman. As in the *Birds,* the present chorus addresses
the audience without abandoning its role: it is "we, the
women," who speak for themselves and not on behalf of
the author. As an exception, their expressed wish, that the
State ought to distinguish between the mothers of scoundrels and those of worthy sons, strikes us as a ghost of the
old Aristophanic sermons.

The other *stasimon* (947–1000) is a ritualistic prayer,
one of the most beautiful that Aristophanes has ever written. Perhaps the order: "Form a circle!" with which they
start their dance, was part of the procedure in the Thesmophoria; all the same, we share the opinion that incanta-
tional dances in Attic Comedy had, by tradition, circular
shape, a reminiscence of their religious origin. In fact, this
choral interlude is the best example of a circular dance
that we find in Aristophanes.[13] It begins with a hymn to
Demeter and Persephone, executed with arms interlinked,
light steps and quick rhythm; then it changes into a slow
ceremonial march, as the women sing to Apollo, Artemis,
Hera, Hermes, Pan, and the Muses. Subsequently, the
"ivy-crowned" Dionysus is summoned by the women to
join their dance, and the god becomes the invisible *exarchon* who leads their ecstatic whirling around the orchestra:

Iô Bacchos
                    Coronal of ivy
                                        Wild Master
                    Leap for us
Lead us
                    Spin for us in the dance

Descend O child of Sémelê thou
        Tumultuous Flame
O son of Zeus come down upon us now
                    —*Evion evion evohé!*—

In song cascading
From hills where the Maenads chant Dionysos' name:
  Kithairon shudders with music a shout
      Bursts from the stone
The upland thickets howl in the nymphic rout
      —*Evion evion evohé!*—
        Of the cortège advancing
As the smitten god strides on to join the dancing.

HERALD:

Gentlemen, Ah beg you will be so kind as to direct me
to the Central Committee. Ah have a communication.

Re-enter MAGISTRATE

MAGISTRATE:

                    Are you a man,
or a fertility symbol?

HERALD:

                    Ah refuse to answer that question!
Ah'm a certified herald from Spahta, and Ah've come to
talk about an ahmistice.

MAGISTRATE:

                    Then why
that spear under your cloak?

HERALD:

                    Ah have no speah!

MAGISTRATE:

You don't walk naturally, with your tunic poked out so.
You have a tumor, maybe, or a hernia?

HERALD:

        No, by Kastor!

MAGISTRATE:

                    Well,
something's wrong. I can see that. And I don't like it.

HERALD:

Colonel, Ah resent this.

MAGISTRATE:

                    So I see. But what *is* it?

HERALD:

A scroll
with a message from Spahta.

MAGISTRATE:

Oh, I've heard about these scrolls.
Well, then, man, speak out: How are things in Sparta?

HERALD:

Hard, Colonel, hard! We're at a standstill. Can't seem
to think of anything but women.

MAGISTRATE:

How curious! Tell me, do you Spartans think that
maybe Pan's to blame?

HERALD:

Pan? No. Lampitô and her little naked friends. They
won't let a man come near them.

MAGISTRATE:

How are you handling it?

HERALD:

Losing our minds,
if you want to know, and walking around hunched over
like men carrying candles in a gale. The women have
sworn they'll have nothing to do with us until we get a
treaty.

(Lines 980–1106, translation by Dudley Fitts)

But is the god really invisible? There is evidence that
his wooden statue was always standing in some part of the
theatre overseeing the performances.[14] Was the chorus addressing that statue? Did the women carry it to the center
of the orchestra and dance around it, crowning the
wooden Bacchus with ivy and enlacing his body with garlands of vine?

The *Women at the Thesmophoria* is the first among the
comedies that we have so far examined whose Arguments

and *didaskalia* are missing. We are therefore in complete ignorance at which of the two festivals it was produced and what its fate was. It is also strange that posterity was not too eager to preserve it. It is the poorest Aristophanic comedy insofar as manuscripts are concerned. (While each of the other comedies exists today in 28 MSS. at least, this one survives in two only, the Ravenna and the Munich.) Among the eleven Aristophanic plays which passed safely through the Scylla and Charybdis of time, the present one nearly shared the fate of those that were lost.

Between 410 B.C. and 405, the comic poet reworked the same theme in a play called the *second Women at the Thesmophoria*. It may have been a sequel to the first one, leading, after the Nesteia day of the first, to the Calligenia day of the second—the goddess Calligenia, in fact, spoke the prologue—a parody, perhaps, of the Euripidian nurse often used for this function. From the fragments we deduce that the plot remained practically the same: Agathon again appeared, the *Antiope* of Euripides was in its turn parodied, a comic slave was active, Elaphion or another *fille-de-joie* performed an oriental dance, and some man was again disguised as a woman.[15] Furthermore, a list of almost fifty items related to women's fashion and beauty paraphernalia, existing in a long fragment, should be studied by all modern specialists of feminine glamor (Fr. 330).

In 408 B.C. the *Plutus* was written; not the one we know, but the first, by twenty years its younger.[16] It must have been, as the surviving *Plutus,* a philosophical allegory on wealth and need, extremely appropriate in those poverty-stricken years. The subject was not a new one: Cratinus had presented a comedy called the *Riches* (*Ploutoi*) about thirty or forty years earlier. In the time of Pericles, however, the problem of wealth and poverty was not as significant as in the present days of political and economic bankruptcy. Between the two Aristophanic *Plu-tuses,* there must have been a marked difference in dra-matic technique. The first would preserve somehow the ancient form of Attic Comedy—the regular *stasima,* the *parabasis* and the traditional invectives. The second, writ-ten in another theatrical period and deprived of all these devices, inaugurates, as we shall see, a new dramatic style.

Most of the lost comedies posterior to the *Lysistrata* have, judging from the titles, feminine choruses. The *Seasons* and the *Lemnian Women* treat a social and reli-gious topic—the superstition of the Athenians and the plethora of imported foreign gods—a phenomenon char-acteristic of the moral instability of those days. "Our city has become Egypt instead of Athens," the poet laments in the former of the two plays. The seasons of the year in the comedy bearing that name are presented as priestesses of the goddess Athena. She is, as likely as not, the play's her-oine, having as her antagonist the Phrygian god Sabazios, who was also mentioned in the *Lysistrata* (388) as idolized by Athenian women. The play's most beautiful fragment (Fr. 569) is a praise of the city's market and of the rich harvest of the Attic soil, perhaps only a sad remembrance of the opulent past.[17]

The craze for imported divinities, marking the twi-light of the native ones, is also dealt with in the *Lemnian Women.* Here the action takes place on the island of Lem-nos and the protagonist is, presumably, Artemis—or, more correctly, her Thracian counterpart Bendis. The plot seems to have been a parody of the legend of the Ar-gonauts, whose landing on that island had inspired Aes-chylus, Sophocles and Euripides each with a tragedy. Which one Aristophanes satirized is not difficult to guess, knowing so well his feelings about the youngest of the three tragic poets. In this play the Aristophanic *bees* ful-filled their biological destiny: after using the Argonauts for the needs of procreation, they annihilated them.[18]

The *Phoenician Women,* another Aristophanic comedy of that period, must have been a parody of the well-known Euripidean tragedy recently produced. A similar satire was the *Danaïds,* written probably shortly before the *Frogs.* Here he makes fun of the miserable theatrical companies of older times, those of the so-called *ethelontes,* who performed in shabby costumes and in the shameful absence of any artistic respectability (Fr. 244). His purpose must have been, as in his older *Proagon,* to criticize contemporary drama undergoing a gradual decline along with its mother city.[19]

All things considered, literary satire, which now absorbed Aristophanes almost completely, was not a new genre. When our playwright was still a child, Cratinus had presented his comedies *Didaskaliai* and *Euneides,* where men of letters living and dead were either featured or mentioned. Crates and Pherecrates had done the same. Yet of all their creations as well as of all the Aristophanic works mentioned above, the only comedy which has survived as a unique and incomparable example of literary criticism is the *Frogs.*

The time when this play was written should be seen as a historical milestone and also as a dead end in the evolution of human culture. In 406 B.C. the death of both Euripides and Sophocles occurs, and in 404 B.C. the fall of Athens. The *Frogs* is performed in between two equally fatal events: the end of Tragedy and the end of Democracy.

Chapter XIV

The *Frogs* and the End of Tragedy

Who more modern than he?
Max Beerbohm, *Around Theatres* [1]

In June, 407 B.C., Alcibiades arrives at the Piraeus harbor in great secrecy; he is uncertain about his reception at the hands of his countrymen, whom he had betrayed eight years ago. The Athenians, however, rush to the harbor to hail him, kiss him, and crown him with olive leaves. They justify his former behavior by saying, as Xenophon reports, that he was "forced to serve his hateful enemies, risking his life daily" (*Hellenica*, I, iv).

Aristophanes had never liked Alcibiades. He had blamed him for his youthful exhibitionism, his impostures, his dreams of glory, his arrivistic tendencies, and his treachery.[2] Now he sees his homecoming with a pessimistic eye. "I hate the citizen," he will say in the *Frogs* (1427–30), "who is slack in serving his country but energetic in harming it." He could not help, however, agreeing with the majority that Alcibiades was a necessary evil: "Since we reared a little lion in our house, now that he is grown we have to do as he pleases" (*Frogs*, 1431–32).

The restoration and deification of Alcibiades will be precarious. He creates a hostile climate around him and soon loses the people's trust. After suffering a defeat in a sea battle near Ephesus, he feels his position shaken and

208

leaves Athens for the second and final time. He retires to his lands by the Hellespont; and from there he will watch, without participating in, the decisive battles of Arginusae and of Aegospotami.

In March, 406 B.C., news comes from Macedonia that Euripides is dead. The tragic poet had left Athens two years earlier, following the production of his *Orestes*. Embittered, perhaps, by his continuous lack of official recognition, wounded, perhaps, by the unyielding Aristophanic attacks, he had accepted an invitation from King Archelaus, the famous patron of the arts, to visit the North, together with his fellow poet Agathon. In the Macedonian capital Euripides must have supervised the production of some new plays. He also wrote there his ultimate tragedies, the *Iphigenia in Aulis* and the *Bacchae,* which he never saw performed. He died, according to legend, devoured by wild dogs.[3]

No ancient chronicle tells us about the Euripidean messenger who galloped from the north to report the poet's death; the only thing that we learn from his *Life* is how the old Sophocles reacted to the news. During the *proagon,* which took place on the first day of the City Dionysia, Sophocles, honoring his fellow poet's memory, appeared on the stage in mourning garments, surrounded by actors who did not wear their traditional wreaths. And the public, the biographer says, shed tears.

Within the same year the nonagenarian Sophocles died too, "calmly and easily, as he had lived." He expired either while reciting a passage from the *Antigone,* or while eating grapes. In any case, it was Dionysus himself, either with his special art or his favorite fruit, who brought a happy death to his worthy servant.[4]

These two irreparable literary losses must have passed almost unperceived in an Athens panicky at losing the war. The swansong of its naval supremacy is the Battle of Arginusae. In a desperate clash off the Lesbian coast, in which former cavalry men had become sailors and even slaves were given arms to fight, the Athenians defeated the Peloponnesian fleet. Besides giving a feeling of hope, this victory had another fortunate issue—the emancipation of the slaves—because all those who survived this battle became free and acquired all the rights of citizenship. Aristophanes applauds wholeheartedly: "It is the only reasonable thing you have ever done," he tells his compatriots *(Frogs,* 697). The Arginusae, however, had an unhappy repercussion as well. The victorious generals were tried and condemned for not rescuing their drowning men. Only Socrates, who happened to be among the jury, raised a voice of protest.[5]

In this sad year, which begins with the death of Euripides, passes through the Arginusae, and ends with the death of Sophocles, Aristophanes composes his *Frogs.* Neither the significant battle nor the court martial that followed cast their light or shade on his comedy. On the other hand, the deaths of the two tragic poets, that of Euripides in particular, constitute the main plot. The magnet of Euripides attracts the satirist even from the underworld. As in his earlier play he had ascended to Olympus to find Peace, now he descends to Hades to find Euripides. It is, after all, his last chance, before the memory of the late poet's tragedies fades; because Aristophanes is certain that the author of *Medea* will not survive his plays. Therefore, the *Frogs* is intended as Euripides' theatrical epitaph and, at the same time, his definitive critical evaluation. Produced at the 405 Lenaea, under the name of Philonides, this comedy presents some outstanding features:

  1. It is Aristophanes' fifth comedy, among those we know of, to receive first prize.[6]

  2. It is his only comedy performed twice—not in a

rewritten but in the same version—as an honorary distinction for the author.[7]

3. It displays almost all the defects of which Aristophanes accuses other playwrights: vulgar jokes, bastinades, whimpering slaves, puns on Heracles, and so forth.

4. The dramatist is more Bergsonian than ever, in deriving laughter from mechanical repetitions either of words or of actions.[8]

5. He uses two choruses, not both visible, perhaps, but anyway two.[9]

6. He offers his last *parabasis;* it is an incomplete but nonetheless orthodox address to the audience.

7. The comic *agon* is not in the beginning of the play, as heretofore customary, but at the end.

8. He demonstrates his conception of the world of the dead.

9. He restores the theatrical god Dionysus as protagonist.

10. For the first time, the comic slave becomes equal in importance with the comic hero. This is, we presume, a theatrical after-effect of the emancipation of the slaves after Arginusae. Thus the slave Xanthias, who had been featured in the past years as auxiliary laughing stock, now shares with the god the glory of the lead. In this new capacity he will engender a long dynasty. "Without the slaves," Engels has said, "there would be no Greek state, art, and science." Without the slaves, we may add, there would be no Greek laughter after the close of the fifth century B.C. Xanthias will be followed by the Carion of *Plutus;* and the playwrights of the Middle and New Comedy will inherit a ready-made character, around whom they will build some of their best inventions; the Romans will imitate them, bestowing the spiritual gifts of the Greek slave on the primitive *maccus* of the local Atellan farce. In the dramatically sterile centuries to come the only man

able to amuse the crowds of Athens, Alexandria, Rome, Antioch, and Constantinople will be this very same Xanthias, *alias* Mimus, Pantomimus, Acrobat, Juggler, or Court Fool. Even later, when drama will rise again from the altar of Christian churches, the shrewd Xanthias will take the aspect of Vice or Devil, who tempts Virtue and is punished for his wickedness. Eventually, the Xanthias family tree will spread into numberless branches: the Italian branch of Arlecchino, Brighella, Pulcinella, Crispino, and Scapino; the branch of the Spanish *gracioso;* the English branch of the intellectual Fool, and so forth.[10]

The Xanthias of the *Frogs* is not yet the inventive and devil-may-care slave who conspires to rob his master. We should rather see in him a faithful Sancho Panza who tries to cope with his fanciful knight or a Sganarelle who grumbles in vain over the risky exploits of Don Juan. Nevertheless he is as clever as few Aristophanic free citizens have been so far. And he appears even more so because the playwright has paired him with a foolish master. It looks as though the conservative Aristophanes is signaling the twilight of masters and the dawn of slaves.

When the play begins (the scholiast thinks that we are at Thebes, the home town of Heracles and, in a way, of Dionysus too) [11] the comic pair make their appearance. Dionysus has donned Heracles' lion-skin and carries a club bigger than himself. The servant follows him, riding upon a donkey and carrying an enormous bundle. (We are prone to wonder about the aspect of this donkey; if it was a real one, then we probably have to imagine the dogs in the *Wasps* as real too; it would be more reasonable to visualize Xanthias riding on a choregic actor, or two actors, disguised as a donkey.)

The year was for the theatre god an *annus mirabilis,* because not only comedy but also tragedy was honoring him. Euripides, the poet who had discarded the Dionysiac spirit for the Socratic, had recognized in his last play, the *Bacchae,* the omnipotence of the god.[12]

That Euripides is the comedy's target is obvious from the very start: a playful stichomythia between Dionysus and Xanthias, whether the donkey or the rider bears the weight of the bundle, is a parody of his own dialectic (19–32). The god and his servant knock at the door of Heracles' house. Out rushes the enormous and terrifying killer of the Centaurs, who, seeing his own caricature standing in front of him, remains dumbfounded. "Do you see," Bacchus whispers to his slave, "how I scare him?" But soon after the two Heracleses, the giant and the dwarf, embrace each other and sit down to chat.

Dionysus now exposes the purpose of his journey. In Athens, after the death of Euripides there is a great lack of poets; only numbskulls are left. "As I was sailing, therefore," the god says, "for the Arginusae, I read the *Andromeda* and felt an immense longing for Euripides, as one feels sometimes for beans" (52–54). That is why, he says, he took the decision to descend to Hell to find the tragic poet and has come to Heracles who can advise him how to get there. The strong man, with a sense of unsuspected humor, suggests three ways: to hang himself, or to drink hemlock, or to jump from a high building. None of these appeals to the comic hero; so Heracles proposes a less deadly way, the one taken by Orpheus, Odysseus, and himself, when they visited the kingdom of Pluto.[13]

Our two clowns reach now the Acherusian lake (180). The old ferry-man, Charon, agrees to row Dionysus across for two obols. He profits shamelessly, because the usual fare (which, according to custom, was put into the mouth of the dead) was only one obol. Besides, the boatman refuses to take Xanthias: "No slaves," he says, "unless they have fought at Arginusae." As Xanthias has not fought, he has no rights and must go to Hell on foot. Master and servant separate, and the boat pushes off, with the god of wine extremely awkward in handling the oars.

How was this rowing across the lake presented in the ancient theatre? Perhaps the clue should be sought in the boats of the Dionysiac festivals, those boats which had no bottoms, and whose oarsmen, pretending to row, marched pushing them along. It is also possible that the motion of the boat, if motion there was, was furthered by some stage machinery. Yet the best conjecture is to accept this scenic sequence as a characteristic example of the abstract technique and of the suggestive power of the Greek theatre: namely, that there was no other device involved but the expressive mimicry of the two actors.[14]

As the boat approaches the farther bank, the song of the Frogs is heard (209 f.). The first of the two choruses of the play makes a sensational appearance with a concert of piercing *brekekekex koax koax*. We emphasize the Frogs' presence, though most editors prefer them invisible; they contend that only their singing was heard, because the dancers would not have time to change costume to reappear as the second chorus and the *choregos* would never have agreed to pay two choruses. Despite those practical arguments, it seems improbable that Aristophanes would have given his comedy the name of an absent chorus. We, therefore, prefer to give faith to that dubious *parachoregema* (second chorus) mentioned in the oldest manuscripts.[15]

In the famous refrain *brekekekex koax koax* the knowledge of most people about Attic Comedy begins and ends. Besides, it is the only example of Aristophanic onomatopoeia to be found in a modern Greek dictionary. Foreign observers, on the other hand, have commented extensively on this croaking. For instance: "The common frogs of Greece have a note totally different from that of the frogs of the northern climates and there cannot be a more perfect imitation of it than the *brekekekex koax koax* of Aristophanes." Or: "the frogs of the nineteenth century have probably been faithful to the pronunciation of their race in former times . . . One set of them, perhaps the tenors. . . . kept singing *brekekekex,* whilst the softer wooing of the ladies is uttered always as *koax koax koax.*" [16] The *Frogs'* chorus is, in our opinion, a satire on contemporary poetasters whose poems contained an overflow of croaking or whose dramatic productions did not leave any other acoustic memory than a monotonous and ill-sounding *brekekekex.*

Now Charon's boat debarks Dionysus on a damp and dark marshland. (Both darkness and dampness should be imagined by the spectator because neither was the orchestra muddy nor could the stage machinists turn off the Attic sun.) In spite of his lion-skin, the wine god trembles with fear. "Xanthias, where are you?" he calls in a shaky voice (271). And the cunning slave, who has just arrived by the footpath, is amused by his master's fear and frightens him still more with various bits of farcical behavior. At last, the pusillanimous god, forgetting both religious protocol and theatrical convention, rushes to the front rows, where the priest of Dionysus Eleuthereus occupies the seat of honor, and screams: "Save me, O priest of mine, and I promise to drink with you tonight!" (297).

We cannot help marveling how unscrupulously the playwright ridicules the poetic Dionysus, "who nurtured me." Of course, to present gods with their weaknesses, which made them funnier and at the same time more human, was an old Greek literary tradition. What is astonishing, however, in the present case, is that Bacchus becomes a fool in the sacred precinct of his own theatre and in the course of a festival honoring him. We might explain the phenomenon by saying that the Greeks resented excessive soberness and that they accepted any antidote provided that it did not disturb natural harmony. In fact, they did not mock Dionysus during sacrifices or litanies, where they glorified him with religious ecstasy as their "ivy-crowned king." During the moments of mirth and hilarity, however, they laughed in his company. In those moments he was the "drinker," "night-wanderer," the "dance-lover," the master of orgiastic revelry.[17] The phallic rites and the invectives were his own customs, the *komos* belonged to him and Comedy was his offspring. It would have been an insult against him, therefore, if his revelers were reluctant to tease him. They knew that, being a divine humorist, he enjoyed laughing at himself. No other line gives the character of Dionysiac grandeur so epigrammatically as the one uttered by Xanthias: "How could my master not be a true nobleman, since he knows nothing besides drinking and making love?" (*Frogs,* 739–40).

With the sound of flutes and the smell of burning torches (316) the second chorus of the comedy makes its formal entrance, white-clad. It is a chorus composed of dead Initiates, of souls of men inducted into the Eleusinian mysteries. With a prayer to Iacchus, the deity of rejuvenation and vigor, they formally exclude from their sacred dances "all those whose thoughts are not pure": namely, those who do not love true art, those who for their own profit kindle the fire of war, judges who are bribed, and all kind of malefactors, including those orators who moved that the comic poets' fees should be reduced.[18] On the other hand, Aristophanes includes a posthumous praise of his great bygone rival, the beast-smashing Cratinus (357).

The Initiates, after dancing in a circle and singing hymns—"Iacchus, dance lover, lead the dance with me!"

—leave the orchestra for the happy fields where roses bloom (400). At the same time Dionysus knocks at Pluto's gate, announcing himself as the mighty Heracles. The person who opens the door, however, happens to be Aeacus, one of the judges of Hades, who has a word or two for the sometime abductor of Cerberus. Two exhilarating farcical scenes follow: in the first (479–589), Dionysus and Xanthias each wants to get rid of the compromising lion-skin by putting it on the other; in the second (605–74), Aeacus, beating both of them alternately, tries to discover which of the two is the real god. Finally, not being able to solve the riddle, he goes into the palace to consult Pluto: "Why didn't you think of that before beating us black and blue!" Dionysus shouts after him. Now the Initiates reappear in the orchestra for an incomplete *parabasis*. It is Aristophanes' last existing address to the audience (675–737). His message is not dictated by indignation against political or literary personalities, but only by pity for his unfortunate country. The playwright advises "equality" among citizens and "forgiveness" for those who were led astray as, for instance, the participants in the abortive government of the Four Hundred. "Let us make," he preaches, "all men our brothers" (701). Then he proceeds to his famous monetary parable—that bad money chases out the good—which twenty centuries later Thomas Gresham will expound to Queen Elizabeth of England.[19]

A short scene of hilarious drunkenness between Xanthias and a slave of Hell (738–813) has no other reason for being except to prepare us for the great literary battle which is about to start. We learn that Aeschylus had occupied of old the throne of tragedy in Hades, but as soon as Euripides arrived all the scoundrels who abound in the underworld ("as well as the upper world" Xanthias interjects, glancing at the audience) crowned him as king. And now the two tragic poets are violently disputing for the throne.

"And Sophocles?" Xanthias asks. "When he came here," the slave answers, "he embraced Aeschylus and left the throne to him, saying that, if Aeschylus wins the round, he will accept him as his superior; but, if Euripides prevails, then he will battle him for supremacy." Sophocles had died after Aristophanes had already composed this comedy and therefore his role is limited to a few last minute insertions.

In great pomp, Pluto and Persephone, the rulers of the Underworld, make their appearance; as the Lenaea takes place in January, it is natural for Demeter's daughter to be in her winter domicile, where, according to the legend, she only stayed six months. Dionysus reappears with them, as the arbiter of the contest. Last, the two combatants enter: the imposing Aeschylus in a long, magnificent tunic and the nervous Euripides wrapped in his rags. The Initiates surround them, to be the witnesses of the historical encounter and at the same time to stir up, if necessary, the two opponents.

This poetic contest is the basic *agon* of the comedy (830–1480). It is the longest *agon* ever written by Aristophanes, covering 650 lines of the 1533 in the play. We would divide it into five main parts:

1. *Introductory debate.* Euripides attacks with marketplace rhetoric while Aeschylus keeps a contemptuous silence—similar to his famous silent heroes.[20]

2. *Comparison of their literary contributions.* Aeschylus praises the moral grandeur of his dramatic characters, Euripides the realistic genuineness of his. Euripides accuses the bombast and verbosity of his rival, Aeschylus the cheapness and immorality of the other.

3. *Comparison of their prologues in form and content.* Here we have the famous *lekythion a-polesen* ("he

lost his jug") that Aeschylus inserts into every Euripidean prologue to prove that they are all made in the same pattern.

4. *Comparison of their choral songs, in meaning and melody.* Here triumphs the word *toflattothrat,* devised by Euripides to emphasize the exaggerated verbal noise of the Aeschylean style. Aeschylus, on the other hand, parodies his rival's modernistic poetry, using the *ostraka,* a vulgar musical accompaniment, instead of the lyre.[21]

5. *Comparison of individual verses.* Dionysus takes the scale and weighs the two poets' verses like cheese. Aeschylus wins by putting a line from his *Glaucus Potnieus,* "chariot upon chariot and corpse upon corpse," which, as Dionysus explains, becomes the weightiest line ever written; and Aeschylus shouts: "Let him sit on the scale himself with his children and Cephisophon and all his books and I will outweigh him with just two lines of mine." [22]

The literary contest is satirical, often approaching parody, but never arbitrary. Aristophanes' critique is genuine and he can solemnly sign all his arguments without any scruple. In fact, these arguments are so masterfully selected that the rivals come out of the clash besmirched and yet triumphant. The dramatic judge Dionysus cannot, therefore, make up his mind which of the two deserves the throne of tragedy. "The one I consider wise, the other I love," he declares (1413). It is strange how reserved the comic poet appears in his anti-Euripidean feelings. Euripides had died only ten months ago and obviously death has raised him in the public esteem. So Aristophanes had to be careful.

The comic *agon* must have an outcome, however, and so its last phase becomes political. The tragic poets are invited to express their opinion of Alcibiades and their views on the country's welfare. When even those answers fail to bring an issue to the dilemma, Dionysus, like most dramatic critics, decides to crown arbitrarily "the one that my soul desires"; and he chooses Aeschylus (1468–71).

So the old tragic champion wins on points and not by knocking out his opponent. The god of the dead—and Aristophanes—install him on the throne of eternal poetry. As Athens, however, needs Aeschylus for his wise and virtuous counsels, Pluto gives him leave to return to the living. The departing poet appoints Sophocles as regent, because he estimates him as "second in wisdom." Whereupon holding Dionysus' hand, he starts on his ascending journey accompanied by the joyous songs of the chorus (1482 f.).

Thus we behold the god of the theatre, who had gone to the underworld in quest of Euripides, return to earth with Aeschylus: not because he finds him a superior poet but because Athens needs his patriotic sentiments.

It is interesting to note that Aeschylus' opinion about the safety of Athens is a nostalgic reminiscence of the political wisdom of Pericles. In the axiom, "Trust the fleet" (1465), he echoes Pericles' advice in the first year of the Peloponnesian War (cf. Thucydides). Our comic poet, who twenty years ago condemned the "Olympian" statesman longing for the good old days that were no more, now, disappointed by democracy's unworthy descendents, returns to the political principles of the dead leader. After all, the Periclean age has by now become part of Aristophanes' "good old days." Comic invective has no meaning whatsoever unless in the present tense.

Many opinions scattered here and there in the Aristophanic plays or fragments embody the comic poet's critical attitude toward his tragic contemporaries. The duel in the *Frogs,* on the other hand, contains a compact and integral literary study. Let us examine Aristophanes' basic view about the three major tragic poets, without including any commentary which is not strictly his own!

Aeschylus

1. *His character.* Aeschylus is a serene poet, the Zeus and the lion of Greek literature. He was in his life a brave Marathon warrior and a spiritual offspring of the Eleusinian mysteries.[23] He is called "Bacchic king" because he, of all tragic poets, is nearer to the old Dionysiac worship. His greatest virtue is sagacity, his greatest defects, fiery temperament and warlike passion, warlike, nonetheless, only against the barbarian aggressors. Possibly he does not possess the knowledge and intelligence of Euripides, but the fecundity of his mind is tremendous: he creates his own ideas, borrowing from nowhere. His heroic and bombastic style often makes him appear as preposterous or sophomoric; but these are characteristics pertaining to Homeric heroes as well, who, like his own, were animated by a giant's breath. His luxuriant mane and his wild eyebrows give Aeschylus a mythological aspect.

2. *His literary style.* His chief value lies in his thundering and impressive words, most of them improvised. His dramatic heroes seem to roar, and his verses sound like galloping war horses; yet, sometimes, they appear more like oxen because of their excessive heaviness. His lines flow unrestrained like torrents; nevertheless, they betray an immense inner tension: his lungs suffer much until they exhale the great volume of his poetry. Sometimes he does not control his writing and that leads to riddles; more often, his poetry is full of strange words, composite and long, like the *hippalectryons,* the *tragelaphs,* and other verbal monsters, which do not sound at all like real human speech. His lust for words has many times led him to unnecessary repetitions and pleonasms.

His choral poetry continues the tradition of Orpheus, Homer, and the old lyric poets, but he imitates no one. Above all, he self-consciously avoids copying his contemporary Phrynichus. Not rarely there is a certain monotony in his stasima; and yet, the best choral songs written until now are his.

Aeschylus is, furthermore, a creator of ferocious heroes, displaying spears and helmets and souls "wrapped sevenfold in bull's hide"—such as Achilles, Cycnus, Memnon, and other valiant knights.[24]

Eros is completely absent from his tragedies.

3. *His social influence.* He taught the Greeks to be brave and bellicose, disciplined, always striving for victory, always having Marathon as their ideal. He believes that a poet must conceal evil and never demonstrate it. If teachers are the guides of boys, poets are those of young men; they should, therefore, say only honest things. Orpheus taught of sacred mysteries and how to avoid murder; Musaeus, of witchcraft in case of illness; Hesiod, how to cultivate the earth; and Homer, the virtues of armament and warfare.[25] Aeschylus imitated their example and created virtuous heroes like Patroclus and Teucer, who lift the spirit of every citizen and make every one wish to rival them. His counsels and examples, especially those in his *Persians,* could now save Athens and make stupid people see reason. The big words Aeschylus uses are indispensable to the great ideas that tragedy must embrace.

Euripides

1. *His character.* He is a clever man but the need to show off his wisdom too often becomes a purpose in itself. As an adherent of Socrates, he has made wisdom his profession, aiming impressively at the enlightenment of the public.

2. *His literary style.* Contrary to Aeschylus, who cre-

ated like an inspired poet, Euripides resorts to theorems, epigrams, obscure stylistic tricks, and literary preciousness. He gathers his material from a thousand books, frequently borrowing from other poets, even inferior ones, and from folklore of every origin. He has a penchant for fallacies and trivialities and his writing betrays a demented person. His power of words, however, saves him; for he is an artisan of phrases and delights in working out verbal intricacies. His poetry appears like a patchwork, sometimes successful and sometimes only as good as garbage.

His versification is based on recipes. All his prologues are of the same mold, as we can well judge from those of *Meleager, Melanippe, Hypsipyle, Phrixus, Oeneus, Iphigenia among the Taurians,* etc. His choral songs are usually cheap and vulgar and his melodic devices are similar to the "twelve love-tricks of the notorious whore, Cyrene."

He may have boasted that he "abolished the vagueness" of tragedy, by explaining in his prologues everything related to the hero; but, on the other hand, he made tragic style artificial, heavy with far-fetched aesthetic rules, scholastic dialectic, and pretentiousness. In order to give a realistic image of life and move his public to tears, he presents pitiful heroes, shabby or lame. For the sake of realism again, he gives speech to housewives, slaves, laymen, little girls, and old crones, and fills the theatre with a lot of common household objects.

3. *His social influence.* He preaches, like Socrates, that there are no gods. He, too, believes in abstract ideas: to Ether, to the Language, and to the Brain. He made men skeptical and they began to avoid temples and sacrifices. He boasts that he taught the Athenians to think, to observe, to understand, to doubt, to suspect evil, to have perception of all things: in two words, that he made Logic and Intellect the cornerstones of tragic art.

He insinuates that all men were idiots and that he was the first to open their eyes; while, in reality, he made them speak superficially; from honest and generous, he made them perverse and fraudulent, idlers of the marketplace and bad citizens neglecting their duties. Although he believes that a poet's purpose is to improve the citizens, Euripides has influenced the private and public morality of the country disastrously. Athens was suddenly filled with talkers and bureaucrats who cheat the people; young men have abandoned sports and now polish their behinds by sitting in sophistic seminars.

His influence was especially injurious to women. He brought on the stage procuresses (like Phaedra's nurse), women who give birth in temples (like Auge), others who fall in love with their brothers (like Canace), and intellectuals (like Melanippe) who wonder "if life is death and death is life." As a true aphrodisiac poet, he presented women lovesick and made many Athenian ladies take poison out of shame for Stheneboea's behavior.[26]

Of the two poets, Aeschylus is the one more beloved by the public, though Euripides is considered a wise man. The works of the former will live eternally, while those of the latter have already died along with him.

Sophocles

Aristophanes does not have many things to tell us about Sophocles, because neither the life of the "happy" poet nor his work gave an excuse for theatrical invectives. Sophocles is respectfully treated by all Attic Comedy writers. Of all his contemporaries, the comic Phrynichus has, in fact, given us the best praise of him (see note 3).

Aristophanes considers Sophocles as second in tragedy after Aeschylus, calls his poetry "honey dripping" (*Gerytades*), and stresses the mildness of his character. Among the benefits of peace—fruits, feasts, music, etc.—he places the melodic odes of Sophocles (*Peace,* 530–31). Only once is there an arrow loosed against him, concerning his avarice: "Even now, old and rotten, he would be able to sail the sea on a straw if there was a chance of some profit" (*Peace,* 695–99).

Another thing to remember is that, at the time of the *Frogs,* Greece was suddenly left without Tragedy. And this, for a nation that, during a whole century, had lived under the poetic stimulus of Phrynichus, Aeschylus, Sophocles, Euripides—even minor poets like Iophon or Agathon—was unquestionably an overwhelming blow. Thanks to this comedy, Jaeger says, "we can see what tragedy meant to the Athenian people." [27]

The *Frogs* won the first prize. For this play, however, the scholiast tells us, Aristophanes was not crowned with ivy alone; his victory was not exclusively a comic poet's victory, but also a triumph, delayed perhaps but definite, of an Athenian patriot. The comedy was presented for a second time, and Aristophanes was crowned with the sacred olive of Athena as a national benefactor (*Life*). It seems that his countrymen were especially impressed with his advice that "We should make all men our brothers and restore the honor of our citizens" (*Frogs,* 701–2).

Thus, the *Frogs* had a theatrical fate just the opposite of that of the *Clouds.* Did this happen because Aristophanes showed greater understanding for Euripides than he had shown twenty years ago for Socrates? Or, because the genre of literary satire had in the meantime become more familiar to the public? The chorus of the Initiates tells Aeschylus and Euripides: "If you suspect that on account of ignorance your intricate speeches won't be appreciated by the spectators, don't have such fear. They have been trained to such things. And each one carries the poet's text with him and learns well" (1109–18). The Athenian audience may not have literally carried text books, as at the matinees of the Comédie Française; still it seems obvious that literary insinuations did not miss their thrust.

While in Athens the *Frogs* was defeating the *Muses* of Phrynichus and the *Cleophon* of the comic Plato,[28] in Sparta, war preparations were in progress. So, in the autumn of 405, the two Lacedaemonian kings, leading an enormous army, arrived in Attica, and, simultaneously, the general Lysander with three hundred ships, blockaded the harbor of Piraeus.

We cannot say how long the siege of Athens would have lasted and what its fate would have been, if the Athenian fleet had not been doomed to destruction at Aegospotami near the Hellespont. At that naval battle Athenian domination was forever sunk, making the *Frogs'* year the last glorious one in the history of the city.

The siege lasts four months. The inhabitants bury during the day those dying from famine and spend sleepless nights thinking of the reprisals that will be inflicted upon them. In those days of despair and repentance they give political amnesty to the old rebels, thus restoring the honor of the citizens, as Aristophanes had advised. They also recall from exile the general Thucydides, the chronicler of the relentless war which is now tragically coming to an end.

Athens falls in March 404 B.C., in that period of the year usually dedicated to the City Dionysia. The victorious allies propose to kill the male population of the city and sell the women and children as slaves. The motion is made by the Thebans and the Corinthians, who twenty years earlier had been invited by Dicaeopolis as good friends to his peaceful market. The Spartans, however, are proven magnanimous; they declare that their intention is by no means to enslave a city which in bygone years had saved all Greece from the Persian menace. If we are to believe a certain legend, the conquerors were moved to pity by someone who sang a passage of the Euripidean *Electra;* the fate of the unhappy princess, destined to live in a miserable hut, made them merciful toward the once princely city. What is characteristic, even in legendary vagueness, is that the much-scorned tragic poet becomes once more, as in Sicily ten years before, the redeemer of his country.[29]

Chapter XV

Transition to the Fourth Century B.C.

A law was passed and the chorus, deprived
of its right to wound, was silenced.

Horace, *Ars poetica*, 282 [1]

In the ten years (404–394 B.C.) which bridge the Peloponnesian War with the Corinthian War and the *Frogs* with the *Assembly of Women,* some three or four of Aristophanes' lost plays may have been written. We do not know how the playwright spent his late forties and early fifties, or what his state of mind and general mood were. No opinion of his has reached us about the Thirty Tyrants who ruled Athens after its fall; nor do we possess any dirge of his about the unhappy fate of his city. We see him evolve from fifth-century passion to fourth-century apathy, without a word of comment on that ruefully significant transitory period. Since Attic Comedy had lost its political vigor, however, and the *parabasis* had atrophied, even if his work of those years had survived we would not know much about his personal affairs. On the other hand, no chronicler informs us about his attitude toward the oligarchical tyrants, as they do in the case of Critias, for instance, or Socrates (Xenophon, *Memorab.,* II).

The Peloponnesian War had lasted twenty-seven years. Aristophanes had fought against it for twenty-three. He devoted to it his most powerful pages and his most creative days. So, now he must have suddenly awakened to an appalling reality. For his fellow citizens this defeat signified the end of glory, national pride, prosperity. For him, it signified all that and something more: the end of an illusion—the most precious illusion that an author can have—that his words shall bear fruit.

During this decade of his life another unhappy event casts its heavy shadow over him: the condemnation of Socrates. The philosopher drinks the hemlock in March, 399 B.C. Three years later *Socrates' Apology,* the first work of the young Plato, appears. In this book, the old sage is quoted as saying to his judges: "I have had many accusers complaining to you and for a long time; these are my dangerous accusers. . ." (18b). He does not remember their names, he adds, "unless one of them happens to be a comic poet" (19c). This comic poet also will be recalled during Socrates' last moments in prison (*Phaedo,* 69d).

Whatever the impression created by the *Apology* on the Athenians, it should have been anything but favorable for Aristophanes. No matter what his opinion about Socrates may have been, to be listed among the "dangerous accusers" of a great personality in a shameful trial was anything but gratifying. And we would not be too far from the truth, perhaps, if we saw in these two happenings—the death of Socrates and the *Apology*—the main causes of his new creative inertia.[2]

The plays suggested as written during those years are not more than four. (1) The *Fryers,* whose title alludes to the social parasites who live by eating other people's food. The rich protector of the arts and notorious playboy, Callias, as well as the famous sophist Prodicus, were among the characters. (2) In the *Telemesses,* so-called from the name of a tribe of prophets in Asia Minor, Aristophanes attacked, perhaps as he had done in the *Polyïdos,* the charlatans who exploited the Athenians with false inter-

pretations of dreams and portents. (3) The *Daedalus,*
whose hero was beyond doubt the mythological inventor,
father of Icarus, and architect of the Labyrinth. The fragments mention wheels and levers, statues and machines.
Possibly this comedy was written in 393 B.C., when the
long walls of Athens were being rebuilt with financial
help from Persia (cf. Fr. 188). (4) The fourth comedy of
this period may have been the *Gerytades.* Scholars who
conjecture its approximate date also suspect that it was a
lampoon on mediocre artists and literary ignoramuses.
Dionysus is here again the leading character, but this time
he descends to Hades to bring back the topmost exponent
of each of the three arts: dithyramb, tragedy, and comedy.
Sophocles, Euripides, Cephisophon, and the poet Cinesias
are mentioned again, and Sannyrion appears as a new
name in the field of comedy writing.[3]

Old Attic Comedy follows the fate of Athens; they both
decline together.

The first wound was inflicted upon comedy by the
Thirty Tyrants who forbade the *parabasis* and the mention of real persons; obviously, that restriction deprived it
of its most significant trait. Four years later another decree (proposed to the government by Cinesias, who had
been for long comedy's target) hit its very soul, the chorus. This gradual decay was mainly due to financial reasons; the poverty-stricken city could not boast any longer
of potential *choregi* to undertake the expenses of a large
chorus. Inevitably, comedy was left "sans teeth, sans eyes,
sans taste."[4]

Its last glow is the *Assembly of Women* (*Ecclesiazusae*). In this play, there is no *parabasis,* yet the comic
chorus, although curtailed, is still active. The plot deals
with a new adventure of the laborious Aristophanic beehive. This time, the bees pretend to be drones (or, to be

historically precise, the male actors pretend to be women who in their turn pretend to be men; in other words, over the feminine masks imposed by theatrical convention they hang the beards demanded by the comic plot).

Some modern critics have discovered a rather tired Aristophanes in this comedy. Gilbert Murray, for instance, wonders how Sophocles and Euripides had retained their vigor into their old age, while Aristophanes shows signs of decline before his sixties.[5] We do not share this view. First of all, we should bear in mind that the work of a comic poet was more exhausting than that of a tragic one. His plots did not carry him away to the impersonal world of mythology but brought him at every moment face to face with contemporary life. They were plots painful to his conscience and liable to cause him troubles with his fellow citizens. The comic poet was a combattant in the strict sense of the word and, therefore, an easier victim of frustration and fatigue. Besides, neither the *Assembly of Women,* nor even the later *Plutus,* reveal an exhausted Aristophanes. Fatigue and frustration would be diagnosed in these plays if self-repetition and routine were the prevailing symptoms and not innovating impetus and evolutionary effort. The form and mood of theatre art had changed, along with the general way of living and the disposition of the people. The elasticity that Aristophanes achieves, in his desire to adjust himself to the new trends, reveals not an exhausted but an altogether indefatigable idiosyncrasy.

We should, furthermore, remember that most of his fellow playwrights in tragedy, comedy, or literature in general, died before their century expired;[6] Sophocles and Euripides did not live to see the downfall of Athenian grandeur, much less so Cratinus and Eupolis. With the death of Socrates, the last great contemporary of Aristophanes passes from the scene. Alcibiades, Agathon, Democritus, and Thucydides have preceded him. Of the great classic generation, our comic poet has remained the sole significant survivor. His past is heavy and his duties demanding. In those transitory years, he, alone, in Athens represents Dionysiac vigor and Attic nobility. Inexhaustible reveler and phallus-carrier, he dances his way in a one-man procession into the rationalistic and anti-Dionysiac fourth century. To accomplish this he had to harness new horses to his old chariot of Laughter.

The mirth inherent in the *Assembly of Women* is not unrelated to the recovery, in 395 B.C., of Athenian independence, thanks to a new alliance which united Thebans, Corinthians, and Athenians against Sparta; if the play was written between 393 and 392 B.C., Persian financial aid had also invigorated the economy of Athens.

In its outer form, this comedy resembles the *Lysistrata*—women triumph once more at the expense of men. In its inner character, however, it is more akin to the *Clouds,* for here, too, the dramatic satire aims at the philosophic ideas of the times. If the *Clouds* attacked the sophists in general, embodied in a fictive Socrates, the *Assembly of Women* aims anonymously at Plato's extremist theories. The heroine of the play, Praxagora, proposes a political system which is a distillation, one might say, of the fifth book of Plato's *Republic:* a socialistic system abolishing family and private property.

The similarity between Praxagora's and Plato's theories are more than striking, although the *Republic* will not appear in book form until ten or even twenty years later. We may well suppose, however, that the philosopher's lectures were known from word of mouth or reproduced in student manuals even before the teacher decided to publish them. Plato had left Athens after the publication of the *Apology* to travel abroad, and had returned to Athens about 395 or 394 B.C. to establish his Academy. It is possible that he had divulged, as early as those days, the communistic doctrines which would later be incorporated in his book. From these very doctrines Aristophanes harvested the idea for his new comedy, which we can see as an indirect counterattack against Plato and his calumniating insinuations in the *Apology*. It is not beyond belief, on the other hand, that this Aristophanic comedy had its effect on the edited form of the *Republic;* for Plato mentions there "the invectives of certain wits," referring possibly to the present dramatic satire.[7]

The play begins in the early dawn. Praxagora creeps out of her house, disguised in man's clothes, and delivers a hymn to her lantern, which helps her make love in secret or steal wine from the cellar (1–18). As Lysistrata, twenty years earlier, this dynamic Athenian matron has to wait for her sisters to arrive at their clandestine meeting. The next one to appear is also dressed as a man, holding a stick and a lantern; the same goes for the third one and for the whole chorus that presently make their entrance (43). We cannot be certain as to whether the comic chorus had preserved the original twenty-four members or if they had already been reduced in number.

The *parodos* is executed silently, to the rhythm of the flute—there is no song. When all the women have surrounded her, Praxagora asks if they have prepared everything according to plan. Yes, they reply: they have oiled their skins to make them darker, they have stopped shaving their bodies to let their hair grow as men's, and they all carry artificial beards with them, as agreed. Their plan is to go to the Pnyx as a crowd of male citizens, and to vote in the People's Assembly for a government of women.

Lest their sex should be betrayed, and it is very easy, they admit, for a tunic to blow open, rehearsal is necessary. This rehearsal of masculinity is the comedy's first episode (130–288). Two bearded women deliver speeches, as politicians do, while Praxagora coaches and scolds them like a nervous director. Then she climbs on the rostrum herself and rehearses her political sermon against the frivolity, fickleness, and self-complacency of men, concluding with a motion to make women leaders of the state, since they are superior to men in every respect. This political speech, the last ever to be written by Aristophanes, seems light and merry when compared to his earliest one, the passionate long speech of Dicaeopolis (*Acharnians,* 497–556); it looks as though the roaring lion has given place to an acrobatic ape.

When the chorus departs in manly step for the Pnyx (289–310), some husbands begin to appear. First of all, Blepyrus, Praxagora's foolish spouse, dressed in a subtle feminine vestment and Persian slippers. He is doubly dismayed, both by his wife's mysterious disappearance and by a stomach ache which got him up from bed in search of clothes and shoes in order to go outside and satisfy his need. As soon as he crouches by the outer wall for that purpose, a neighbor interrupts him; he, too, is dressed in woman's clothing and is looking for his wife. Blepyrus waits patiently for the neighbor's departure before resuming his business. He is still striving, when another neighbor, Chremes, one of the few conscientious Athenian citizens who still attend the Assembly, returns from the Pnyx. Overwhelmed by astonishment, he tells Blepyrus about the strange thing which happened there: a bearded young man, with a white skin and a soft voice, made the motion that the government should be turned over to the women, and a majority of pale-faced, similarly bearded persons passed the motion, as being "the only experiment that hasn't been tried yet." Therefore, now women govern.

In masculine march the chorus makes its second *parodos* (478). "Now that we have won," they say, "we can change our clothes and get rid of these scratchy beards." Here a technical problem arises: very few lines separate what the chorus say as men and what they say as *women*. How was the transition possible without an intermission? Possibly Bleyprus, at last relieved, executed a mute scene while the women changed. Another guess is that the chorus changed on stage, in one of those wordless dances that the *Assembly of Women* and the *Plutus* are full of. In fact, the word *chorou* (chorus interlude) is often substituted for the traditional *stasima* in the plays of this period.

With the reappearance of Praxagora and chorus in all the grace and charm of their sex (520), the *agon* takes place between the state's new leader and her husband. This stichomythia offers a novelty: it begins in a conversational tone of private character, which forecasts the dialogues of the New Comedy:

> BLEP: Where have you been Praxagora?
> PRAX: What does it matter, sweetheart?
> BLEP: What does it matter? Listen to that!
> PRAX: You don't think I was with a lover?
> BLEP: Perhaps with more than one.
> PRAX: That can be proved.
> BLEP: How?
> PRAX: Smell, is my hair perfumed?
> BLEP: Bah! You mean a woman doesn't make love without perfumes?
> PRAX: At least I don't. (520–26)

The *agon* culminates in Praxagora's announcement of her political program:

> All goods will become owned communally and everyone will have a share. There will be no rich or poor but all will live on the same profits. There won't be a

few people possessing great land while others die
without a grave . . . Etc. (590–94).

Normally, at the end of the *agon* (729), the *parabasis*
would interrupt the action; but again *chorou* is substituted. (This word, appearing in the Ravenna MS., suggests either that the *parabasis* was lost or that the chorus
executed a mute dance.) In any case, here the first part of
the comedy, the Theory, ends and the second, the Practice, begins.

The first episode showing the effects of the new policy is a duel of arguments between two men, who could be
called the Just Citizen and the Unjust Citizen (746–876).
Again we are struck by the resemblance of style between
this scene and some of Plautus or Terence, not to mention, of course, Menander. The second episode
(877–1111) ridicules the theories *in extremis* on free love.
The women, realizing that they do not all attract men
equally, had decreed a new law: "If a young man desires a
young woman, it is forbidden that he mates with her unless he first makes love with an older woman." So now an
old crone and a pretty girl quarrel over a young man.
They sing to each other their insults and to the man their
affections. The old woman, well powdered and painted,
uses all her wiles in coloratura to win the man. The desperate girl sighs for her love, but is finally obliged—*dura
lex sed lex*—to give up. Thereupon a second shrew makes
her appearance, who, being older and uglier than the first,
claims priority. Subsequently, a third plague, even more
repulsive than the other two, rushes in like a toothless tornado and grabs the man for herself. The scene ends with a
parody of a tragic lament by the unfortunate male.

The comedy closes in the old Aristophanic tradition
with a gay *exodos* and an optimistic anticipation of victory. It is, however, the most gluttonous finale of all those

written by the poet so far, for the simple reason that we are entering now the *delicatessen* period of Middle Comedy. The hero's *kordax* does not celebrate good harvest or peaceful bliss, but an unrelated-to-the-plot eating and drinking orgy. The old *komos,* which traditionally closed all Aristophanic comedies, used to smell of olives and wine; this one smells of the frying pan. In a hungry delirium the chorus sings the longest word ever written by our poet, the longest word, no doubt, that world drama has ever spawned: it is composed of 169 letters and describes the menu of the banquet (1169–75).

> Plattero-filleto-mulleto-turboto-
> cranio-morselo-pickleo-acido-
> silphio-honeyo-poured on the-topothe-
> ouzelo-throstleo-cushato-culvero-
> cutleto-roastingo-marrowo-dippero-
> leveret-syrupo-gibleto-wings. (Rogers' transl.)

What is the overall impression left on us by this "unusual" comedy, as a scholarly Byzantine bishop calls it? It is, I think, that of a witty theatrical satire, full of funny inventions and diffused mirth. Of course, it does not compare too favorably, as far as poetic verve is concerned, with the *Birds;* but the art of the theatre follows an evolutionary course and a good dramatist has to adjust continuously to the currents of the time. A new period of Attic Comedy—Middle Comedy—has already started and the *Assembly of Women* is at the turning point. It still conserves many traits of the older Aristophanic drama, floating at the same time on the new wave.

We ought to give special consideration to the fact that this comedy introduces, even if in an embryonic state, the theatrical *love couple.* The mutual passion of the amorous young pair sighing over the contrarieties of fate will become hereafter the emotional nucleus of almost every dramatic plot. Therefore, we should see the *Assembly of Women* as the last crop of the Old Attic Comedy bringing the winter of the fifth century to an end. With the *Plutus,* the fourth century of the theatre begins.

To compare this *Plutus* with the old militant plays of Aristophanes, such as the *Peace,* is to compare little art with big. There is, in fact, a contemporary statue by Cephisodotus presenting a tiny Plutus in the hands of a big-sized Peace.[8]

The hero of the last surviving Aristophanic comedy is not an Athenian who leaves his home for a crusade in heaven, birdland, hell, or even the Pnyx. His adventure begins and ends in his small backyard. Evidently the personality of the Aristophanic elder has diminished. On the other hand, the personality of the Aristophanic slave has expanded. The Xanthias of the *Frogs* has now become more emancipated; he is the real protagonist, the moderator, the ringmaster of the theatrical game, and as such he delivers, all by himself, the Euripidean prologue of the comedy; he will also participate in the *parodos* song, in which no actor so far has even taken part; and in many instances he will replace the chorus leader in his function of commander-in-chief.

The transition of the Old Attic Comedy to the Middle is an eloquent proof that, usually, nonaesthetic reasons create aesthetic revolutions. Aristophanes was obliged to eliminate his choral songs and dialogues merely for economic and political causes, of which mention was made earlier. His ancient biographer wants us to believe that he was the first innovator in this field, i.e., the father of Middle Comedy, but the opposite may also have been true, as in the case of Shakespeare, who in his later years will turn to idyllic fantasy in order to compete with fashionable younger playwrights. The comic poets known as representing the Middle Comedy—Antiphanes, Alexis, Eubulus, Timocles, Anaxandrides and others—may have started their careers before 388 B.C., year of the *Plutus*. Aristophanes, however, succeeded more than Shakespeare in outshadowing his young rivals, because of all the dramatic output of that period posterity preserved none but his *Plutus*.

This play is the comedy of Athenian poverty or, better say, its tragedy. "There is potential tragedy in Aristophanes and there is potential comedy in Sophocles," T. S. Eliot believes.[9] It is no coincidence, on the other hand, that man's financial troubles will become, henceforward, the basis of comedy plots and that the *Plutus,* named after the god of wealth, is at the very origin of this phenomenon.

The tragedy depicted in this play is the tragic complaint of every honest Athenian: "For being honest and god-fearing I have sunk into poverty" (28–29). The plot is no more than the skeleton of an allegory: Chremylus, a farmer of Attica, asks the Delphic oracle whether he should bring up his son honestly, to make him a failure, or dishonestly, to make him a success. Apollo advises him to invite into his house the first man he will meet on the street. This man happens to be an old, grumbling, and totally blind tramp, who stubbornly maintains a famous Aeschylean silence. When, eventually, he reveals that he is Plutus, the god of wealth, blinded by Zeus in order to distribute his goods indiscriminately, Chremylus decides to cure him and henceforward make good men rich and bad men poor.

This cure is accomplished at the Asclepios sanctuary. Carion, the slave, paints a picture of the whole procedure (653–747) which is a masterpiece of sarcasm on popular superstitions and middle-class habits. Surprising though it may be, comedy even in this stage retains its *agon:* it takes place between Chremylus and Poverty, a hideous old woman who furiously reacts to Plutus' rehabilitation (415–86). She says:

> If all of you possess wealth, then who will take care of arts and letters? Who will make locks, clothes, ships, carriages, shoes? Who will chop wood, wash linen, knead bread, build houses, plough the fields—since you will all sit back on your riches—

The old farmer answers that, naturally enough, all this will be done by the slaves. (Slavery had not been abolished even after Arginusae, and it still existed in Praxagora's communistic paradise.) As a more down-to-earth socialist than Praxagora, however, Blepyrus proceeds into a moving apology for the poor: even when the poor man is asleep, he contends, mosquitoes, fleas, and other insects buzz around him as if saying "Wake up and starve!" The *agon,* therefore, is cut short by Blepyrus, who would rather enjoy the idleness of wealth than poverty's creative energy.

The second part of the play (802–1209), after Plutus' recovery from blindness and his return to the society of good men, is composed of a few episodes introducing social parasites like those that we met in the *Peace* and in the *Birds.* The farcical verve reaches its zenith when Hermes, the gods' messenger, comes to protest on behalf of the Olympians, because men, having become rich, do not pray to the gods any longer. There is a vivid dialogue between the two servants, the divine Hermes and the mortal Carion, in which, finally, the god requests from the man a job in his master's household. He is by no means the only one to leave the celestial halls attracted by earthly riches; we learn that even Zeus the Savior "is wandering around somewhere" seeking food (1188–89).

The comedy ends with a wordless *exodos,* in which presumably the farmers celebrated with a dance the just distribution of wealth. Aristophanes had offered the Athenians, as a counterbalance to actual poverty, a comforting pipedream of wealth.

The Argument informs us that the play competed with four other comedies, signed by playwrights Nicochares, Aristomenes, Nicophon, and Alcaeus. Although those names mean nothing to us, we note that, instead of three, five comedies are presented at the festivals, as was customary before the outbreak of the War. The choral *stasima* having waned and the chorus reduced, dramatic performances are now half as expensive, and Athens can afford five entries at the festival.[10] What is noteworthy about the *second Plutus* is that, with this play, the comic chorus takes its final bow. More than a hundred years earlier, the theatre had started as a chorus; eventually, the chorus had accepted the actor; then, the actor elbowed the chorus out of the way, until he finally pushed it out of the theatre completely.

The *Plutus* is the last comedy that Aristophanes will present under his own name. His is already over sixty and he wants to promote his son Araros in theatre business. He lets him, therefore, produce his *Aeolosicon,* a dramatic allegory written soon after the *Plutus.* (The ancient *Life* states, though, that even the *second Plutus* was staged by Araros.) As for the *Aeolosicon,* we surmise that it featured the god of the winds (Aeolus) as a cook (Sicon) and that it parodied the Euripidean tragedy *Aeolus.* The plot, however, is not half as interesting as is the information given to us by the scholars that, in this comedy, *the chorus was finally abolished.* The *Aeolosicon* was performed twice; either the same play, as had happened with the *Frogs* or a revised version, as was the case of the *Peace,* the *Clouds,* the *Plutus* and possibly the *Women at the Thesmophoria.*[11]

We are inclined to believe that Aristophanes' son was successful as a producer, because two years later (385) he put his name to another of his father's comedies, the *Cocalos,* the last known title in the Aristophanic canon. The inventor Daedalus is again, as he was in the *Daedalus,* the hero of the dramatic satire, which takes the spectator to king Cocalos' court, or, more appropriately, brings king Cocalos to the spectator's courtyard; the mythological characters have become ordinary everyday men, to comply with the new comic style. According to an ancient myth, this Sicilian ruler had invited king Minos to his palace, where his daughters drowned the guest in his bathtub to punish him for his unfriendly behavior to Daedalus. To what extent Aristophanes drew his material from this myth we do not know.[12]

Mythology will become the common recipe for Middle Comedy. The theatres in the first half of the fourth century will be filled with the adventures of Aphrodite and Adonis, Odysseus and Circe, Pan, Heracles, Zeus, and their mistresses. Needless to say, all these gods and demigods will behave like Athenian shopkeepers. The bourgeois dream has replaced the Dionysiac vision.

Comic allegories on mythological subjects were established by the *Plutus,* the *Aeolosicon* and the *Cocalos.* Another element inherited from Aristophanes, and destined to become the most popular subject-matter of the new theatre, is the contrast between wealth and poverty. Furthermore, the role of the *sikon* (the cook) will dominate the Athenian comic stage, where, to recall Persius' dictum, "master of the arts is the belly." [13]

The dramatic intrigue most fashionable in those times is the one which begins with the seduction of a young girl and ends with the recognition of a foundling. Even this stock-pattern is apparently an invention of the elderly Aristophanes. "He first showed the way of the New Comedy in his *Cocalos,* where from Menander and Philemon he got the example for their dramaturgy," the biographer tells us. If this is true, then the worthy son of Old Attic Comedy leaves on his death two young daughters, Middle Comedy and New Comedy. The younger one, growing-up, will reign throughout the last century of Greek dramatic poetry.

Aristophanes is led by Charon across the Acherusian lake and the dark marshlands of the *Frogs* sometime after 385 B.C.; the date of his death is as uncertain as that of his birth. It may be true or not, that Plato honored his passing away and prophesied his immortality with the following epigram:

> *The Graces, looking for a temple that would never fall, found the soul of Aristophanes.*[14]

Chapter XVI

The Posterity of Aristophanes

*"The beautiful should not be only life and
only form, but living form."*
Schiller, *Aesthetics*

Every great man is at the mercy of the crowd; and for every great author, the masses will eventually bring a verdict of either eternal life or death.

The memory of Aristophanes has passed through recurring waves of fashion which sometimes brought him safe to harbor and sometimes sunk him. The sailing of the Dionysiac poet through the centuries has been unsteady, and men were shown as fickle in evaluating him as his contemporaries had been. He was called by Cicero a "most clever poet," then, by Voltaire "a vulgar buffoon," to become in Gogol's words "the father of all comedy," or in Hugo's "a pigmy."

It is interesting to follow some of the stages of his survival, both in the library and in the living theatre. Only four opinions of his contemporaries about him have been preserved: (*a*) The oldest is the critical epigram of Cratinus, which we mentioned in our chapter on the *Clouds*. (*b*) Then comes Eupolis' libel, calling Aristophanes a plagiarist, in connection with their collaboration on the *Knights*. (*c*) The invectives of Eupolis and the comic Plato about his colossal statue of Peace. (*d*) Last, the lam-

244

pooning by three fellow writers—Ameipsias, Aristony-
mus, and Sannyrion—that he sweated for the glory of his
straw-men, Callistratus and Philonides.[1]

These are about the only fifth-century relics. The
fourth century is comparatively richer, thanks chiefly to
evidence given by Plato. Plato's attitude toward the author of the *Clouds* looks somewhat enigmatic. Basically,
Plato understood and admired the comic poet. Some of
the arguments to support this are: (*a*) his famous epigram
about the Graces, if genuine; (*b*) the story, according to
which he advised the Sicilian tyrant, Dionysius, to read
Aristophanes in order to understand the Athenian government; (*c*) information that Aristophanes' plays were found
beside Plato's deathbed.[2] None of the above, however, can
be taken too seriously.

On the contrary, unimpeachable evidence of admiration is found in the *Symposium,* where the author attributes to Aristophanes the most fascinating discourse on
love next to the Socratic one. He accepts the comic writer
as a genuinely artistic and original creator, and the prose
that he puts in his mouth is the same bright Attic speech
of the Aristophanic comedies. A still more laudatory comment is the statement of the inebriated Socrates that Aristophanes' only true preoccupations are wine and love.
Plato must have had in mind the poet's own praise of Bacchus: "He is a noble soul, for he cares about nothing else
but drinking and love-making" (*Frogs,* 739–40).

It was natural for Plato to admire, and perhaps envy
too, the comic author. He, himself, was an imitator of Sophron and Epicharmus and had also written a tetralogy
for the theatre, which Socrates advised him to destroy.[3]
Even his *Dialogues*—that very special form he gave to his
essays—were a comfortable refuge offered by the successful philosopher to the unsuccessful dramatist. Furthermore, whenever in those *Dialogues* some hilarious atmo-

sphere is desired, Plato borrows freely from Aristophanes. The *Euthydemus* echoes the *Clouds;* the intellectual reunion at Callias' house, described in the *Protagoras,* presents a cast of three high-brow sophists and a chorus of adherents, that could marvelously fit any Aristophanic scene; Agathon's portrait, given in the *Symposium,* is in no way contradictory to the one painted in the *Women at the Thesmophoria.* The famous hiccup of the *Symposium* is also a thoroughly Aristophanic gag; and the parable of the *androgyna* could find its place in any of his plays. More generally, the longing of the Platonic Aristophanes for the good old days, his conservatism, his fantasies, the mingling of serious and comic in his discourse, as well as his total lack of "philosophic" thought, compose a lively literary portrait.

The philosopher not only understood the playwright but agreed, in the main, with his political views and his despairing attitudes toward democracy. In C. M. Bowra's words, "Plato refused the greatness of Periclean Athens and rejected its basic belief that its citizens, as free and responsible men, could make significant decisions." [4] In Aristophanes' passionate iambics against political degeneracy, the forceful protest which later bore the *Republic* as its fruit, already existed.

Speaking of the *Republic,* even there Aristophanes' influence is not absent. In the creation of his ideal state, Plato appears as a second Peithetairos, and builds, more methodically of course but no less utopianly, a second Cloudcuckoo City. What is certain is that he embraces Aristophanes' views about the decline of music, lyric poetry, tragedy, and statesmanship.

Now let us turn our attention to the capital subject of Socrates' condemnation. In Plato's *Apology,* the old sage reminds the court that they had already heard many another unfounded accusation against him "in the comedy of Aristophanes." Plato seems to insinuate that the *Clouds* had occasioned the thunderstorm.

While writing the *Symposium* (some twelve years after the *Apology*) Plato still has not forgotten the libelous *Clouds*. In the long encomium that Alcibiades embroiders around his teacher, we perceive hints of an indirect yet quite conclusive answer to the *Clouds'* author, sitting among the guests. And everywhere through the dialogue, Plato misses no chance to stress the superiority of the philosophically minded over the plain men of letters —Socrates and Alcibiades often triumphing at Aristophanes' expense. And when, at the break of dawn, the banquet is over, the old philosopher, very much awake, starts a new day, while Aristophanes is already snoring: a proof, in Plato's view, that philosophy rather than comic poetry is keeping the human mind awake.

Another humiliating hint is Plato's choice of Aristophanes as the typical representative of Comedy, against the much inferior and somewhat ridiculous Agathon, instead of a Sophocles or a Euripides as the typical representative of Tragedy. We also come across the aphorism, that "whosoever laughs at Socrates' teaching can be nothing but an illiterate." That summarizes, perhaps, Plato's final policy toward the comic poet. If, in the *Apology,* he had taken him seriously, in the *Symposium* he does not. Between the two works, Plato has matured and can see things as Socrates himself would have seen them. The master used to accept theatrical attacks as if they were dinner-jokes; Plato pays off the jokes, therefore, with a literary dinner.

Another fact explaining the change in Plato's feelings is that, in the time of the *Apology,* Aristophanes was still alive and could defend himself. When the *Symposium* was written, the comic poet was already dead. And it seems that Plato wished to bring him closer to his beloved teacher, uniting the two men in a posthumous reconciliation.

Aristotle mentions Aristophanes only once, in that paragraph of the *Poetics* where he explains the three aspects of imitation. The tragic imitation of Sophocles and the comic of Aristophanes have, Aristotle says, one thing in common—they both imitate a human action (III, 2). From this juxtaposition we may well suspect that the lost Aristotelian essay on Comedy might have used Aristophanes as a canon of comic playwriting, in the same way that his preserved essay on Tragedy has used Sophocles.

Nevertheless, the peripatetic philosopher seems more familiar with his contemporary Middle and New Comedy. "The ludicrous is either a fault or a vice, quite inoffensive," states he in his definition of Comedy (V,i), a definition which does not apply to Aristophanic drama. Imagine the indignation of the author of the *Knights* or the *Clouds,* if someone called "inoffensive" the crimes of demagogues and the sins of the sophists, which to him were no less than synonymous with his country's decay. On the contrary, the fictitious characters of the Middle and the New Comedy are quite "harmless" laughable people; the Braggart Soldier of the fourth century only terrorizes backyards, while the Lamachus of the fifth had led a whole city to disaster. It becomes almost obvious that Aristotle considered the Middle and the New as the definitive forms of Greek comedy. In the *Ethics* (1127 b. 33) he states that: "In the old comedies, the comic is achieved through vulgarity, while in the new ones, by insinuation; and this difference, insofar as decency is concerned, is not a minor one." In other words, he tries to ostracize Aristophanes, for the sake of his inferior successes, in the same way as European critics of the seventeenth century will dethrone Shakespeare in favor of Racine or Dryden.

The same mentality is more-or-less characteristic of the Alexandrian scholars, who zealously annotate Aristophanes' works but, when literary or dramatic perfection is asked for, they unroll Menander.[5]

It is curious that Plautus, though imitating, and quite frankly so, New Comedy models, revives no less the spontaneous, almost primitive hilariousness of Aristophanes. And this is one of the reasons why the respectable critics of Christian Europe will rather vote for Terence, who duly retains Menander's decorum, than for the uncouth Plautus. Thus, from the Ptolemies to Queen Victoria, Menander and Terence will be the most appraised of ancient comedy writers. In the meantime, however, through twenty-two centuries of papyri and litterati, the overlauded Terence will have only six of his comedies saved while the disreputable Plautus, twenty-one. Similarly, Menander will reach our days almost completely ruined, while Aristophanes has a decent revenue of eleven plays.

In the Hellenistic days appear the first Scholiasts and commentators of Aristophanes. Mention should be made of his namesake, Aristophanes from Byzantium, who wrote verse summaries of all his plays; Aristarchus and his pupils, Didymus and Heliodorus, who reconstituted lines and punctuation; Platonius and Andronicus, possible authors of the Arguments and the *Life* of the comic poet. The last important Scholiasts probably lived in the first century of our era. Thanks to all those grammarians and to their humble copyists, Aristophanes can boast today of being the richest Greek author in scholia, next only to Homer and Pindar.

In the first century A.D., our main source of information on Greek art is Plutarch. Reading his fragmentary *Comparison between Aristophanes and Menander,* we perceive that the Aristotelian conception about the supe-

riority of the New Comedy has become even more solidly
rooted:

> There is a vulgar, theatrical and common quality in
> Aristophanes' language, and not at all in Menander's.
> The man in the street is caught by his writing, but the
> man of culture offended. I mean especially the an-
> titheses and rhymes and similarities of sound. . . .
> Then in his choice of words we have the tragic and
> the comic, the grand and the common, obscurity and
> ordinariness, pomp and elevation mixed with bab-
> bling and nonsense to make one sick. . . . And I can-
> not see wherein that cleverness that he boasts of lies,
> in the words or the characters. Even what he does
> represent he distorts for the worse. His rascals are not
> like fellow-creatures, but malignant beings; his rustics
> not simple but idiotic; his laughter not playful but
> full of scorn, his treatment of love not gay but lasciv-
> ious. The man never seems to have written for de-
> cent readers.[6]

It has been contended that the above passage belongs
to a literary dialogue, of which only the pro-Menander arguments survived, while the pro-Aristophanic ones were
lost. Be that as it may, the surviving ones are enough to
complete a smashing critique against Aristophanes and
against Ancient Comedy generally.

The two scholars who have stored in their various
writings the greatest number of fragments from Aristophanes' lost comedies both belong to the second century
A.D. The *Onomasticon* of Julius Pollux and the *Deipnoso-
phistai* of Athenaeus contain fabulous treasures, not only
of unknown texts but also of technical information about
ancient theatre customs.

Lucian, more or less their contemporary, obviously
was an ardent admirer of the author of *Plutus*. He ap-

pears, as a matter of fact, quite Aristophanic in his *Dialogues of the gods* and in his *Dialogues of the dead,* where almost all the caricatures of divine or historical personalities emerge as reminiscences from the Aristophanic gallery. In this respect, Lucian's works typify the last rictus of the Ancient Attic Comedy.

When in the middle of the second century A.D., Hadrian built a new Athens, there were no more comic poets on the market, only second-rate script-writers of spectacular shows. Literature and spectacle had divorced.

More particularly interesting is the fact that, in the fashionable Roman mime-plays of those times, the spirit of personal invective, which had vanished since Aristophanes, now made a striking reappearance. In comic mime-shows, flourishing in the last years of the Empire, living people often become the targets of satire. In spite of its spiritual decline, the theatre had rediscovered its social purpose. Not seldom Roman censorship was obliged to exercise its veto on the besmirching of illustrious patricians or statesmen, even sometimes the emperor himself, upon the stage.

Christianity, in the early centuries of its existence, is also a topic of lampooning. Many of its customs, especially baptism, attract parody—much in the same way that the ancient Thesmophoria or Anthesteria spurred Aristophanes' sense of humor. There can be no doubt that the *mimi* and the *pantomimi* stood, in matter of theatrical art, much higher than the history of the first Christian chroniclers wants us to believe. Thanks to their theatre, something of the glow of Aristophanes' social comedy came back into existence, after four centuries dominated by comedies on private life.

Now the question arises, were Aristophanes' plays actually performed during those four centuries? There is no positive information available. We know only that Eurip-

ides' tragedies and Menander's comedies were performed, not only in Athens but also in Alexandria,[7]
Pergamum, Antioch, and the Sicilian cities. It is difficult,
however, to imagine a likely fate for the plays of either
Aeschylus or Aristophanes, where the real protagonist was
the Chorus, departed long since. Also, we must not forget
that, after the twilight of the fifth century theatrical architecture had undergone changes. Hellenistic and Roman
theatres were adjusted to the new dramatic technique: the
stage became high and deep, while the orchestra was reduced to almost half of its former area. The main action,
therefore, was now concentrated on the stage, while the
dancing interludes taking place in the orchestra were of
secondary importance.

So perhaps we ought to accept the implication that,
after the death of Aristophanes, the Ancient Comedy survived as a literary curiosity rather than as a form of dramatic tradition. If any Aristophanic play was performed at
all, it must have been the *Plutus,* which had inaugurated,
as we have seen, the new theatrical trend. Even after the
prevailing of Christianity, this comedy must have seemed
not only easy to stage but even helpful to the religious
cause, because of its disrespectful attitude toward the ancient gods.

Quite surprisingly, the Byzantine centuries, though
bubbling with religious fanaticism, are a period of Aristophanic worship. Most of the church fathers discover a remarkable kinship between the comic poet's scourge and
their own. St. John Chrysostom, a keen student of Aristophanes' works, borrows the poet's language and style for
his own flaming orisons against his opponents. The interest in the pagan comic master remains unextinguished
during the five hundred years which separate the saga-
cious patriarchs, Chrysostom and Photius. The last mentioned has preserved innumerable Aristophanic fragments

and scholia for our use. Curiously enough, in Photius' times (ninth century) the spirit of Aristophanes is revived even beyond parchment rolls. Emperor Michael III likes to organize Bacchic orgies and to stage in the Palace of Constantinople parodies of religious ceremonies. He either dons the patriarchal robes and mimics the holy mass, or he gives the prelate's role to his court jester Grylos, and has him lead a religious litany, riding on a donkey, while church psalms are mingled with obscene ditties. These Ghelderodian festivities not only prove that the spirit of torrid farce was not absent from Byzantium, but also ring an echo of most genuine Aristophanic burlesque.

Hesychius, Stobaeus, Stephanus, Zonaras, and Tzetzes are among the most important Byzantine authors who have contributed to Aristophanes' immortality. The *Suda* has retained for us a short, but not very authentic, life of the comic poet. Another life and critical study was written by Thomas Magister, a monk, who declared, seventeen centuries after the Greek playwright's death, that "No one has ever appeared to equal Aristophanes."

The fall of Constantinople (1453) saw the archives of classic Greek Comedy pass, along with other literary treasures, to Italy. A noteworthy Byzantine immigrant to Venice was Marcus Musuros, a twenty-eight-year-old scholar, who was commissioned by Aldus Manutius to edit the first printed edition of the comic poet. So, in 1498, the *editio princeps* of the Aristophanic plays makes its appearance and the comic vein of Ancient Greece is transferred from calligraphic manuscripts to print. Aristophanes is the first Greek dramatist to be printed, four years before Sophocles, five before Euripides,[8] and twenty before Aeschylus.

The *editio princeps* contains only nine comedies of the 44 (including four spurious) which the poet wrote. The eleven known comedies will be assembled in the second edition, the *Junta,* in Florence in 1515.

It seems that the most famous comedies in Byzantine times were the *Frogs* (78 mss. existing today), the *Clouds* (127 mss.) and the *Plutus* (148 mss.). Of each of the other comedies we possess 28 mss.; of the *Women at the Thesmophoria* only two. One cannot help wondering what happened to the rest of the forty or more comedies which apparently the poet wrote. How did they perish? Burnt with the Alexandrian Library? Sunk between Greece, Egypt, and Italy? Destroyed by Christian vandalism? Or, more prosaically, in a monastic stove, to warm the feet of some pious monk on a cold Byzantine night? . . . We shall never know.[9]

The discovery of the dynamic and original personality of Aristophanes made an astounding impression on the European literary minds of the fifteenth century. That signaled the beginning of a long period of reprinting, translating, and studying of the Attic playwright. Italy had made the first step; France and Switzerland followed; Dutch editions will prevail during the seventeenth century and German ones in the nineteenth.

Even before Aristophanes appeared in print, however, to invade European libraries, his satiric vein had invigorated, directly or indirectly, many authors as well as showmen. Of course, the medieval writers of moralities or interludes had never read him. Still, as it had happened with the Roman mimes, their audacity and urge for social satire made them, though unconsciously, his artistic descendants. During the Middle Ages, audiences were in no position to appreciate subtle literary parodies but could very easily grasp caricatures of judges, astrologers, priests, fake doctors, or even, more vaguely, the rivalry between Good and Evil, God and Satan, Virtue and Vice—a true survival of the *agon* of ancient Greek comedy.

An interesting example of such an Aristophanic survival in medieval France is a play by the troubadour

Adam de la Halle, called *Le Jeu de la feuillée*. It was written in 1277 and staged by the author in his home town Arras. It was performed in the open air on a festive day; it combined lyricism, fantasy, and political satire; it referred to real, living people, and ended in a collective *komos*.

Two centuries later, the *Farce of Maître Pathelin* presents the parody of a trial, amazingly similar to that of the *Wasps*. The defendant's imitation of a sheep's *baa* is not far from the *au au* of the Aristophanic dog-defendant. (However, Cratinus was responsible for the first sheep's cry in world history—*bee*.)

The oldest among the great authors of the Renaissance to show a notable Aristophanic influence are Erasmus and Rabelais. Erasmus admired the language and moral purpose of Aristophanes and, as St. Chrysostom had done, drew ideas and vigor from the ancient poet's texts. In Rabelais' *Gargantua,* on the other hand, we find the parody of a war caused by a few biscuits, while the Lamachus spirit reappears in King Picrocholus and his braggart generals. We also meet some army trumpeteers who, in peaceful times, fill their trumpets with grapes—as the helmet-makers and spear-sellers of the *Peace* adjusted their trade to the necessities of peaceful life. In *Pantagruel,* a comic trial takes place, where Judge Bridois renders his verdict while playing dice, as Philocleon rendered his while eating soup. A little further, we come across the Bell-Island, whose joyful inhabitants are birds—"big, beautiful and good-mannered, resembling the men of my country, drinking and eating like men, digesting like men and sleeping like men." Finally, the hymn to the divine wine-bottle ("O thou Bottle, full of mysteries") belongs to the same family with Praxagora's hymn to the Lantern or Dicaeopolis' hymn to the Eel.

We are told that Rabelais had a copy of Aristophanes

in his library; and, though he himself confessed his preference for Lucian, nonetheless his outspokenness, and earthly primitiveness, as well as the colorful pandemonium of people who fill his pages, make him—as his fellow writer DuBellay said—"the man who resurrected Aristophanes." [10]

During the Renaissance our playwright's immortality is mostly secured by the least representative of his plays, the *Plutus*. In France, Ronsard translates part of the comedy and performs it in the company of some friends. In Germany, Hans Sachs and, in Spain, Pedro Simón Abril adapt it. In England, Thomas More salutes Aristophanes as one of the pioneers of humanism. After all, Utopia is not far from Cloudcuckoo City.

An important event in the sixteenth century was the birth of improvised comedy, the Commedia dell'arte. Its basic subjects being love and money, it reminds us of the New Comedy rather than of the Ancient. Nevertheless, most of the stock characters of New Comedy had their origins in Aristophanes. The founder, for instance, of the dynasty of all the *Capitani,* with their crests and sabers, is no other than Lamachus; the original *zanni* were Xanthias, Carion and the Sausage-Seller; the earliest *Pantaloni* were the various Philocleons and Strepsiadeses; and the first *Dottore* was by all means our familiar Aristophanic Socrates. This observation leads us to a much more significant fact. The established comic characters of the European theatre originated as caricatures of *real* Athenians living in the fifth century B.C.

There are more elements in common between the theatre of Aristophanes and that of Arlecchino: such as— stage machines that carry air-borne characters, gay and often indecent dances resembling the *kordax,* various provincials who speak with a funny, regional dialect, and, generally, all the traditional gags, such as drinking, shaving, drenching, disguising, changing sexes, beating, even demonstrating the artificial phallus, as the sketches of Jacques Callot and other pictorial evidence of the period testify. In an Italian scenario of the seventeenth century we also find "ostriches dancing."

In the times when the improvised comedy brought new theatrical life to Italy and France, the England of Elizabeth and the Spain of Philip II were going through an equally brilliant theatrical era.

Shakespeare, knowing "little Latin and less Greek," was, of course, unable to contact Aristophanes, still untranslated into English. At any rate, his drama has little in common with Attic comedy. Wherever we discover certain similarities (Falstaff disguised as a woman brings memories of Mnesilochus), they should be attributed to the influence of the Italian comedy. The comparison, on the other hand, between the *Birds* and *A Midsummer Night's Dream,* attempted by some critics, is not particularly successful, the only point in common between the two plays being an atmosphere of fantasy surrounding the world of action.

The only Shakespearean scenes bearing an Aristophanic flavor can be found in two of his early plays: the Nine Worthies interlude in *Love's Labour's Lost* and the Pyramus and Thisbe sequence in the *Dream.* They have much in common with the Greek poet's burlesques of Euripidean tragedy. Also, it has been suggested that in his lost comedy, the *Danaids,* Aristophanes made fun of ludicrous strolling players of antiquity.

Ben Jonson, with his academic education, must have been more familiar with the Attic playwright. In fact he mentions him in an essay called *Discoveries on Persons and Things:* "Aristophanes offers a rich harvest because he does not only surpass Plautus and all the others in comedy but he expresses peculiarly all the dispositions

and the views of the ridiculous." This very same disposition is expressed in Jonson's own *Staple of News* and *The
Poetaster*. The former has been often compared to the
Plutus. The latter belongs to a phase of the so-called War
of the Theatres which, in 1602, had roused the managers
and playwrights of London against each other—more or
less as a similar war had once brought Aristophanes
against Cratinus and Eupolis. In *The Poetaster,* on the
other hand, the heroes are Jonson himself and his fellow
dramatists, Marston and Dekker. Dekker, in turn, attacks
Jonson in his *Satiromastix,* where "he is discovered in his
study, with a burning candle and scattered books, composing a wedding ode"—a scene astonishingly like those (in
the *Acharnians* and the *Women at the Thesmophoria*) presenting Euripides or Agathon in their moments of creative ecstasy.

Jonson's comic heroes usually typify social evils, not
differing in this respect from the crowds of Aristophanic
parasites. Sir and Lady Politick Would-Be, for instance,
might well have been among the undesirable visitors to
birdland. The same goes for Sir Epicure Mammon and
Lady Argyrion.

Jonson's customary dramatic pattern is also compara-
ble to the Aristophanic—a central intrigue, used as a pretext for a long chain of comic episodes and interludes.
The English poet states in his prologues that, in his plays,
"no thrones fall down creaking for children to laugh";
that his heroes "neither break eggs or swallow pies"; and
that he does not "steal jokes from other tables." It is, almost word by word, the ancient Greek chorus boasting
about the originality and good taste of Aristophanes.

Jonson's Spanish contemporary, Lope de Vega,
praises the Athenian comic authors for having attacked
sin and vice. He gives somewhat more practical advice to
his readers, however, "Never make your satire open and

explicit, because it is known that for that very reason comedies were forbidden in Greece and Italy." This prudent advice he tries to follow himself.

About the same time, Paris cultivates letters in "the manner of the Ancients." Boileau's *Art Poétique* condemns Greek comedy, where "poisonous tongues and shameless buffoonery devoured wisdom, intellect and honor." And he continues by accusing Aristophanes, as Voltaire will later do, on the ground of the *Clouds* and Socrates' death. He seems relieved when he relates that, finally, the law forbade attacks against real persons on the stage,[11] and he hails the period of the New Comedy, when "fury" and "bitterness" were driven off the ancient orchestra:

> *Le théâtre perdit son antique fureur;*
> *La comédie apprit à rire sans aigreur . . .*

Happily, the three great dramatists of those times—Corneille, Racine, Molière—in spite of their friendship with Boileau, never succumbed entirely to his commands. Molière, of course, has been often referred to as Aristophanes reincarnated. Still, it was the tragic Racine who, in his only comedy, *Les Plaideurs,* chose to imitate the *Wasps.* The Aristophanic satire on courts appealed to him as being "worthy of the seriousness of Scaramouch" (i.e., Tiberio Fiorelli, the Italian actor).

His consciousness of dramatic respectability, however, and his fixation on the Aristotle-Horace-Boileau code caused Racine scruples similar to those of his heroines. "In spite of the sparkling wit," he writes, "that I found in this author [Aristophanes] my feelings do not allow me to use him as a model . . . . I would rather imitate the strict method of Menander and Terence than the absolute freedom of Plautus and Aristophanes." And he proceeds to this unexpectedly humoristic remark: "Even those who wholeheartedly enjoyed the production of *Les Plaideurs* feared that they had laughed illegally. They thought it improper of me that I hadn't made them laugh by more serious means! . ."

For his own security, Racine calls his comedy a "translation." It is, though, a much different play. As he used to graft the tragedies of Euripides with the spirit of Versailles, in the same way, Racine gave Philocleon's story a Gallic touch. The trial's parody, however, exists in his play intact; so does the fanatic judge Dandin (Philocleon); his son, Léandre (Bdelycleon); the Secretary (Sosias); the servant Jeannot (Xanthias); and, naturally, the accused dog. Having already paired his own Hippolyte with the fair Aricia, he now marries his Bdelycleon with a young bourgeoise. In general terms, *Les Plaideurs* is a very successful comedy; and Schlegel is perhaps right in assuming that, had Racine been involved more systematically with the comic genre, Molière would have found a dangerous rival. The Aristophanic adaptation, however, remains the only comic child of the French tragic poet.

All of Molière's plays were written on the pattern of the New Comedy, which the author of *Scapin* had inherited through Plautus. From the Italian improvised comedy, however, he took certain elements—such as satiric ballets and parodies—whose roots lay in the Aristophanic theatre. Apart from this, Molière's comic situations often remind us of equivalents in Aristophanes. Lessing points that out; and Heine proclaims that both the Greek and French comic poets mock not only ephemeral persons and things, but the eternal weaknesses of mankind.[12]

In Strepsiades there is the protoplasm of Jourdain and a microscopic Georges Dandin. And all of Molière's gerontions belong to the family of the grumbling Aristophanic elders, though lacking their shrewdness and their adventurous spirit. His sophisticated ladies do not differ essentially from those in the *Assembly of Women,* nor is Tartuffe a complete stranger to Socrates, the impostor. Alceste, the misanthrope, who longs for "a remote place" is another Peithetairus who seeks a quiet country far from the Athenians. The insipid versifiers, Trissotin and Oronte, are the various Aristophanic Kinesiases; and the Hôtel de Rambouillet generates *Les Precieuses ridicules,* as the sophist schools had prompted the *Clouds.* We may as well add that the fragments of the *Amphiaraos* make us suspect some Athenian imaginary invalid, and that the lost *Triphales* presented an ambiguous personality like that of Don Juan.

There was a natural affinity between the two geniuses, for Molière had never studied Aristophanes. Yet both the Frenchman and the Athenian placed the purpose of dramatic satire much higher than mere laugh-producing. Their courage, therefore, often sent them fighting against "Heracles' fury," against the mighty and the great of this world. Guided by the same revolutionary temperament, both had repeated clashes with authority and both suffered repercussions. On the other hand, the artistic attacks raised against them by envious fellow authors were not few. Another common point between them was that they identified their views, both the conservative Aristophanes as well as the royalist Molière, with the people's feelings. Their public was their master, their pupil, their family. And, as many passages from their comedies reveal, their fellow countrymen embraced them with the same adoration and hit them with the same ingratitude.

There is an essential point of contrast, however, between the two clowning reformers: Molière's ideals concern human character, those of Aristophanes, human fate. The spiritual scope of both outgrows the boundaries of bourgeois mentality; but the Frenchman's hero is the individual, while the Greek's is the masses.

Most English critics of the Restoration admired the Greek classics. Dryden complained that "So long as Aristophanes in the old comedy and Plautus in the new are extant, while the tragedies of Euripides, Sophocles and Seneca are to be had, I can never see one of these plays which are now written but it increases my admiration of the ancients." [13] Although, following the fashion, he mentions Seneca and ignores Aeschylus, Dryden shows considerable perspicacity about ancient comedy.

In general terms, however, the playwrights of the period were too shallow to have much in common with the passionate Attic style.[14] Aristophanes' sting is more evident in Pope or Swift than on the stage.

The eighteenth-century English theatre has an accomplished Aristophanic representative in the person of Henry Fielding. In his youth, the author of *Tom Jones* had translated the *Plutus*. Among his twenty-six comedies, produced at the Haymarket, the most famous is a parody on the heroic drama of the day, called *Tom Thumb, A Tragedy*. His political burlesques, *Pasquin* and *Historical Archive of 1736*, were daring attacks against Prime Minister Walpole, who on this account was induced to institute the Lord Chamberlain's censorship on drama.[15]

We should mention, as a minor scion of the Aristophanic family, Sheridan's *Critic, or The Rehearsal of a Tragedy*. It is a take-off on contemporary tragic performances, strongly reminiscent of Aristophanes' burlesques on Euripides.[16] In those years, when lampoons and pamphlets were in vogue, there lived a man nicknamed "the English Aristophanes." He was the actor Samuel Foote, an excellent mime and composer of satiric skits which ridiculed people and things of contemporary life.

About the same time, on the other side of the Channel, Palissot wrote two theatrical pamphlets against the philosophers—Rousseau, D'Alembert, and Diderot—"a la mannière" of the ancient *Clouds*. "Ah, M. Palissot, so you present the philosophers on the stage!" Voltaire answered in a fit of anger; and immediately he counterattacked with a comedy, *The Scottish Woman.*

Voltaire was among the most ruthless enemies of Aristophanes. It is rather surprising, because the Voltairic salt tastes much like the Attic one. We must remember, however, that we are in the Century of Reason and Philosophy; and quite naturally, for Voltaire, the really great Greek personality is Socrates and not the comic poet who derided him. When reading the word *atheism* in the *Philosophical Dictionary,* we are apt to think that Voltaire himself, and not Socrates, had a bill to settle with the author of the *Clouds:*

> We wouldn't have permitted this comic poet, who is neither comic nor a poet, to give his farces at the fair of Saint-Laurent. He seems to me vile and more despicable than Plutarch portrays him. . . . This was the man who from afar prepared the poison with which infamous judges put the most virtuous man in Greece to death. . . . The tanners, cobblers and seamstresses of Athens applauded a farce that showed Socrates hoisted up in the air in a basket announcing that there was no God and boasting of having stolen a coat while teaching philosophy. A nation whose bad government authorized such infamous license thoroughly deserved what happened to it, to become slaves of the Romans and, today, of the Turks.[17]

Thus Voltaire in his article on Aristophanes; by the way, he was a passionate enemy of Shakespeare as well.

Among French philosophers, the most enlightened on theatre matters was Diderot. Against the general academic views, he believed in the transcendent value of farce and in its social purpose. "Not every man can write a good farce," he declared. "That needs a special kind of gaiety. Its characters are like the grotesque figures of Callot who preserve only the essential human traits. Not everyone is capable of distorting humorously his opinions." Diderot also thought that a satiric author, like Aristophanes, was a "divine gift" for any government that knows how to use him, because "when he takes in his charge the various exalted people who disturb society and exposes them publicly, then even prisons are unnecessary."

The words of the French encyclopedist demolish definitively a centuries-long fallacy about the aesthetic prerequisites of theatrical laughter. From this historical moment on, the bisection of the theatre into theatre which amuses the people and theatre which satisfies the intelligentsia ceases to exist. Accordingly, the wild fascination of Aristophanes emerges with striking life from the palimpsests of the New, Roman, and Italian comedy.

While still in the eighteenth century, we ought to mention two theatre men who contributed in their way to the posthumous glory of the Attic spirit. The one is Beaumarchais, who in 1784 gave us the *Marriage of Figaro*. He is the first playwright since Aristophanes, who, with a jolly comedy full of brio and ballets, assaulted the country's political life. A protesting cry against social inequity is uttered, almost in the same breath, by Figaro and by Dicaeopolis.

The second one is the young Goethe who, inspired by Aristophanes' other side, the literary one, wrote his *Birds,* a paraphrase of the Greek play of that name, aiming at Klopstock and his adherents. It was produced in the Court of Weimer and the author himself played the part of Peithetairus, improperly translated as Treufreund. In the epilogue, Goethe rendered Aristophanes what was Aristophanes', calling him "the indomitable favorite of the Graces." In his *Faust,* besides, Goethe uses a thoroughly *parabatic* prologue, where he discusses dramatic problems. And in the Walpurgis Night interlude there is a hilarious parade of contemporary personalities of the German literary world.

The Romantic poets discover in Aristophanes many of their ideals: the restless, never satisfied spirit, the violent passion, the merging of lyricism and satire, the undisciplined flow of dramatic imagination, the visionary hero who raises himself against a slumbering world, and, finally, the back-to-nature element. Coleridge writes: "In Aristophanes, comedy is poetry in its most democratic form, and it is a fundamental principle with it rather to risk all the confusion of anarchy . . . than to destroy the independence and privileges of its individual constituents —place, verse, characters, even single thoughts, conceits and allusions, each turning on the pivot of its own free will." [18]

Shelley, mesmerized by his admiration for Aristophanes, composes his greatest fiasco: *Oedipus; or, The Swellfoot Tyrant,* a burlesquing of contemporary events, with a chorus of pigs.

The first literary work, since Plato's *Symposium,* to use the Greek comic poet as a character is, we believe, Robert Browning's *The Apology of Aristophanes* (1875). Browning admired Euripides and his purpose in writing this poem was to prove that Euripidean tragedy was a superior genre and that it answered the enigmas of life much better than the negative and catalytic Aristophanic comedy. The Victorian poet takes us to Athens in the times when Euripides' death had just occurred. Balaustion, a young woman of Rhodes, and her husband meet Aristophanes who comes tipsy from a banquet just after his triumph with the *Women at the Thesmophoria.* They invite him to their home where a literary debate takes place. Aristophanes defends his anti-Euripidean polemic, while Balaustion counter-argues and finally reads aloud the entire *Mad Heracles* of Euripides, in Browning's own translation. Aristophanes is not convinced, however, and leaves the house meditating on a new comedy plot, the *Frogs* (written, in fact, five years later!).

Browning's exploitation of the subject is naïve and, at times, forced. What is touching, however, is his perfect knowledge of the Greek poet's plays and his attempt to paint, in his famous portrait-manner, an Aristophanes of flesh and blood. One pictures the hero taking his aperitif at some Athenian Savoy or strolling in a Hyde Park below the Acropolis.

A more fervent admirer of the Attic playwright was another Victorian, George Meredith. "We may build up a conception of his powers if we mount Rabelais upon Hudibras, lift him with the songfulness of Shelley, give him a vein of Heinrich Heine, and cover him with the mantle of the Anti-Jacobin, adding (that there may be some Irish in him) a dash of Grattan, before he is in motion." [19]

Among the French romantics, the most brilliant devotee of our playwright was Musset. As we have seen (chap. IV) he publicly attacked the prime minister of the day, by advising him to take lessons from the plays of Aristophanes. Because, he says, "for him no veil concealed good and evil; his verses did not spare cruel truths." In his *Essay on Tragedy,* Musset praises the poetic talent of the Athenian comic writer, and declares that his debate between the Just Reason and the Unjust is "the most serious and superb scene ever heard on a stage." It is not improbable that it was Musset himself who made Georges Sand sensible to Aristophanic fascination. We have a free adaptation of hers of the *Plutus,* where the novelist's romantic touch becomes obvious. She gives Chremylos a daughter and has her young heart beat for a poor slave.

Contrary to Musset, Victor Hugo, in his Prologue to *Cromwell* (1827), appears rather blind to the charms of Greek comedy. Among his various aphorisms we read that "the ancient grotesque is timid and tries always to hide." Where he gets that notion it is difficult to say. "Beside the Homeric colossi, beside Aeschylus, Sophocles and Euripides, what are Aristophanes and Plautus? . . . Homer drags them behind him as Heracles dragged the pygmies . . ." (What pygmies?)

In Germany, Tieck saluted Aristophanes as a true forerunner of the romantic school, and his follower, Augustus von Blatten, writes two satiric comedies in the Greek manner. Anzengruber, a later playwright, will borrow from the *Lysistrata* the theme of a sexual strike.

The great critic of Romanticism, A. W. Schlegel, had placed the Attic poet on a high pedestal, since the very early years of the nineteenth century. Thus, this century will become, for scholars and for poets alike, a period of unconcealed admiration for Aristophanes. The double quarantine of indecency and timeliness, so negatively active in the long past, no longer keeps the comic poet out of the European repertory. Coincidentally, scientific scholarship becomes passionately interested in his work. With the help of a whole alchemy of collations, comparisons, juxtapositions, interpretations, argumentations, and comments, Brunck, Bekker, Dindorf, Bergk, Meineke, Kock, Blaydes, and many others will accomplish a miraculous restoration of the ruined Aristophanic monuments.

Two Germans—Heine and Nietzsche—perhaps the most vigorous personalities in the whole Teutonic literature of this century, will become the most fanatic preachers of Aristophanic worship.

In Heine's case, we witness the pathetic insistence of the Jewish poet to see his bitterly satirical self as a reincarnation of Aristophanes. Contrary to Hugo or Browning, he considers the comic poet's world-theory as much superior to that of the tragic's. The comedies are essentially, he believes, "tragedies with jokes." Praising Aristophanes, he berates Voltaire, whom he calls an inferior satirist, able to expose only contemporary and not eternal human weaknesses. We owe Heine the most wonderful epigrammatic comment ever written, perhaps, about Aristophanes: "That profound world-destructive imagination which underlies every Aristophanic comedy and from which, as from a fantastic, ironic, magic tree, bloom the rich branches of thought, with their nests of singing nightingales and clambering apes." [20]

Heine's fixation for his Attic master's genius was so intense that, even in his last days, sick and lonely in the rue d'Amsterdam, he wrote: "Alas! I feel heavy upon me the irony of God! The great Poet of the Universe, the celestial Aristophanes, wanted to show the little earthly German Aristophanes that even his strongest sarcasms were nothing but weak jokes compared to His. He is incomparably my superior in satiric mood and in comic spirit." [21]

Nietzsche, recognizing in Aristophanes the ideal representative of the Dionysiac spirit, overturns the old accusation about the comic poet's criminal influence on the fate of Socrates. He, on the contrary, accuses the Socratic adherents of besmirching Aristophanes' memory. In the *Birth of Tragedy* (1871), by repeated references to the *Clouds* and the *Frogs,* Nietzsche belittles Socratic reasoning and Euripidean realism, which he considers as the causes of Greek decline. "The sure and penetrating instinct of Aristophanes," he writes, "diagnosed the truth, when it combined in a common object of hatred Socrates himself, Euripidean tragedy, and the music of the newest dithyrambs and saw in these three phenomena the stigmata of a corrupted civilization."

It would not be superfluous to note a survival of

the Aristophanic spirit apparent in the works of three great painters of the eighteenth and nineteenth centuries —Hogarth, Goya, and Daumier. Hogarth's Rake is a brother to the young man with the curly hair, crazy for horse races, disrespectful to ancestors and tradition, running after fashion and living a lazy life on borrowed money, the hero of the *Banqueters,* the *Clouds* and perhaps other lost plays. In Goya, the hatred of war is not very different from that which appears in the Aristophanic etchings; choruses of vultures and monsters devour the peasants of devastated Spain, who seem to murmur the same lamentations as the war-afflicted Acharnians of old. Both in Aristophanes and in Goya, however, the joyful blessing of peace creates a colorful contrast to the blackness of war: the Spanish carnivals, the blind-man's-bluff, the dummies, the field-games, all belong to the Dionysiac festivities celebrated by Dicaeopolis in his peaceful island amid the wild sea of war. Finally, in Daumier's work there emerges a whole host of gloomy periwigged Parisian Philocleons and robed Wasps of the Palais de Justice.

In the middle of the nineteenth century we come across the first Aristophanic performances. The reason for this delay is not only the fact that accurate translations had not yet been made, but also the prejudice that Aristophanes, being a Greek, belonged mainly to archaeology. As there is superstition concerning the excavations of ancient tombs, there is a similar one, at least among theatremanagers, for the excavations of unknown dramatic texts.

One of the first official performances in the theatrical archives is the *Clouds* presented at the Odéon in Paris in 1843. At about the same time, Dumas père has his shortlived Théâtre Historique decorated with a portrait of Aristophanes as representing ancient comedy, and without sharing any more this honor with either Menander, Terence or Plautus. In 1867, Emile Deschanel publishes his book, *Étude sur Aristophane,* which is the first modern monograph on Aristophanes and one of the liveliest ever written. In the same year, Anatole France mentions the Greek comic poet, first in order, among the robust humorists of history, because "he knows how to shift from the most primitive exultation to the most perfect lyricism with the dexterity of a drunken demi-god."

Some years later, the comedian Coquelin, the original Cyrano, refers to Aristophanes enthusiastically. He also has the opportunity to utter the Greek poet's name in those lines where Cyrano's nose is compared to that of an animal, "called by Aristophanes hippocambele-phantocamelos . . ."—an animal nonexistent, let us add, in the Aristophanic zoo. At the end of the century, Maurice Donnay, famous for his revues at the Chat Noire, concocts a free adaptation of the *Lysistrata,* making this play very popular with the French public of the Belle Epoque.

Having sailed safely as far as the twentieth century, Aristophanes is recognized both by artists and by critics as one of the most original personalities of classic literature. Relying on up-to-date archeological conclusions, they are able to view, in a completely new light, the form that theatrical performances had in antiquity. Still more important is the fact that modern dramatic convention has come much closer to the Greek, than any other theatrical style had ever been. No one can agree anymore with Schlegel, that "the parabasis must be considered as something absurd and unfit to the essence of a dramatic performance because the dramatist must always hide behind his characters." On the contrary, the critics of our times realize that "something similar to the dramaturgy proposed by Brecht had been practiced by Aristophanes." [22] Even at the very beginning of our century, Max Beerbohm, astonished by the freshness and timelessness of Aristophanes, had exclaimed "Who is more modern that he?" [23] And no intelligent reader or spectator of the Greek playwright has since denied it.

Depending on each particular viewer's sphere of interest, Aristophanes has become a striking figure in four main capacities:

a) *As a historian*. He not only complements—even though extravagantly—Thucydides in his chronicles of the Peloponnesian War, but he is also the only fifth-century author to give a three-dimensional image of public life in ancient Athens. We owe to him (granted the notorious liberties enjoyed by comic poets) the most first-hand information about Greek courts, education, financial systems, diplomacy, religious festivals, literary activities, political assemblies, theatrical productions, even the architecture and functions of the ancient theatre. Satirists, as well as cartoonists, are in a way the best chroniclers of an era.

b) *As a political editorialist*. He is the first in history. His plays have the same social purpose as newspaper editorials have today.

c) *As a literary critic*. He is also the earliest that we know of. His essays on contemporary writers are of unique value.

d) *As a theatre man*. His style and spirit are inherent in nearly everything creatively original that the twentieth-century theatre has produced.

Inspired modern playwrights and directors, even whole theatrical movements—especially those which have appeared in the postwar years of economic troubles and pessimism—have rekindled the Aristophanic idea. The merging of the musical revue and the political sermon, so characteristic of ancient Attic comedy, has become once more alive in the gloomy and uneasy times when the enlightened writer's voice, more than the bankrupt politician's, was expected to awaken the people's conscience.

Most of these theatrical phenomena were, much like Aristophanes' plays, antimilitaristic and antibourgeois manifestoes. Sometimes partisan, more often humanistic.

Mayakovsky and Meyerhold salute the success of the October Revolution—and later expose its shortcomings —with satiric pageants. Romain Rolland writes a parody on justice with a chorus of flies. In the German Expressionistic theatre, the passionate protest of the authors against the order of things resounds, and everyday life is sarcastically distorted. Piscator's Epic theatre is purely *parabatic;* it uses the stage as a platform for political criticism. In the dramas of Ernst Toller, the proletariat invades the stage with the symbolic significance of a chorus. Kaiser's gas workers and O'Neill's sea-men, the gentlemen in tails in the Ballet Joos, Marc Blitzstein's oratorio singers, the Union members who are waiting for Lefty, O'Casey's crowd enclosed within the Gates, the Jules Romain's characters of *Donogoo,* who build a new Cloud-cuckoo City, the prospectors of Mahagonny, and Genêt's Blacks—to use but a few examples—are the modern Knights and Acharnians, the active descendants of the farmers and soldiers of Attica, who, as in the ancient plays, utter the people's indignant protest. In most of those spectacles, either dramatic or satiric, the choruses sing or speak in rhythmical prose—the modern equivalent of the Aristophanic iambs and anapaests.

The popular opera and the dramatic ballad, proposed by Brecht for theatrical expression, is a form as undisciplined, as anarchical and as "nicht-Aristotelische," as Aristophanes' drama was.

T. S. Eliot calls his earliest dramatic effort, *Sweeney Agonistes,* "fragments of an Aristophanic melodrama," because it has the form of a musical parody of all the popular modern media of entertainment. On Eliot's traces and on those of the Germans, Auden and Isherwood wrote a charming allegorical farce *The Dog beneath the Skin,* a lyrical play where a flimsy central idea and many independent episodes aim at the respectability and absurdity of modern civilization. Yet, though belonging to the genuine Aristophanic tradition, the British authors were too exhausted by their own culture to possess any of the passion or spontaneity of the Athenian comic poet. That is only natural, in a country where Dionysus is represented primarily by gin.[24]

In 1933, dedicating his book on Aristophanes to Bernard Shaw, Gilbert Murray wrote:

> To my old friend, G. B. S., lover of ideas and hater of cruelty, who has filled many lands with laughter and whose courage has never failed.

It is rather odd that the most prolific comic playwright of our century, who might have been named the modern Aristophanes, never reveals any particular disposition to identify himself with his ancient colleague, much less to use him as a guide. Nevertheless, in his long introductions, Shaw very often tackles subjects favored by Aristophanes. They both were choleric entertainers, they both hated war and despised heroes, loved to parody fashionable dramas, and Shaw used Sardou as Aristophanes had used Euripides. The battle of the sexes is a common theme to both, although the Irishman contemplates it more as a social than as a sexual fact. He, like Aristophanes, often has the feminine genius triumph over masculine mediocrity, making even his superman a woman. We could add that longevity, a subject often treated by the author of *Methuselah,* was very probably Aristophanes' theme in the *Amphiaraos* and in the *Old Age.* As for their anthropological parables, Shaw draws from Darwin what Aristophanes drew from Hesiod.

In spite of the manifest admiration for Aristophanes

in our century, his stage career has not yet been too rich; theatre chronicles mention few significant productions of plays. Of all his comedies, the *Lysistrata* has so far had the lion's share. The performance which first bestowed preeminence upon it was the one Max Reinhardt staged in 1908 on the small stage of his Kammerspiele. His intention was, it seems, to adjust Aristophanes to the modern theatrical style, rather than discover an appropriate one for him, as he later did for Sophocles and Aeschylus.

In Soviet Russia, where Commissar Lunacharsky declared that Aristophanes would take a permanent place in the proletarian theatre, the most famous *Lysistratas* were staged by Komisarjevsky in 1917 and by Nemirovitch-Danchenko in 1923. The first was a stylized performance, omitting *stasima* and *parabasis* and stressing the farcical erotic element rather that the serious one of peace. The second *Lysistrata,* done in the musical studio of the Moscow Art Theatre, had music by Glière and shared the repertory with Bizet, Offenbach, and Le Cocq. Played for 200 performances, it gave rise to many artistic and political feuds. Some called it an important event in the cultural life of the capital, others "the Cherry Orchard burned down." To this last criticism, Nemirovitch-Danchenko replied that the modern theatre "needs no neuroses and fogs but loud laughter, rich colors and spiritual enthusiasm," adding that on the stage of the *Lysistrata* a "sunny Attic joy" is predominant. Contrary to Komisarjevsky, he not only retained the choral part of the play but used singing and dancing in abundance. The modernistic tendencies of the dances, however, made certain Soviet critics discern "a spirit of decadence."

Second in the Russian repertoire comes the *Assembly of Women.* We read that in a 1910 production, choreographed by Fokine, "the illustrious dancer Olga Preobrajenskaya executed a barefoot Greek dance in the Isadora Duncan style." [25]

In France, the 1927 production of the *Birds* by Charles Dullin, at his famous little Théâtre de l'Atelier, signaled the first important presence of Aristophanes in that country. The success was repeated during the following decade with the *Peace* and the *Plutus,* scored by Auric and Milhaud. Dullin took many liberties with the ancient author. In the *Peace,* for instance, playing the part of Trygaeus, he advanced toward the public and made a speech on the past and the present, declaring his deep wish for a universal peace and asking every spectator's help.

In the production of the *Birds* at the Atelier, the decor by the young painter Coutaud was made of steel, paper, and waxed cloth. The American designer, Donald Oenslager, also visualized a cubistic birdland made of steel and birds costumed as aviators. Abstract scenery was used in 1930 by Norman Bel Geddes in a production of the *Lysistrata,* which became one of the season's hits. A critic wrote that "the only reason it didn't receive the Pulitzer Prize was that the author was dead and resident of another country." According to another viewer: *"Charlie's Aunt* is recognized as a marvel of longevity; but what can one say of *Lysistrata,* first performed in the year 411 B.C. and alive today?" [26]

In the playwright's own country, Greece, his comedies started to be translated into the modern idiom only as late as the middle of the nineteenth century. Throughout the last part of that century, he became a favorite subject with classic professors, many of whom went so far as to imitate him in plays of their own.

His first stage revivals took place in the Roman Odeon of Herod Atticus in Athens. There, in 1868, the *Plutus* was presented in modern Greek and the *Clouds* in the original. Yet Aristophanes will not become a popular hit until 1956, when the National Theatre inaugurates annual performances of his comedies at the Summer Festival of Epidaurus. Ever since then, two or three Aristophanic comedies are performed every year to a packed and wildly enthusiastic theatre.

At the end of one of those performances at Epidaurus, when the public was streaming down the pine-covered slopes, humming the tunes and repeating the jokes they had just rejoiced with, the author, sitting alone in the empty theatre, still vibrating with the voice of Aristophanes, began to write this book.

Notes

1. Plato's *Symposium* was probably written a little after 385 B.C. As for the event commemorated therein, it dates back to 416 B.C., when Agathon celebrated his first tragic victory (cf. Athenaeus, 217a). The dialogue is narrated by Aristodemus. The speakers at the banquet are Phaedrus, Pausanias, Eryximachus, Aristophanes, Agathon, Socrates and, apparently unscheduled, Alcibiades. When Plato wrote it, most of the banqueters were already dead—very likely, Aristophanes too (see also Chapter XVI).

2. A. W. von Schlegel, *A Course of Lectures on Dramatic Art* (trans. J. Black, 1846). Cf. Lecture XI.

3. *Kento:* a literary composition made up of scraps from various authors.

4. *Hilarotragoedia:* literally gay and lively tragedy. *Emmeleia* was the dancing in tragedy.

5. A. Schopenhauer in *The World as Will and Representation.*

6. H. Bergson, *Le Rire,* p. 3. He notes that we may laugh at an animal, but only because we have detected in it some human attitude or expression. Nor must we forget that Aristophanes had a superb model in the *Fables* of Aesop.

7. The approximate dating of the three periods of Attic Comedy could be as follows:

A. *Old Comedy* (political and allegorical subjects with allusions to contemporary persons and problems) begins in 486 B.C. (Chionides' first victory) and ends in 404 B.C. with the fall of Athens and the restrictions imposed on the comic chorus. (*See* Chapter XV.)

B. *Middle Comedy* (mythological and allegorical fantasies) takes over from the Old and, after half a century (404–340 B.C.), gives place to the New

C. *New Comedy* (sentimental comedy on contemporary everyday life) begins about 340 B.C. (Macedonian conquest of Greece, Lycurgus' financial administration, Philemon's debuts in playwriting) and expires ca. 290 B.C. when Menander dies and the mime authors of Alexandria and Tarentum flourish.

No manuscript of any complete Attic Comedy, besides Aristophanes' eleven plays, has survived. And of Menander's 105 or 109 reported works one, the *Dyscolos,* was discovered as late as 1957. The *Dyscolos* has been published in two editions with English and Greek texts and commentaries: edited by E. W. Handley (Cambridge, Mass., 1965) and by Warren E. Blake (American Philological Ass'n., 1966); in addition the manuscript also contained *The Woman of Samos* and about half of *The Shield,* both of which have been edited and translated by Lionel Casson (New York, 1971). From all the other Greek comedies—well over a thousand—only fragments have reached us, quoted by Plutarch, Athenaeus, Pollux, Hesychius, Stobaeus, Photius, and including, of course, the prolific anonymous scholiasts.

8. W. Dindorf suggests 44 genuine Aristophanic plays (*Aristophanis Comoediae,* 1838). His opinion corresponds with that of the anonymous author of the ancient *Life* of Aristophanes, who considers the comedies *Niobos, Poetry, Islands,* and *Zeus Shipwrecked* or *Twice Shipwrecked* as erroneously attributed to the poet. Of the eleven integral plays, the *Plutus* has survived in 148 mss, the *Clouds* in 127, the *Frogs* in 78, and all the others in 28, except the *Women at the Thesmophoria,* of which we possess only two.

9. E. Coquelin, the first Cyrano of the stage, used to say that "the vulgarity to be found in Christian farces (of the middle ages) outshadows Aristophanes." Since 1961, when *The Living Aristophanes* was written, licentious drama and povocatively pornographic spectacles have indeed become a norm in the theatre.

10. H. Granville-Barker lamented the fact that "little more than a skeleton" has survived from the Greek theatrical technique (*On Dramatic Method*).

11. In the course of our present study we shall explain most of these technical terms. Yet, though theoretically we seem to know their meaning, we are in complete darkness as to their true character, aim, and aesthetic value.

12. George Bernard Shaw, "The Sanity of Art" in *Major Critical Essays* (London, 1932), p. 283.

13. *Karaghiozes:* Greek shadow-drama of oriental origin, popular during the Turkish occupation of Greece and after its liberation (1821). The stock characters are Karaghiozes, the cunning tramp,

Hadjiavates, the parasite, Veli Gheka, the bragging soldier, Barba Yorgos, the grumpy elder, Sior Nionios, the gallant from Zante, Stavrakas, the Athenian idler, et al. Sometimes legendary personalities like Achilles or Alexander the Great, or heroes of the Greek Independence participate in the action.

14. Christophoros Nezer, the late comic genius in my Aristophanic revivals in Epidaurus, was telling me that, having once been compelled to perform with mask, he could control neither his acting nor his voice. The same was true for the other actors too: the mask petrified their senses. Needless to say, the public's response was analogous.

15. *The Assembly of Women,* 1155–56 (translation by B. B. Rogers). The comedy was performed about 392 B.C., when the playwright was almost sixty.

16. The author saw this all-Black production in a Broadway theatre in the late forties and enjoyed it immensely.

CHAPTER I

1. The information "he belonged to the Cydathenaeon Deme of the Pandionis Tribe" is given both by the ancient *Life* (Venetian MS) and by Thomas Magister, grammarian of the fourteenth century. The "Rhodian" descent (from the town of Lindos) is only hinted at by the biographer, but is taken for granted in the *Suda* (tenth century), where, also, are mentioned rumors that Aristophanes' family came from another Rhodian town, Camiros, or from Egypt, and that the poet was a naturalized Athenian. All three sources agree as to Philip's name.

2. Zenodora's name appears only in Thomas Magister.

3. Here are some opinions about Aristophanes' date of birth, based (*a*) on the ancient sources, (*b*) on the date—427 B.C.—of his first play, and (*c*) on the poet's own statements to be found in his plays: 452–448 B.C. (Rogers), 450 B.C. (Croiset), 448 B.C. (Nicoll), 446–444 B.C. (Murray), 445 B.C. (Norwood), 444 B.C. (Pickard-Cambridge).

4. The Periclean constructions on the Acropolis began ca.450 B.C. (cf. J. B. Bury, *A History of Greece,* p. 367). The *Oresteia* was produced in 458 B.C. (Argument on *Agamemnon,* scholiast on *Frogs*) and Aeschylus died about two years later. When Aristophanes was born, Sophocles was forty-five and Euripides thirty. Anaxagoras (born ca. 500 B.C.) lived in Athens from ca. 460 to ca. 430

B.C.; when accused of impiety he left prison for exile. Protagoras (born ca. 485 B.C.) frequented Sophocles and Socrates and he also was obliged to leave Athens on an impiety charge. The father of History, Herodotus, was in Attica until 444 B.C. Simonides of Ceos had died ca. 486 B.C. The Poecile Stoa or Painted Portico in the Agora had been decorated by Polygnotus ca. 470. He was the first painter to use perspective. Myron flourished 460–440 B.C., Polycletus, 450–420 B.C.

5. Argument, *Oedipus.*

6. The accusations against Phidias, indirectly aiming at his chief and friend, were: (*a*) that he had pocketed part of the gold appropriated for Athene's statue, and (*b*) that on the goddess' shield he had portrayed Pericles and himself. The sculptor exculpated himself only from the first charge (*Peace,* 605–11; Plutarch, *Pericles,* 31, 32; Diodorus Siculus, XII, 39).

7. Aristophanes' references to lines of Homer and Hesiod are very frequent. Homer was the most quoted poet of antiquity and his works, the basic knowledge for all Greeks (cf. Plato, *Republic,* 606o). The curriculum of the Athenian schools suggested in this chapter is founded on general impressions from various sources.

8. *Odyssey,* X and XI; *Iliad,* III; *Odyssey,* VIII.

9. Magnes, after Chionides, the second poet of Attic Comedy, flourished about 475–440 B.C. Pratinas, a senior contemporary of Aeschylus, was a specialist of the satyr drama. His son, Aristias, carried on the family tradition as far as 467 B.C.

10. The age at which Athenian children were allowed to attend performances is discussed by Pickard-Cambridge in *The Dramatic Festivals of Athens,* pp. 268 f.

11. Cf. *Birds,* 685 ff.

12. Aesop, the legendary creator of fables, lived about the middle of the sixth century B.C. (Herodotus, II, 134). Aristophanes mentions him or his works: *Wasps,* 1446 f.; *Peace,* 129 f.; *Birds,* 471 f.; *Lysistrata,* 695.

13. On the dithyramb cf. Herodotus, I, 23, Euripides, *Bacchae,* 523 f.; poets chiefly associated with the dithyramb are Arion, Simonides of Ceos, Bacchylides, and Pindar.

14. Pickard-Cambridge, op. cit., p. 260.

15. C. A. Elton has translated three fragments of Archilochus and E. Diehl (*Anthologia Lyrica Graeca*) has reprinted others. Cratinus had written a comedy called *Archilochi,* and Aristophanes uses his hymn to victory, *tenella callinicos,* in the *Acharnians*

(1229 f.) and in the *Birds* (1764). Heraclitus placed Archilochus next to Homer as educator of the Greeks.

16. Aristotle says that "of all meters the iambic is the most suitable to speech . . . We frequently use iambics when conversing" (*Poetics,* IV, 14). On the iambic poetry of Archilochus, cf. Lesky, *A History of Greek Literature,* pp. 110 f.

17. Semonides of Amorgos or Samos lived in the seventh century B.C. Hipponax of Ephesus (fl. ca. 540) was the inventor of the "limping iamb" (the *scazon* or *choliambic* meter).

18. Alcaeus of Mytilene (seventh–sixth century B.C.) fought the tyrants Myrsilus and Pittacus with his poems.

19. Archilochus, Fr. 65 (Diehl); Alcaeus, Fr. 39 (Diehl); Aristophanes, *Peace,* 649.

20. In 438 B.C. Euripides, competing with the *Cretan Women, Alcmaeon in Psophis, Telephus,* and *Alcestis,* was defeated by Sophocles.

21. For wages and Pericles' law about aliens, see J. B. Bury, op. cit., pp. 349–50.

22. The ancient *Life* tells us that Cleon "accused him of alien descent . . . Twice and thrice indicted, he (Aristophanes) was cleared of the charge and manifestly established himself as a citizen, overruling Cleon . . ." In the courtroom, according to the same source, Aristophanes quoted Telemachus' words, that "no man can be sure who his father is and has to take his mother's word for granted" (*Odyssey,* I).

23. Scholiast on Plato's *Apology.*

24. Thucydides, II, 27; Plutarch, *Pericles,* XXXIV.

25. Some "thought him an Aeginetan, considering the fact that he spent most of his time there" (*Life*).

26. Aristophanes mentions Aegina also in the *Frogs,* 363, and in the *Wasps,* 122, but with no allusion to his connection with the island.

CHAPTER II

1. Similar ritualistic customs were, in fact, the fountainhead of Christian Drama. The dialogued *quem quaeritis* trope (ninth century A.D.) is considered as the first expression of the theatre in our era. The phenomenon had an earlier occurrence in the churches of the Greek orient. (Cf. A. Nicoll, *World Drama,* p. 141; J. Lindsay, *Byzantium into Europe,* passim; A. Solomos, *Saint Bacchus,* passim.; Karl Young, *The Drama of the Medieval Church.*)

2. Among many books written on primitive rites, Professor Malinowski's studies, along with those of Karl Jung, hold an important place. Our knowledge has, furthermore, been enhanced by documentary films and folkloric dancing companies from Africa and Asia touring the world; not omitting, of course, all the revelatory reports that have appeared in the pages of the *National Geographic* and other magazines.

3. Even the American black of the twentieth century has retained this capacity. There was a marvelous illustration of religious frenzy in King Vidor's classic film, *Hallelujah* (1929).

4. About the Dionysiac *mania,* there are some interesting pages in Nietzsche, *Die Geburt der Tragoedie,* I, II; also in W. Jaeger, *Paideia,* pp. 352 f. Aristotle discusses mania in poets (*Poetics,* XVII, 2) and Plato in actors (*Ion,* passim).

5. The controversy about the Dionysiac origins of drama begins with the much quoted *"What does it have to do with Dionysus?"* (Plutarch, *Symp. Quaest.,* I, i, 15). Cf. Herodotus, V, 67; Virgil, *Georgics,* II, 380–84; Pickard-Cambridge, op. cit., pp. 74 f. and 112 f.; and M. Bieber, *The History of the Greek and Roman Theatre,* pp. 1–17. Also W. Ridgeway, *The Origin of Tragedy,* passim, and G. E. Else, *The Origin and Early Form of Greek Tragedy,* Chap. I, passim. Aristophanes calls comedy *"trygoedia,"* from *trygos,* vintage (*Acharnians,* 499).

6. Athenaeus has referred to a practice according to which Greek chorus-masters made their choruses drink wine before a performance (*The Deiphosophists,* II). According to Horace, the actors of Thespis had their faces "painted with wine-lees" (*Ars Poetica,* 275–77). Every artist, says Nietzsche, is "exalted by Dionysiac intoxication to a mystical renouncement of his own self" (op. cit., II).

7. On the metamorphoses of Dionysus, consult R. Graves, *The Greek Myths,* 27. The god transformed Learchus into a stag, the pirates into dolphins, the daughters of Minyas into bats, etc.

8. Bacchus, as a transplant of the Egyptian Osiris, is mentioned by Herodotus (II, 42). According to the same historian, the Greeks learned the Dionysiac rituals from a certain Melampus, who had imported them from Egypt (II, 49). For the identification of Dionysus with Triptolemus and Bacchus, see Pickard-Cambridge (op. cit., p. 33). In the imaginary reconstruction of the Hermes of Praxiteles, the god is supposed to hold the baby Dionysus—having only recently joined the Olympian pantheon—and to offer him grapes.

9. The best Aristophanic examples of Bacchic odes are to be found in the *Women at the Thesmophoria* (954–1000) and the *Frogs* (316–413), the latter in connection with the Eleusinian rites.

10. The *phallus-pole* custom was also brought from Egypt (Herodotus, II, 48). Havelock Ellis agrees with Nietzsche that "the true Hellenes were sturdy realists enamored with life, . . . holding in highest honor the sexual symbol of life, which Christianity, with its denial of life, despises" (On "Nietzsche," in *Affirmations,* p. 15).

11. The *exarchon* or *exarchos* was the ancestor of the *first actor,* not of the *coryphaeus* or chorus leader. Thespis was the first (and only) actor in his plays; so were Phrynichus, Choerilus, and Aeschylus. The latter introduced the *second actor* and Sophocles the third (cf. Aristotle, *Poetics,* IV, 13).

12. The so-called Ichernofert Stele, which gives the outline of a religious mystery in eight episodes, dating ca. 1868 B.C., as well as the Pyramid Texts and other findings, provide us with enough information—besides Herodotus—to sustain such a theory (Cf. G. Freedley and J. A. Reeves, *A History of the Theatre,* pp. 1–7).

13. This brief summary of the Dionysiac Festival procedures follows Pickard-Cambridge (op. cit., pp. 1–103). Cf. also Bieber (op. cit., pp. 51–53).

14. Aelian tells us that Socrates went to the Rural Dionysia of Piraeus to see a play by Euripides (*Varia historia,* II, 13). The best photographic panorama of an ancient theatre is still that in P. & D. Cailler, *Les Théâtres Greco-Romains de Grèce,* photographed by I. Bettex (*Style,* Autumn, 1966, No. 1).

15. The *phallophoroi* (phallus-carriers) were crowned with ivy. The masked dancers of the phallic revels were called *ithyphalloi* (Athenaeus, XIV, 16).

16. Dionysus' boat can be seen on various vase-paintings in the Athens, London, and Bologna museums; and, less realistically, on the famous Exekias kylix in Munich.

17. The *archon eponymus* gave his name to the year of his archonship; he also presided over the Great Dionysia and legal suits concerning family rights. The *archon basileus* was in charge of the Eleusinian Mysteries, the Lenaea and the Anthesteria, as well as law-suits on religious matters. Besides those two, there was another archon, the *polemarchos* or military commander and the six *thesmothetai* or guardians of the law.

18. Cf. Plutarch, *Lives of the Ten Orators.*

19. Pickard-Cambridge provides us with good evidence on the Lenaea (op. cit., pp. 22–40).

20. *Inscriptiones Graecae*, II, 2, 2325.

21. In 434 B.C. five comedies competed (*Inscriptiones Graecae*, XIV, 1097). During almost his whole career, however, Aristophanes had to compete with two rival-poets and not with four, as it was customary before the war (Arguments to his plays). Only in the *Plutus* (388 B.C.) have the competitors become five again (Argument, the *Plutus*).

22. Cf. J. B. Bury, op. cit., p. 200.

23. Cf. R. Graves, op. cit.

24. Athenaeus (II). The town of Icaria—today nonexistent— on Mount Pentelicon has been immortalized as the birthplace of three Dionysiac personalities: (*a*) Icarius, the first vintner, (*b*) Thespis, the first tragic poet, and (*c*) Susarion, the first comic poet. None of that, however, has been historically confirmed.

25. Scholiast on *Acharnians*, 243; Pausanias, I, ii, 5.

26. Aeschines, *In Ctesiphonta*, 66–68. Also, the ancient *Life* of Euripides.

27. Men riding upon men disguised as horses (Attic black-figured amphora ca. 550 B.C. in Berlin Museum); men disguised as birds (black-figured oenochoe ca. 480 B.C., British Museum); soldiers riding on dolphins and ostriches (Attic skyphos ca. 480 B.C., Boston Museum). And a great many representations of men in the guise of sileni, satyrs with horsetails, and so forth.

28. Cf. Kock, *Comicorum Atticorum Fragmenta*.

29. Did the Greek playwrights pretend that it was "night" when the sun was blazing in mid-sky, or did they arrange their theatrical time according to the real time of the performances? . . . Here are some hints from Aristophanic comedies: The *Wasps* begins at "dark dawn" (216); so do the *Clouds* (3), the *Women at the Thesmophoria* (5) and the *Assembly of Women* (20). In the *Acharnians* we are told that it is almost noon (40). The *Wasps* ends in the late evening or early night (1478). In the Underworld scene of the *Frogs*, it is dark as hell (273–315). Finally—an evidence for the time of the performances—the chorus of the *Birds* tells the spectators that, if they had wings, they might fly home for lunch after the tragedies and return in the afternoon for comedy (786–89).

30. The first dithyramb contest was won by Hypodicus in 508 B.C.

31. Named after Pandion, legendary king of Athens.

32. Lycurgus mentioned by Apollodorus (III, 5, i); Pentheus in Euripides' *Bacchae,* passim.

33. Ovid, *Heroides* (IX, 53 f.); Lucian, *Dialogues of Gods* (13).

CHAPTER III

1. Aristotle, *Politics* (III). See also G. Glotz, *The Greek City* (Part I, Chapter II).

2. Aldus, *Prolegomena:* "in the archonship of Diotimus."

3. Here is a chronological table of the Old Attic Comedy poets:

a) *Legendary forerunner* (sixth century B.C.): Susarion.

b) *Generation of the Persian Wars* (486–458 B.C.): Chionides (first victory 486 B.C.), Magnes (first victory 472 B.C.).

c) *Periclean Generation* (458–431 B.C.): Ecphantides (first victory 458 B.C.), Cratinus, Crates, Telecleides, Pherecrates, Hermippus.

d) *Generation of the Peloponnesian War* (431–404 B.C.): Eupolis, Aristophanes, Phrynichus the Comic, Ameipsias, Plato the Comic, Leucon.

4. Elsewhere they were called *ethelontes, gypones, autocavdaloi,* also *phallophoroi,* etc. (Athenaeus, XIV, 621, 622). The Dorian humor most familiar to the Athenian poets was the contemporary one from Megara (cf. Ecphantides, Fr. 2; Eupolis, Fr. 246; Aristophanes, *Wasps,* 57).

5. Cf. T. B. L. Webster, *Greek Theatre Production,* pp. 131–37.

6. Athenaeus (XIV, 621).

7. Aristotle, *Poetics* (III, 3, and V, 5); Horace, *Epistles* (II, i, 58); *Suda.*

8. Plato, *Theaetetus,* 152e.

9. On Phormis or Phormos and Sophron, cf. *Suda* and Kaibel, *Comicorum Graecorum Fragmenta.* Rhinthon of Syracuse was the creator of the popular (in Hellenistic times) *hilarotragoedia* or travesty on tragic myths (fl. ca. 300 B.C.). Theocritus (about 325–267 B.C.) was born in Syracuse and lived both in Alexandria and Sicily; he was famous for his *idylls,* many in dialogue form. Herondas or Herodas (about 300–250 B.C.), from Cos or Miletus, was a writer of *mimes.* They were all influenced by Sophron.

10. A. Artaud, *The Theatre and Its Double* (translated by M. C. Richards), p. 92.

11. *Phlyax,* pl. *phlyakes:* farcical plays or actors—or both—

contemporary with the Middle Attic Comedy (Athenaeus, XIV, 621 f.).

12. The Marmor Parium or Parian Chronicle (Oxford) was discovered in 1627. It gives valuable dates down to ca. 260 B.C. About Susarion, see Pickard-Cambridge, *Dithyramb, Tragedy, Comedy*, pp. 183–87.

13. Titles and fragments of the Attic playwrights in Kock, op. cit. On their victories, consult also G. Norwood, *Greek Comedy*, passsim. Aristotle's essay on Comedy is missing from the surviving version of the *Poetics*. The Stagiritan mentions, however, Epicharmus, Phormis, Chionides, Magnes, and Crates. There is no word about Susarion. He also says that Athenian Comedy was originally "improvised" and that being studied insufficiently, its origins were forgotten (*Poetics*, V, 2).

14. Tzetzes (in Kaibel, op. cit.). Aristotle, fifteen centuries earlier, could state nothing of the kind (*Poetics*, V, 2).

15. The Morychidean decree issued in 440 B.C. (Scholiast on the *Acharnians*, 67; Xenophon, *On the Government of Athens*, II, 18). "The precaution shows that the situation was critical; though the restraints were drawn as soon as possible, for they were contrary to the spirit of the time. Henceforward the only check on the comic poet was that he *might* be prosecuted before the Council of Five Hundred for 'doing wrong to the people' . . . The Old Comedy is a most telling witness to the greatness of Athens" (J. B. Bury, op. cit., pp. 384–85). What remains a fact is that those who mostly suffered from the arrows of uncensored comedy were the greatest men of the Golden Age: Pericles, Phidias, Socrates, Euripides, even the venerable Aeschylus.

16. We know more about the *Dionysalexandros* than any other Cratinian comedy thanks to the Oxyrhynchus Papyri (published by Grenfell and Hunt, 1904). There was a gag in that play—Dionysus disguises Helen as a goose—which will be remembered, perhaps, by Aristophanes when he disguises the Megarian girls as pigs (*Acharnians*, 738 f.).

17. About Crates: Aristotle, *Poetics*, V, 3; Kaibel, op. cit.; also the *Knights*, 537–40.

18. According to O. Navarre, the oldest surviving *proskenia* or stage-buildings belong to the first half of the third century B.C. (*Représentations dramatiques en Grèce*, p. 13). The only pictorial evidence of the comic stage in the fifth century that we possess, says Webster, is a red-figure oenochoe representing Perseus climbing a small wooden staircase (op. cit., pp. 7, 20, 180, plate 14).

19. The episodes mentioned are from Aeschylus' *Prometheus* and *Eumenides*, Euripides' *Medea, Suppliants,* and his lost *Androm-eda,* respectively.

20. Many excellent studies on the possible development and technique of the Greek theatre have been written in recent years. The authors are particularly indebted to Pickard-Cambridge's *The Theatre of Dionysus in Athens.* An outstanding work is also Margarete Bieber's *The History of the Greek and Roman Theatre.*

21. The fallacious conception of two separate areas was based mostly on Vitruvius (*Architecture,* Book V, Chapter 6) and Pollux (IV, 123) and a few hints from other ancient authors, including Aristotle (*Poetics,* XII). Hoepken first published his views in 1884 (*De Theatro Attico Saeculi* a.C.quinti); Doerpfeld since 1886 in many works.

22. Doerpfeld believed in a one-level acting area. Other authorities, like Navarre, Mazon, Nicoll, Webster, though agreeing as to the nonexistence of a regular stage, suggest that there might have been a low wooden rostrum, of two or three steps, in front of the proskenion.

23. In *Architecture et Dramaturgie,* p. 155.

24. See note 18.

25. Cf. Pickard-Cambridge, *The Theatre of Dionysus in Athens,* pp. 126 and 134 f.

26. Cf. Pickard-Cambridge, *Festivals,* pp. 177–212.

27. Cf. *Acharnians,* 408–9; *Knights,* 1326; *Peace,* 174; his lost *Daedalus,* Fr. 188.

CHAPTER IV

1. Thucydides (I, 146). Heralds carrying the caduceus were messengers only between belligerents. All the descriptions of war events in this book are based on the histories of Thucydides, who was an eye-witness.

2. Argument to the *Medea.*

3. Plutarch, *Pericles,* 31, 32.

4. *Ibid.* Compare Socrates' words about the slanders of comic poets in Plato's *Apology* (19, b, c). C. M. Bowra says that "Athenian democracy may sometimes have suffered from it [comedy], but the assumption that it was indispensable to a civilized community was in the main a source of strength. A people which can laugh at itself is well armed against many catastrophes" (*The Greek Experience,* Ch. IV). This is the reason, perhaps, they never held the comic poets seriously responsible for the harm done to Pericles' reputation

or even Socrates' life, whose conviction and death was nothing less than a catastrophe to the democratic ideal.

5. Argument to the *Hippolytus*.

6. For stage-machinery, see Chapter III above.

7. *Suda;* Aldus, *Prolegomena.* Murray uses *Daitales;* Norwood, *Banqueters.*

8. We owe the longest fragment of the *Banqueters* to Galen (in Dindorf, op. cit., IV).

9. Pickard-Cambridge, *The Dramatic Festivals,* pp. 85–100.

10. Scholiast on *Clouds,* 29.

11. Letter to Karl Marx, quoted by S. I. Radchig in *Aristophanes, Collected Articles,* published by the University of Moscow (1956).

12. G. Murray, *Aristophanes, a Study,* p. 26.

13. *Acharnians* (377–82 and 502–4); Scholiast on the *Acharnians,* 378.

14. *I.G.* (II, 2–2325); also Pickard-Cambridge, op. cit., p. 86, n. 6 and p. 114.

15. *"Lisez-le, monsieur Thiers,* c'est un rude génie . . ." A. de Musset, *La Loi sur la presse,* a poem (1835).

CHAPTER V

1. "In the presence of foreigners" (cf. *Acharnians,* 502; *Life,* etc.).

2. *Acharnians,* 377–82. All quotations of the *Acharnians* are from B. B. Rogers' translation.

3. Cf. Chapter I, note 22.

4. The *Acharnians,* 1235 lines; the *Knights,* 1408; the *Clouds,* 1510. Among contemporary tragedies, the *Sons of Heracles,* 1050; the *Hecuba,* 1271; the *Hippolytus,* 1459; the *Oedipus Tyrant,* 1464.

5. We cannot be certain whether or not it was Cratinus who inaugurated the "autobiographical" type of comedy. At any rate, in his last play, the *Wine Jug* (423 B.C.), he made himself the comic hero.

6. Pollux, IV, 108–9 (cf. Pickard-Cambridge, *Festivals,* pp. 245–50).

7. The order of the leader for a circular dance is "Get into a circle!" (the *Women at the Thesmophoria,* 954, 968). About the flute-player, cf. Scholiast on *Wasps,* 582.

8. The *proskenion* (or stage-facade) in Aristophanes needs to

have either three doors (or openings) in the *Acharnians* and the *Assembly of Women*, or two doors, as in the *Clouds*, or a single central one, as in the *Knights*, the *Wasps*, the *Lysistrata*.

9. *Acharnians*, 408–9. Since Aristophanes is parodying the device, it is beyond question that Euripides had already been using the *ekkyclema* in his tragedies before 425 B.C.

10. J. Copeau (*Lectures*, 1921).

11. For stock-types in Aristophanes and their traditions, *see also* F. M. Cornford, *The Origin of Attic Comedy*, passim.

12. F. M. Cornford, op. cit., passim; Pickard-Cambridge, *Dithyramb, Tragedy, Comedy*, pp. 213–29.

13. A. W. Schlegel, op. cit., Lecture XI, p. 151.

14. I cannot say that I share the opinion that in Attic Comedy's early years the *parabasis* had its place at the beginning of a play. Its message could hardly be delivered in the still unsettled atmosphere of the opening of a performance. Besides, the sermon should assault the public when the action was already ripe and the concentration absolute. (Perhaps, those who suggested the idea had never seen an Attic Comedy performed.)

15. Schiller saw the ancient tragic chorus as a *living wall* surrounding tragedy, in order to keep it untouched by reality and to protect its poetic liberty (Introduction to *The Bride of Messina*). Something analogous might be attributed to the comic chorus, as well. In the Epidaurus performances of the Greek National Theatre, we introduced the device of twenty-four wooden cubes aligned on the semicircumference of the orchestra, on the amphitheatre's side. There the chorus sat during its passive moments and watched the actors, reacted and commented on the happenings, like a genuine audience.

16. *Acharnians*, 780; *Wasps*, 903; *Birds*, 227 f.; *Frogs*, 209 f. Even in this respect, Cratinus had been a pioneer: in his *Dionysalexandros* (Fr. 43) there was a sheep's cry—*bee bee* ($b\bar{n}$)—which subsequently became the cornerstone of a vast linguistic controversy over the ancient Greek pronunciation.

17. Archilochus' song of victory, on Heracles (cf. Pindar, *Olympian Odes*, IX; *Birds*, 1764).

18. Rabelais, Swift, Voltaire, Jarry, and many others have presented fantastic wars fought for idiotic reasons. The only difference between them and Aristophanes is that his war was real and burning with actuality.

CHAPTER VI

1. Scholiast on *Knights,* 1291. Eupolis' quotation is mentioned by the Scholiast on *Clouds,* 554.

2. The translation is by G. Murray. Eupolis' *Maricas* appeared in 421 B.C. The original *Clouds* was produced in 423 B.C., but the *Clouds* that we possess—where Aristophanes' answer is to be found —was written at a later date.

3. Eupolis, Frs. 94 and 100; and Plutarch, *Pericles,* III.

4. Platonius (in Kaibel, *C.G.F.,* p. 4) says that Alcibiades had Eupolis drowned during the Sicilian Expedition (415 B.C.). Others placed his death in the Hellespont (*Suda*) or in Aegina (Aelian, *On the Characteristics of Animals,* X, 41).

5. I find G. Norwood's remark "The *Knights* is a bad and stupid play" (op. cit., p. 207) not only arbitrary but also absurd. Dramatic works can only be fully appreciated when performed. In Epidaurus a whole theatre of 14,000 spectators of various nationalities enjoyed every word of the *Knights* (cf. Thierry Maulnier, "Contestation à Epidaure," *Le Figaro littéraire,* October 2, 1968; and Aldo Giovannetti, "Aristofane polemico sulla scena di Epidauro," *Il Tempo,* August 12, 1968). Also M. Jean-Louis Barrault has told the author that the *Knights* is his favorite Aristophanic comedy.

6. "Paphlagonian": from Paphlagonia, a country providing slaves; also from the verb "paphlazein," to boil and bubble. The Old Demos is called "bean-eater" (1.41) because the Assembly used to vote with beans.

7. The Athenian cavalry was composed of 1,000 (*Knights,* 225, 731). About their dissension with Cleon, *Acharnians,* 6; Scholiast on *Knights,* 226; *Life.*

8. W. Jaeger, op. cit., p. 367.

9. About the Heliasts and the court systems, see B. B. Rogers, *Introduction to the Wasps,* xx f.; G. Glotz, op. cit., Chapter VI; O. Seyffert, op. cit., pp. 330–33.

10. An oral criticism which I have heard many times from scholars. But even G. Murray thinks that "there is a startling inconsistency in the plot" (op. cit., p. 50).

11. The Parliament or Council of Five Hundred. Norwood calls it the Senate.

12. Cf. Pickard-Cambridge, *Festivals,* p. 203.

13. The Prytaneum (Gr. prutaneion) was the public house where "the State offered hospitable entertainment to foreign ambas-

sadors . . . distinguished generals and victors in the great Panhellenic games" O. Seyffert (op. cit., p. 526). Cf. Aristotle, *The Constitution of Athens*, 43.

14. Alcibiades' political rise begins ca. 420 B.C. Aristophanes mentions him "en passant" in 422 B.C. (*Wasps*, 44–45), but will be more interested in him after 416 B.C.

15. About Apollo in Admetus' court: Apollodorus, *The Library*, III, 10, 4. About Jason the One-sandalled; Apollonius Rhodius, *The Argonautica*, I, 7. Cecrops was the son of Erechtheus and the father of Pandion, the grandfather of Aegeus and the great-grandfather of Theseus, all legendary kings of Athens. A customary surname of Athens was "City of Cranaus," Cranaus being the autochthonous ruler in times immemorial (cf. R. Graves, op. cit., 94).

16. For the metric systems of comedy, consult G. Norwood (op. cit., Chapter VIII); for the *parakataloge*, Pickard-Cambridge, *Festivals*, pp. 153–55. The basic theatrical instruments were the flute (single or double) which accompanied the choral sequences, and the lyre (*cithara, lyra, phormix, barbitos*, etc.) used when an actor sang (*monodia*). There were also auxiliary instruments, such as cymbals, rattles, tamburines, triangles, etc. (cf. N. Dufourcq, *La Musique des origines à nos jours*, pp. 64 f.). The ancient *harmonies* are what we call melodies (cf. Aristotle, *Politics*, V, viii; V, 1340 f.). About the dancing figures: Pollux (IV, 103–5) and Athenaeus (XIV, 629 f.).

17. On costumes, cf. Pickard-Cambridge, *Festivals* (pp. 198–238), T. B. L. Webster, op. cit. (pp. 28–73).

18. Pollux' list of masks (second century A.D.) describes those of the New Comedy. It is probable, however, that some were already in use in Aristophanes' time. Two of them, at least, seem to have been named after real fifth-century comedians: the *Hermonios* mask and the *Servant Maison* mask.

19. The prologue of the *Acharnians* and the banquet scene in the *Wasps* are two instances where more than three actors are necessary. Besides, there is always necessity for extra performers to play the numerous mute parts; those were paid by the *choregus*, who also paid the chorus, and not by the state.

20. Argument II to the *Peace*. After 442 B.C. competitions of comic actors were instituted by Pericles in the dramatic festivals. The split-in-two of the theatre-man (poet-actor) was thus officially accomplished.

CHAPTER VII

1. Voltaire, *Dictionnaire philosophique* (athéisme).

2. *Knights,* 400. The Scholiast says that Aristophanes slanders Cratinus for being a drunkard pissing on his mattress.

3. Argument II of the *Peace.*

4. Cf. G. Murray, op. cit., p. 65, note 1.

5. In Callias' house Socrates meets the sophists Protagoras, Hippias and Prodicus (Plato, *Protagoras*). Sophists are also featured in Plato's *Euthydemus, Sophists* and *Gorgias.* In Attic Comedy, Cratinus in his *Archilochi* (Fr. 2) and Ameipsias in his *Connos* (Athenaeus, V, 218c) had dealt with sophists.

6. B. B. Rogers, *Introduction to the Clouds,* xxi.

7. Although no dates are available, it is generally accepted that Plato began composing his *Dialogues* in the early years of the fourth century B.C. (the *Apology* ca. 396 B.C., the *Symposium* ca. 386 B.C.).

8. Cf. Xenophon, *Memorabilia,* I, ii, iii; Plato, *Symposium,* 223, d; Diogenes Laertius, *Life of Socrates,* passim.

9. "You, O Athenians, have killed Socrates the sophist," Aeschines, "Against Timarchus" (345 B.C.).

10. Plutarch, *On Education,* XIV.

11. The theory about Meletus and Anytus in Argument I of the *Clouds.* But in the *Apology* (XIII), Meletus is called "so young," twenty-four years after the production of the play. The theory about Archelaus is in Argument V. A recent, brilliant study by Leo Strauss is wholly devoted to these two great personalities: *Socrates and Aristophanes* (New York and London, 1966).

12. Plato, *Symposium,* 213–15.

13. Plato was born ca. 427 B.C. He frequented Socrates from 407 to 399 B.C., that is, barely eight years.

14. Socrates fought at Potidaea, Delium, and Amphipolis (Diogenes Laertius, op. cit.). Also cf. Alcibiades' description of Socrates' military activities in the *Symposium,* 220, a, f.

15. Arguments of the *Clouds* and Scholiast on line 552.

16. Cf. F. M. Cornford, op. cit., II, 62.

17. The *Clouds* could also be meant as an attack on the sophists Prodicus and Protagoras. The first, with his parable of Virtue and Vice fighting for Heracles, perhaps gave Aristophanes the idea for the two Reasons debate; on the other hand, the formula "to make the lesser reason seem the greater" was a slogan attributed to

Protagoras. The only accusation brought against Socrates in the play that should be taken seriously is the one referring to the philosopher's atheism (cf. Xenophon, *Memorabilia*, I).

18. *Laws* (*Nomoi*) and *Riches* (*Ploutoi*) by Cratinus, *Cities* (*Poleis*) by Eupolis, *Islands* (*Nesoi*) by Plato the comic.

19. B. Brecht had seen the famous Chinese actor in Moscow in 1935 (cf. *Schriftin zum Theater 4*). The line 344 on the Clouds "having noses," may be interpreted as "having Xanthippe's (Socrates' wife's) nose" or as "having nipples" or as "have penises" (they were played by male actors); anyway, not as the "meaningless joke" that Wieland has suggested.

20. In the closing scene of the *second Clouds* (the surviving version) there is, in the oldest manuscripts, the word *EPM* . . . , indicating Hermes as the speaker, without any spoken lines following.

21. Cf. B. B. Rogers, the *Clouds*, note to line 1484.

22. Aelian, *Varia Historia*, II, 13; Plutarch, *On Education*, XIV.

23. The judges in the dramatic contests were ten and they were selected by lot. They swore to be impartial, but this was not always true; they were, it seems, often influenced by the clapping, yelling, and whistling public. At the end of all the dramatic performances, each judge threw his ballot into an urn. The archon drew out five ballots. On those five the verdict was based.

24. Kock, op. cit. Also Scholiast on *Knights*, 400.

CHAPTER VIII

1. Callistratus handled "the political comedies, while those against Euripides and Socrates were given to Philonides" (Aldus, *Prolegomena*). Among the productions that we know of, Callistratus was responsible for the *Banqueters,* the *Babylonians,* the *Acharnians,* the *Birds,* the *Lysistrata,* and possibly the *Merchant Ships;* Philonides for the *Clouds,* the *Proagon,* the *Amphiaraos,* the *Frogs* and possibly the *Wasps* and the *Women at the Thesmophoria.* Aristophanes personally produced the *Knights,* and his son Araros, the last three plays — the *Plutus,* the *Aeolosicon* and the *Cocalus.*

2. Argument II of the *Wasps* and Scholiast on line 61.

3. The comic poet Telecleides had written about "man-devouring courts" (Fr. 2). Cleon's relations with the judges, cf. *Knights,* 255–56, and also B. B. Rogers, *Introduction to the Wasps,* xix ff. It should be seen as an ironic coincidence that in the *Clouds,* Aris-

tophanes attacked Socrates and in the *Wasps,* a year later, he attacked the very courts which one day would condemn Socrates to death.

4. Cf. Chapter I, note 22. There is also mention of Athenian courts in *Clouds,* 208; *Birds,* 40–41 and 110.

5. Cf. V. Ehrenberg, *The People of Aristophanes,* Chapter IX.

6. Cf. Menander's comedy, *The Arbitration.*

7. The tragic poet Phrynichus (not to be confused with the much younger comic one) was older than Aeschylus, had his first victory ca. 510 B.C., and is reported as having introduced feminine characters in tragedy for the first time (*Suda*). He was especially remembered for the excellence of his choral songs (cf. *Birds,* 748–51).

8. *Maître Pierre Pathelin,* French farce (ca. 1460 A.D.), the *Marriage of Figaro* by Beaumarchais (1784), Racine's *Les Plaideurs* (1668).

9. Philocleon's parody on tragic dancers may have been something like Chaplin's masterful burlesque on classic ballet in *The Kid.*

10. *Wasps,* 1536–37. An actor dancing his way out of the theatre along with the chorus must have been an Aristophanic innovation—or a parody on some contemporary tragic innovation—also a proof that actors and chorus mingled in the orchestra.

11. "It was produced under the archonship of Ameinias at the Lenaean Festival of the city during the second year of the 89th Olympiad, and won first Philonides with the *Proagon* Leucon with the *Ambassadors* third" (Argument of the *Wasps*). The last part of the didascalia may be restored (*a*) either, "and won. Philonides with the *Proagon* (second), Leucon with the *Ambassadors* third," (*b*) or, "And Philonides won with the *Proagon,* Leucon . . . etc." (Rogers and Murray are for the first reading, Norwood for the second.)

12. For instance: "the feeblest of Aristophanes' plays" (A. W. Schlegel, *A Course of Lectures on Dramatic Art and Literature,* XII); "a delightful, indeed a haunting play" (Norwood, op. cit., p. 224).

13. Lines 64–66 probably refer to the failure of the previous year's *Clouds.*

CHAPTER IX

1. Cf. Kock, *C.A.F.,* and Blaydes, *Aristophanis Comoediae. Fragmenta* (including Frs. 266, 275). There is a proverb used by Aristophanes only in these two plays, which suggest a certain time af-

finity between them. The *Tents* must be slightly posterior to Cratinus' *Wine Jug* (423 B.C.) as containing Aristophanes' answer; but in 422 B.C. there were the *Wasps* and *Proagon*. So, a probable date for *Tents* is 421 B.C. The date of *Centaur* or *Dramas* is even less certain. It might have been produced before the *Wasps* (cf. Scholiast on *Wasps*, 60). The comedy *Dramas* also appears in conjunction with the spurious *Niobos*.

2. After 423 B.C. Cratinus produced no more plays. Norwood roughly dates his life 490–420 B.C.

3. Plutarch, *Nicias*, IX; Thucydides, V, 15.

4. Aeschylus fought at Marathon and Salamis; Thucydides was a general during the Peloponnesian War; Socrates fought in the same war as a plain soldier. According to the *Suda*, dramatic poets were legally exempt from military service, after Eupolis' death during a naval expedition; yet this cannot be earlier than 415 or 411 B.C., unless the lexicon is mistaken and there was such an exemption in effect from the beginning of the war.

5. Archilochus, Fr. 6; Alcaeus, Fr. 49; Dionysus, *Iliad*, VI, 130 f.

6. Sophocles, *Antigone*, passim; Thucydides, V, 10 ff.

7. The beetle flew to heaven and took his revenge on the eagle, who had carried off his offspring. The fable was told by Aesop to the people of Delphi who had wanted to kill him; thus he saved his life (Scholiast on *Peace*, 129; also *Wasps*, 1446).

8. Argument II of the *Peace* (compare Samuel Pepys: "7 January 1667. Saw *Macbeth* which . . . appears a most excellent play in all respects but especially in divertisement . . .").

9. Apollodorus is mentioned in Argument II of the *Peace*. This Aristophanic actor should not be confused with either Apollodorus of Gela or those of Carystus and Tarsus, all dramatic poets of the fourth and third century B.C.

10. Torelli and Vigarani, famous stage-designers of the seventeenth century A.D. who worked mechanistic miracles in the Italian and French theatres.

11. We surmise that the body-tights, the padded belly, the leather phallus, and the footwear of the comic choruses were standard in all plays. The mask and costume varied according to each comedy, but, as likely as not, were homogeneous for the whole chorus, because its twenty-four members belonged as a rule to the same species: Acharnians, wasps, flatterers, centaurs, laws, etc. I do not agree with the commonly accepted view that the *Peace* chorus was composed uniquely of Athenians and that the Spartans, Thebans,

Megarians, Corinthians, etc. mentioned were *choregic* actors (cf. Norwood, op. cit., pp. 232–34).

12. "He was ridiculed for having produced Peace's colossal statue, by Eupolis in his *Autolycus* and Plato in his *Victories*" (Scholiast on Plato's *Apology*).

13. Aristophanes mentions *stones* (361), *levers* (299, 307), *machines* (307) and *ropes* (437). In lines 294 and 315 the Greeks are told to pull the goddess *out;* in 307, to pull her *up.* And there is a continuous action of pulling, during 80 lines of verse consisting in "pull, pull, pull . . . yo ho, yo ho," etc.

14. There is a rich folkloric element in the festive songs and dances of these farmers; and it is interesting to notice how much they resemble in ideas, images, and even metrical structure, not only some modern Greek village-songs, but also the Spanish *soleas,* so wonderfully reproduced by Lorca in his plays. (So the word "fiesta" is not casual.)

15. The Argument has survived in a frightfully corrupted condition, full of linguistic, syntactical, and spelling errors. After mentioning the victory of Eupolis over Aristophanes and Leucon, it goes as follows: "the drama was acted by Apollodorus . . . won Hermes Leocrotes." This Leocrotes might have been some actor interpreting Hermes. Yet, the "won" might as well stick to the preceding word, thus: "Apollodorus defeated the Hermes of Leocrotes." Pickard-Cambridge believes that the Argument refers to the second *Peace* and should be read: "Hermon the hypocrites won" (*Dramatic Festivals,* 126).

CHAPTER X

1. We learn that Aristophanes' second son, Araros, staged his father's *Plutus* in 388 B.C. (*Life*) and that he often competed both with his own and with his father's plays (Scholiast on Plato's *Apology*). One of his comedies was the *Birth of Pan* (Middle Comedy). If we assume that he had begun his career at twenty-five, ca. 390 B.C., he must have been born ca. 415 B.C. and his elder brother, Philip, ca. 417 B.C. So the wedding of our poet can be approximately dated between 420 and 418 B.C.

2. Cf. Kock, *C.A.F.,* and Blaydes, *Aristophanis Comoediae Fragmenta;* G. Murray, op. cit., pp. 138 and 265.

3. Arguments V and VI.

4. For Socrates' magnanimous attitude, see Chapter VII, note 22; about Plato's views, Chapter XVI.

5. Victor Hugo, "Preface" to *Cromwell* (1827). Kant, *Critique of Judgement,* Book II, 54.

6. Agriculture is mentioned in Fr. 294 (cf. Norwood, op. cit., pp. 332–34).

7. In the *Farmers'* fragments, war with Sparta is mentioned and also Nicias the general. Norwood and Rose date the play after 425 B.C., Murray after 421 B.C.

8. See Note 1. It is an interesting fact that, from the moment Aristophanes becomes a father, he no longer dramatizes his favorite father-against-son conflict. As for his wife—*cette inconnue*—what can we surmise? . . . There is a line from one of his lost plays: "I am ashamed of the woman who neglects her children" (Fr. 907). Could this be taken as a criticism of his own spouse? If yes, then we might deduce that the period of his *feminine* satires (411–406 B.C.) begins with his first marital quarrels.

CHAPTER XI

1. Historical sources: Thucydides, VI; Plutarch, *Pericles,* 20, 21; *Nicias,* 12; *Alcibiades,* 17. Also *Birds,* 145–47 and Argument II of the *Birds.*

2. Argument II of the *Birds.*

3. Cf. G. Murray, op. cit., pp. 138–39.

4. The name appears as *Peisthetairos* (latinized form, *Peisthetaerus*). Rogers accepts it as it is. Others have suggested: *Pisthetairos* or *Pisthetaerus,* i.e., *faithful* to his friends (Meineke, Cornford, Norwood, Pickard-Cambridge). However the rendering, *Peisetairos* or *Peisetaerus* (Van Leeuwen, Blaydes, Rose) and *Peithetairos* or *Peithetaerus* (Kock, Holden, Murray, Ehrenberg), meaning *persuasive* to his friends, fits best the character of the comic hero. About *Evelpides,* the hopeful and optimistic, there is no controversy. I prefer, however, not to use the ill-sounding *Evelpides.*

5. Tereus, king of Thrace, had married Procne, daughter of the Athenian king, Pandion. Seduced by the singing of his wife's sister, Philomela, he raped her. Thereupon, the deserted Procne killed their son, Itys. Tereus was transformed by the gods into a Hoopoe (*epops*), Procne into a swallow, and Philomela into a nightingale. Aristophanes, however, follows a different version of the myth, which was dramatized by Sophocles in his famous *Tereus.* His nightingale is Procne. Cf. R. Graves, *The Greek Myths,* 46. Line 92, "open the wood for me," suggests that the Hoopoe appears through the central aperture of the *proskenion* with the help of the *ekky-*

klema (like Euripides in the *Acharnians* or Agathon in the *Women at the Thesmophoria*).

6. Scholiast on *Birds*, 222. (Cf. Pickard-Cambridge, *Festivals*, p. 265.)

7. The translations from the *Birds* inserted in this chapter are by William Arrowsmith (Ann Arbor, 1961).

8. In the production of the *Birds* at the Ypsilanti Greek Theatre, Michigan, in the summer 1966 (which was directed by the author of this book), the chorus wore four different kinds of plumed costumes. The designer, Eldon Elder, made the birds look like richly feathered Indians and the heroes, Bert Lahr and Jack Fletcher, like two adventurers exploring the Far West. (The chorus was, furthermore, composed of twelve male and twelve female dancers —thus complying with the information given by the Scholiast on *Knights*, 589.)

9. The birth of Love from an egg is not to be found in Hesiod. Aristophanes may have taken it from some apocrypha (or possibly from some Asiatic source), or just created it himself. (The invention is akin to G. B. Shaw's egg in the first part of *Back to Methuselah*.)

10. Heinrich Heine's dictum is quoted by E. Deschanel in *Études sur Aristophanes*, p. 354.

11. Argument II of the *Birds*. Bergk has suggested that Phryni-chus was the author of both the *Revelers* (*Comastai*) and the *Solitary* (*Monotropos*), and that he presented the first under the name of Ameipsias, as Aristophanes had often done. (Cf. Rogers, *Introduction to the Birds*, VII.)

12. Allardyce Nicoll, *World Drama*, p. 99; N. B. Kliatchko, "The Socio-political Tendencies of Aristophanes' Birds," in *Studies on Aristophanes* (University of Moscow).

13. S. T. Coleridge, "Greek Drama," in *Lectures on Shakespeare* (Everyman Library, 1930, p. 13).

CHAPTER XII

1. Thucydides, VII, 85; Plutarch, *Nicias*, 29.

2. Of course, the dating of the *Storks* (*Pelargoi*), the *Heroes*, and *Polyïdos* is only conjectural (cf. Kock, Dindorf, Blaydes).

3. Hierocles, the interpreter of oracles (*Peace*, 1046 f.) was probably a real person. An anonymous oracle-monger also appears in the *Birds* (959). In the *Polyïdos*, besides the soothsayer himself, the characters included Minos and his children, Phaedra and Glaucus. A famous line from Euripides' *Polyïdos*—"Who knows of life

that is aught but death, and death aught else than life beyond the grave . . ." (translation by Norwood)—was lampooned by Aristophanes in his play of the same name (Fr. 456).

4. The *Persians* by Aeschylus (472 B.C.), the *Trojan Women* by Euripides (415 B.C.), *Wallenstein* by Schiller (1799), *Journey's End* by R. C. Sherriff (1928). Alfred Jarry, author of *King Ubu* (1896) and Jaroslav Hasek of the novel, *The Good Soldier Schweyk,* dramatized by Brecht as *Schweyk in the Second World War.* It should be noted that post-World War II avant-garde, antipolemic reviews and musical plays, in London, New York, and German cities, have genuinely and spontaneously recaptured the Aristophanic spirit and verve.

5. Lysistrata: word composed of the Greek words for "disband" and "army."

6. The banquet in Agathon's house took place in 416 B.C.; the *Birds* was produced in 414 B.C., and the *Lysistrata* in 411 B.C. Plato may have known, perhaps, of other Aristophanic parables written in those years.

7. We find a *metastasis* or *epipardos* (second entrance of the chorus) in the *Eumenides,* the *Ajax,* the *Alcestis,* the *Helen,* also in the *Assembly of Women.* I do not agree with some translators or directors of the *Lysistrata,* who separate old and young women from old and young men. The MSS mention two choruses: *chorus of women, chorus of old men* (showing elderly husbands sex-raving is, of course, funnier). As for the separation of the chorus into Athenian and Spartan semichoruses, there is no mention in the MSS, but it appears as aesthetically necessary for the symmetry of the choral sequences.

8. J. J. Rousseau, *Lettre sur les spectacles* (1752). We should note here, perhaps, that the problem of the emancipation of women had already been handled by Aeschylus in his *Suppliants.*

9. Melanippe was Poseidon's mistress. In Euripides' tragedy, her father Aeolus was the villain who ordered her illegitimate children to be burned alive; she displayed her wisdom in pledging for their lives. *Melanippe the Wise* was considered Euripides' most intellectual play, probably influenced by Anaxagoras' theories (cf. Norwood, *Greek Tragedy,* pp. 305 ff.).

10. The hunter Melanion is mentioned by Xenophon (*Cyneget,* I, 2, 7). Timon was a contemporary of Aristophanes (cf. *Birds,* 1549), famous for his misanthropy. He also inspired Lucian and Shakespeare.

11. The Athenian women's love for wine was also a topic of satire in the lost comedy, *Women Getting Hold of Tents*, where the matrons had "the wine-jug as their fellow-spectator" (Fr. 478), and to a great extent in the *Women at the Thesmophoria*. As the whole bulk of Aristophanic production, between 411 and 392 B.C., reeks with antifeminist poisonous vapors, the torturing question arises again: if women were allowed to attend performances in ancient Athens. In other words, was the invective against women meant to divert men alone or women as well? The Aristophanic comedies provide enough evidence in favor of both surmises:

1. *Women did not attend performances:* (a) in the *Acharnians* Dicaeopolis addresses the audience with the words: "O men who watch us . . ."; Evelpides does the same in the *Birds;* (b) in the *Women at the Thesmophoria,* the chorus asks the spectators: "If we are plagues, as *you* think, then why do *you* marry us?" (c) in the *Assembly of Women,* Chremes says that the women accused Blepyrus of being a thief, as well as "all this crowd," and points at the audience (maybe, however, women were sitting separately); (d) in the *Peace,* after a slave has thrown corn to the audience, Trygaeus asks: "Have all taken?" and the slave replies: "Women haven't" whereupon his master explains that "they will receive it from their husbands at night."

2. *Women attended performances:* (a) the last mentioned negative argument could be seen as a positive one as well, if women were sitting, as we have suggested, separately; (b) in the *Lysistrata,* the combined chorus of men and women, addressing the spectators, says: "Whoever among you, be it *man,* be it *woman,* is in need of money . . . we can give from our purses" (though, a little earlier, they had addressed the public: "O men"); (c) in the *Assembly of Women,* Blepyrus enumerates all the everyday occupations that, heretofore, were strictly men's privileges and that have now become women's as well. He does not include "now they will be going to the theatre"; *ergo,* they were already going; (d) we know that women attended the performance of tragedies since Aeschylus' times (they had been frightened by the erinyes in the *Eumenides*) and generally attended the Dionysiac festivals. So, with what logic— Greek and not puritan—would they abstain from comedies? . . . However, the enigma remains.

CHAPTER XIII

1. Conjectural dating of lost Aristophanic comedies probably written in that period: *Polyïdos,* 415–412 B.C.; *Storks,* after 414 B.C.;

Heroes, 413–412 B.C.; *Seasons,* 413–419 B.C.; *Triphales,* 411–410 B.C.; *Lemnian Women,* 410–418 B.C.; *Second Women at the Thesmophoria,* after 410 B.C.; *First Plutus,* 408 B.C.; *Danaïds,* 408–405 B.C.; *Phoenician Women,* 407–405 B.C.; *Fryers,* 405–404 B.C. Cf. Kock, Bergk, Dindorf, Blaydes.

2. Maurice Croiset, *Aristophanes et les partis à Athènes* (Paris, 1906); André Bellessort, *Athènes et son théâtre* (Paris, 1954), p. 302; Aristophanes' *Farmers,* Fr. 108.

3. Sea-battle of Cynossema, revolt of Cyzicus, success at Abydus: Xenophon, *Hellenica,* I, i; Plutarch, *Alcibiades,* passim.

4. Plutarch, *Alcibiades,* 24.

5. Dobree, Rogers, Murray, Jebb date the play 410 B.C., to which view we adhere, against 411 B.C., suggested by Dindorf, Norwood, and the Budé editor of the comedy. (Also, cf. Scholiast on *Frogs,* 53, and Rogers' extensive discussion in *Introduction to the Thesmophoriazusae,* II.)

6. Euripides was born either on the day of the battle of Salamis, 480 B.C. (*Life*), or on the day of Aeschylus' first victory, 484 B.C. (*Marmor Parium*). He received five first victories, the last one posthumously (*Suda*).

7. Schiller in *Dissertation on Naïve and Sacramental Poetry* (passim) contends that Euripides was the favorite poet of his times; Nietzsche, *The Birth of Tragedy,* passim. See also Plutarch, *Nicias,* 29. On his death Thucydides reports the following epitaph: "The whole of Greece is Euripides' tomb; his bones lie in Macedonia, where he died; his country in Greece is Athens; having many times pleased men in the Muses' way, he is lauded by many" (*Diehl,* I, p. 77).

8. The Athenians celebrated the Thesmophoria in the month, Pyanepsion, in a temple situated "above the fountain, Enneacrounos" (Pausanias, *Attica,* XIV, 1). The rituals honoring Demeter lasted four days, each having a special symbolism: (*a*) the Thesmophoria or Anodos (ascent of the women to the temple); (*b*) the Cathodos (descent of Persephone to Hades); (*c*) the Nesteia (fasting and mourning); and (*d*) the Calligenia (resurrection of Persephone and her reunion with her mother).

9. "Comic parody was brought out when the thing parodied was fresh in recollection" (Schlegel, Lecture XI).

10. Euripides' *Palamedes* was produced in 415 B.C., together with the *Alexander,* the *Trojan Women* and the *Sisyphus.* The hero's father was Nauplius and his brother, Oeax; he was a participant in the Trojan War.

11. Compare *Helen,* 56, and *Thesmophoriazusae,* 868; also, for the recognition (*Anagnoresis*), *Helen,* 557–66, and *Thesmophoriazusae,* 905–12.

12. The *Andromeda* was considered in antiquity as one of Euripides' most successful tragedies. Maybe the introduction of Echo as a character, and the sound effects involved, constituted a major novelty. (Cf. Scholiast on *Frogs,* 53.)

13. About circular dances, etc., Pickard-Cambridge, *Festivals,* p. 245, and note 3.

14. Pickard-Cambridge, ibid., p. 58.

15. According to Athenaeus (I, 52) the second version was mentioned by Demetrios of Troezen as *Thesmophoriasasae* (or the Women Who *Were* at the Thesmophoria).

16. Cf. Scholiast on *Plutus,* 173. Why was the *Plutus* rewritten or revised twenty whole years later? Was it solely in order that Aristophanes' son could make his debut as an adapter and a producer? (Cf. *Life* and Argument III of the *Plutus.*)

17. Referring to the invasion of foreign gods, Strabo says: "Just as in all other respects the Athenians continue to be hospitable to things foreign, so also in their worship of the gods; for they welcomed so many of the foreign rites that they were ridiculed therefore by comic writers" (*Geography,* translated by H. L. Jones, Loeb Classical Library, Vol. V, p. 109), and Cicero, that "new gods and night-long vigils held in their honor are attacked by Aristophanes . . . in his play, Sabazius, and certain other gods are condemned as foreigners and expelled from the State" (*De Legibus,* II, 15).

18. Euripides' *Hypsipyle* "was recently produced"—that is, a little before 405 B.C. (Scholiast on *Frogs,* 53). Aeschylus' and Sophocles' tragedies were both called the *Lemnian Women,* though the former had also written an *Hypsipyle.*

19. Euripides' the *Phoenician Women* was presented, according to Kock, between 411 and 404 B.C. and according to Bergk, between 407 and 405 B.C. If Pickard-Cambridge is right in dating it ca. 410 B.C., then the Aristophanic parody must have been produced a year or two after the *Thesmophoriazusae.* The *Danaïds* (or *Daughters of Danaus*) bears the same title as Phrynichus' tragedy of old and Aeschylus' sequel to the *Suppliants.* Neither Sophocles nor Euripides had used that title, as far as we know. Pherecrates' *Crapataloi* was a similar lampoon on theatrical conditions.

CHAPTER XIV

1. Max Beerbohm, *"The Frogs" at Oxford* (February 20, 1909, in *Around Theatres*, pp. 538 f.).

2. Alcibiades is first mentioned by Aristophanes in 422 B.C. (*Wasps*, 44); is perhaps hinted at by the character of Peithetaerus in the *Birds* in 414 B.C.; and was, probably, the central hero of the lost *Triphales* in 410 B.C. A discussion about his policy is also significant in the *Frogs*, in 404 B.C. (1422 ff.).

3. After presenting his *Orestes* in 408 B.C., Euripides left for Macedonia where he wrote his lost *Archelaus*. In his posthumous *Bacchae* he praises Pieria, the king's country. He died during a hunting party with Archelaus (*Life of Euripides*).

4. Cf. *Life of Sophocles*. The comic Phrynichus honors him thus: "The blessed Sophocles, who enjoyed a long life, died, a happy and competent man; having written many beautiful tragedies, he beautifully passed away having suffered no evil" (Fr. 31).

5. Xenophon, *Memorabilia*, I, i, 18.

6. The *Babylonians* (426 B.C.), the *Acharnians* (425 B.C.), the *Knights* (424 B.C.), the *Proagon* or the *Wasps* (422 B.C.) gave him—among the productions we know of—his other first victories.

7. Arguments I and III of the *Frogs*, based on Dicaearchus' information.

8. H. Bergson (*Le Rire*) sees repetition as one of the fundamental elements of comedy.

9. See note 15, below.

10. The god Hermes, who first appears as a comic servant in the *Plutus*, will become the most popular type of Middle Comedy; we get an idea of that stock-type from Plautus' *Amphitryon*, which was based on a play of Middle Comedy. In Menander, the servant is usually called Getas, Pyrrias, Daos or Sicon; Sosias and Xanthias also survive.

11. Heracles was born in Thebes, where his legitimate father, Amphitryon, had found refuge after being dethroned from Troezen. Dionysus' mother was Semele, daughter of king Cadmus of Thebes (Apollodorus, II, 4, and III, 4).

12. Euripides died in the first months of 406 B.C. The Scholiast on *Frogs*, 67, says that, when the poet died, his son produced his posthumous *Iphigenia in Aulis, Alcmeon in Corinth*, and *Bacchae*, probably at the City Dionysia of 405 B.C. The *Frogs* had already been produced two months earlier, at the Lenaea (unless the Euripi-

dean plays were not presented until the City Dionysia of 404 B.C., which seems less likely, because Athens surrendered in that very spring).

13. Orpheus had gone to Hades to rescue Euridyce (*Alcestis,* 357, and Scholiast); Odysseus to comply with Circe's wish (*Odyssey,* XI); and Heracles to perform his twelfth labor, the capture of the three-headed watch-dog Cerberus (Apollodorus, II, 5).

14. It is possible that the *pinakes* were used to show the change of scenery, though the *periaktoi* were not invented as yet. Furthermore, if we must imagine some mechanical intervention, the *ekkyklema* may have revealed the interior of Pluto's palace.

15. Charon says "you shall *hear* the songs of the frogs" (205) and the Scholiast on 209 explains that "neither the frogs nor the chorus are seen in the theatre, but are heard from inside imitating the frogs." Many editors and translators have accepted this, because only 47 lines separate the exit of the Frogs and the entrance of the Initiates. A similar *parachoregema* should also be imagined for the Children's chorus accompanying the elderly Wasps (*Wasps*) as well as for the procession of Libations (*Knights*).

16. Dodwell (II, 45) and Macgregor, *The Rob Roy on the Jordan* (Ch. IX) are mentioned by Rogers (*Frogs,* 209, note).

17. Cf. *Acharnians,* 263–65; *Frogs,* 413.

18. *Frogs,* 367–68. The orator in question made that motion because he was lampooned by the comic poets. The Scholiast mentions the names of Archinus and Agyrrhius; the latter is also mentioned by the Scholiast on *Ecclesiazusae,* 102.

19. *Frogs,* 717–33. Sir Thomas Gresham, financial agent to the Crown, expressed his theory that "bad money drives out good" in a letter to Queen Elizabeth, in 1558.

20. Achilles, Niobe, and other Aeschylean heroes were famous for keeping a mysterious silence before they actually decided to speak. The same is true for the surviving Prometheus.

21. *Frogs,* 1303–6. The *ostraca* were wooden instruments like rattles or castanets.

22. Cephisophon was Euripides' renowned servant and, as insinuated by comic poets, collaborator in his tragedies.

23. *Frogs,* 886–87; Aristotle, *Nicomachean Ethics,* IIII, a.

24. Cycnus and Memnon were Trojan allies killed by Achilles (*Iliad,* VIII); Achilles and Memnon appeared as the heroes in Aeschylus' tragedies *Memnon* and *Psychostasia.*

25. *Frogs,* 1032–36. Orpheus and Musaeus were old, semi-legendary poets.

26. *Stheneboea* was a sister-tragedy to the *Bellerophon;* in it, the heroine had an adulterous love affair with the legendary rider of Pegasus.

27. W. Jaeger, op. cit., p. 377.

28. Argument I of the *Frogs.*

29. Plutarch, *Lysander,* 15.

CHAPTER XV

1. Norwood believes that Horace is confusing dates, the only law against Comedy being the Morychidean one in 440 B.C. There must have been some new official restriction, however, after 404 B.C., to bring about such a notable change in the form of Comedy.

2. Fenelon, the seventeenth-century French author, writes: "Comedy satirizing Socrates made a great impression on the people, and therefore Meletus sued him . . ." As many other European intellectuals, both pagan and Christian, Fenelon considered Aristophanes as the instrument of an anti-Socratic mafia and the *Clouds* as the first step in the philosopher's annihilation.

3. The *Fryers* (*Tagenistai*) is dated 405–404 B.C. by Bergk; it probably had a chorus of parasites, like those in Eupolis' *Flatterers.* The *Gerytades,* also written shortly after the *Frogs,* bears many similarities with that play. A famous Aristophanic fragment about Sophocles belongs, perhaps, to this play: "He licked the mouth of the honey-dripping Sophocles." The *Telemesians* or *Telemeses* is considered a fourth-century product; the same goes for the *Daedalus.*

4. The quotation is, of course, from the Ages of Man Speech in *As You Like It.* Schlegel sees the death of Old Comedy as a violent one, contrary to the natural death of Tragedy (Lecture XII). Cinesias, who was featured in the *Birds* and also in the *Gerytades,* was a bad dithyramb poet, scoffed at by poets (Scholiast on *Frogs,* V, 404), philosophers (Plato, *Gorgias*), and orators alike (Athenaeus, XII). He is supposed to have proposed a law abolishing the *choregia,* the financing of a comic chorus. Norwood rejects the information as a mere blunder (op. cit., p. 28).

5. Murray, op. cit., p. 181.

6. Cratinus had died ca. 422 B.C., Eupolis in 414 or 411 B.C., Sophocles and Euripides in 406 B.C., Alcibiades in 404 B.C., Thucydides in 400 B.C., and Agathon thereabout, Socrates in 399 B.C.— although none of those death-dates, except those of Sophocles, Euripides, and Socrates are known for sure.

7. Plato *Republic* (cf. Rogers, *Introduction to the Ecclesiazusae,* XXI–XXVIII; Murray, op. cit., pp. 186–88).

8. Pausanias, I, 8, 2, and IX, 16, 2. A copy of the statue is in the Munich Glyptothek Museum. Cephisodotus was Praxiteles' father.

9. Quoted in L. Freed, *T. S. Eliot: Aesthetics and History,* p. 20.

10. With the *Laconians,* the *Admetus,* the *Adonis,* and the *Paciphae,* respectively (Argument III of the *Plutus*).

11. "Wishing to introduce his son, Araros, to the public, he let him stage his last two plays, the *Cocalos* and the *Aeolosicon*" (Argument III of the *Plutus*). That there were two *Aeolosicons* we learn from Athenaeus, VIII. Platonius (*On the difference between comedies*) writes: "The choregi disappeared—therefore, Aristophanes produced his *Aeolosicon* which has no choral parts. As there were no choregi appointed and as no food was provided for the dancers, comedy lost its choral parts and the plots were changed—so, this is a typical Middle Comedy play—which has neither chorus nor *parabasis.*"

12. "He first showed the style of New Comedy in his *Cocalos* and, from this start, Menander and Philemon wrote their plays. He introduced seduction and recognition and all the rest that Menander labored upon" (*Life*).

13. A. Persius Flaccus, *Satire I.*

14. This epigram—the eleventh Platonic one in the Greek Anthology—is considered spurious (mentioned by Thomas Magister in his *Life of Aristophanes*).

CHAPTER XVI

1. The information about these four contemporary opinions is to be found in the ancient *Life* and the Scholia on Plato's *Apology.*

2. Sources about Plato's death are the ancient *Life* and Apollodorus.

3. Diogenes Laertius, III, 5, 18; Aelian, *Varia historia,* II, 30.

4. *The Greek Experience,* Epilogue.

5. Callimachus' *Pinakes,* Lycophron's *On Comedy,* and Eratosthenes' *On Ancient Comedy*—which have not survived—were the basic reference works for Byzantine and Roman scholars.

6. Translated by G. Murray, in his *Aristophanes* (Oxford, 1933), p. 214.

7. Ptolemy II (Philadelphus) had instituted dramatic competitions in Alexandria.

8. The *editio princeps* of Euripides is that of J. Lascaris (Florence, 1496) but it contains only four plays; the Aldine edition of Musurus (Venice, 1503) contains all the plays except the *Electra*.

9. The story of the survival of Greek literary texts is a fascinating one; it can be read in L. D. Reynolds and N. G. Wilson, *Scribes and Scholars: a Guide to the Transmission of Greek and Latin Literature* (Oxford, 1968); K. J. Dover's *Aristophanic Comedy* (Berkeley, 1972) has a section (pp. 1–6) on "The Survival of the Text."

10. The Swiss Hellenist, A. Bonnard, is the author of a study, *L'Esprit de Rabelais illuminé par Aristophane*.

11. Boileau, as many other critics before and after him, condemned with the same constipated spirit the *"accès insolent d'une bouffonne joie"* of Greek comedy, and Molière who, they thought, often forgot his subtle self for the sake of the fool.

12. G. E. Lessing, *Hamburg Dramaturgy*, nos. 90–92; H. Heine, *On the History of Religion and Philosophy in Germany*, reprinted in *Prose Miscellanies* (trans. S. L. Fleishman, Philadelphia, 1876), pp. 126–27.

13. John Dryden, "Of Dramatic Poesy," ed. George Watson (London and New York, 1962), Vol. I, pp. 30–31.

14. But we cannot smile at Farquhar's opinion that "we must go higher than either Aristophanes or Menander to discover comedy in its primitive institution, if we would draw any moral design of its invention to warrant and authorize its continuance" ("A Discourse upon Comedy," ed. Louis A. Strauss, Boston, 1914, p. 19).

15. In Bernard Shaw's opinion (Introduction to *Plays Unpleasant*), Fielding was the greatest dramatist who ever practiced his art in England with the only exception of Shakespeare.

16. Influences of *The Rehearsal* (1672) by George Villiers, Duke of Buckingham, on *The Critic*.

17. Entry, "atheist, atheism," in Voltaire, *Philosophical Dictionary*, translated by Peter Gay (New York, 1962), Vol. I, pp. 96–97.

18. *Greek Drama*, lecture, 1818.

19. George Meredith, "An Essay on Comedy and the Uses of the Comic Spirit" (London, 1919), p. 73.

20. From "Count August von Platen and I," reprinted in *The Poetry and Prose of Heinrich Heine*, selected, edited, and newly translated by Frederic Ewen (New York, 1948), p. 379.

21. Heine, "Confessions" from *Memoirs*, Vol. II, p. 260.

22. Eric Bentley, *In Search of Theatre*, p. 148.

23. See Ch. XIV, note 1.

24. Reviewing the Cherry Lane production of *The Dog Beneath the Skin,* directed by Alexis Solomos, Richard Watts, Jr., wrote: ". . . the play scornfully contemplates the madness of Hitler's Germany and the Tory dullness of Baldwin's Britain, it also manages to laugh mockingly, even to the extent of going in for gushy comedy" (N.Y. *Post,* July 23, 1947).

25. I. M. Mahkov (in *Aristophanes, a Study,* published by the University of Moscow).

26. J. W. Marriott, *The Theatre* (London, 1931), pp. 173–74.

Index

Page numbers in italics indicate major discussion of a work.